FROM TRADITION TO IMITATION

Program in Judaic Studies
Brown University
BROWN JUDAIC STUDIES
Edited by
Jacob Neusner,
Wendell S. Dietrich, William Scott Green, Ernest S. Frerichs,
Calvin Goldscheider, Alan Zuckerman

Project Editors (Project)

David Blumenthal, Emory University (Approaches to Medieval Judaism)
William Brinner (Studies in Judaism and Islam)
Ernest S. Frerichs, Brown University (Dissertations and Monographs)
Lenn Evan Goodman, University of Hawaii (Studies in Medieval Judaism)
(Studies in Judaism and Islam)
William Scott Green, University of Rochester (Approaches to Ancient
Judaism)
Ivan Marcus, Jewish Theological Seminary of America
(Texts and Studies in Medieval Judaism)
Marc L. Raphael, Ohio State University (Approaches to Judaism in
Modern Times)
Norbert Samuelson, Temple University (Jewish Philosophy)
Jonathan Z. Smith, University of Chicago (Studia Philonica)

Number 80
FROM TRADITION TO IMITATION:
The Plan and Program of Pesiqta Rabbati and
Pesiqta deRab Kahana

by
Jacob Neusner

FROM TRADITION TO IMITATION
The Plan and Program of Pesiqta Rabbati
and Pesiqta deRab Kahana

by
Jacob Neusner

Scholars Press
Atlanta, Georgia

FROM TRADITION TO IMITATION
The Plan and Program of Pesiqta Rabbati and Pesiqta deRab Kahana

©1987
Brown University

BM
517
.P43
N48
1987

Library of Congress Cataloging in Publication Data

Neusner, Jacob, 1932-
   From tradition to imitation.

   (Brown Judaic studies ; no. 80)
   Bibliography: p.
   Includes index.
   1. Pesikta rabbati--Criticism, interpretation, etc.
2. Pesikta de-Rav Kahana--Criticism, interpretation,
etc. I. Title. II. Series.
BM517.P43N48 1987   296.1'406   87-4664
ISBN 1-55540-113-9 (alk. paper)

Printed in the United States of America
on acid-free paper

For

My dear friend and sometime-student

RABBI ARNOLD RESNICOFF

Chaplain, United States Navy

and for

his wife,

BARBARA,

and daughter

MALKAH

who have graced the lives of my family
and myself
with their love.

Contents

Part One
A SAMPLE OF PESIQTA RABBATI:
PESIQTA RABBATI PISQAOT 1 THROUGH 5 AND 15

*[For as the new heavens and the new earth which I am making shall
endure in my sight, says the Lord, so shall your race and your name
endure;]* and month by month at the new moon, week by week on the
Sabbath, all mankind shall come to bow down before me, says the
Lord; *[and they shall come out and see the dead bodies of those who
have rebelled against me; their worm shall not die nor their fire be
quenched; and they shall be abhorred by all mankind]* (Is. 66:22-24).

A Psalm. A song at the dedication of the house of David. *[I will
exalt you, O Lord, you have lifted me up and have not let my
enemies make merry over me. O Lord, my God, I cried to you and
you healed me. O Lord, You brought me up from Sheol and saved
my life as I was sinking into the abyss. Sing a psalm to the Lord,
all you his loyal servants, and give thanks to his holy name* (Ps.
30:1-4).

On the eighth day the chief of the Manassites, *[Gamaliel son of
Pedahzur, came. His offering was one silver dish weighing a hundred
and thirty shekels by the sacred standard and one silver tossing-bowl
weighing seventy, both full of flour mixed with oil as a grain-
offering; one saucer weighing ten gold shekels, full of incense; one
young bull, one full-grown ram, and one yearling ram, as a whole-
offering; one he-goat as a sin-offering; and two bulls, five full-grown
rams, five he-goats, and five yearling rams, as a shared-offering. This
was the offering of Gamaliel son of Pedahzur]* (Num. 7:54-59).

*[Then Elijah said to all the people, Come here to me. They all came,
and he repaired the altar of the Lord which had been torn down.]* He
took twelve stones, one for each tribe of the sons of Jacob, the man
named Israel, by the word of the Lord. *[With these stones he built an
altar in the name of the Lord]* (1 Kgs. 18:30-32).

Part Two
LITERARY STRUCTURES OF PESIQTA RABBATI
AND PESIQTA DERAB KAHANA

Preface

For the purposes of the studies of Parts Two and Three, which are explained at length in the Introduction, I have retranslated six *pisqaot* of Pesiqta Rabbati, 1 through 5 and 15. I found it necessary to do so because the available translation, cited presently, does not contain a suitable reference system and does not differentiate the components of the document, except in paragraphs. Analysis is possible only when we can readily specify what we analyze and the basis on which we differentiate one passage from some other.

I translate the printed text of Ephraim Zalman Margoliot, with Zeev Wolf, David Luria, and Yeruham Leiner, *Pesiqta Rabbati deRab Kahana*, (reprinted N.Y., 1959: Menorah Institute for Research and Publishing of Manuscripts and Rare Books, Inc.). I consulted the edition of Meir IshShalom [Friedman], in the reprint of Tel Aviv, 1963. This was originally published under the title *Pesikta Rabbati, Midrasch für den Fest-cyclus und die ausgezeichneten Sabbathe* (Vienna, 1860). But I decided not to pretend to compose a "critical text" by comparing the two printed versions, and, for the gross analysis undertaken here, do not deem it necessary. Where my translation differs from the Hebrew text against which a reader may wish to check it, I have tried to render, with the usual, requisite care and accuracy, what I found in the specified printed version. Readers who supply corrections of my translation will enjoy my thanks, and in a future edition, I shall of course improve on what is here with acknowledgement of their help. No translation has ever pleased everyone who claimed to know the original language, nor does any have to. It has only to do its job.

I do not conceive that a translation defines the arena for the creation of a "critical text," and I do not follow the reasoning of those who do. A translation puts into English the Hebrew of an available text. When we have better versions of the ancient documents than are now in hand, there will be new translations of those versions, as they become widely available. Since I translated for the first time the critical text of M. Margulies for Leviticus Rabbah and of Bernard Mandelbaum for Pesiqta deRab Kahana, I can testify to the vast improvement in translation that such a text makes possible. But the text-critics who criticize translations of less than the perfect text (which, to be sure, they have not supplied) seem to me to have made no strong case for their position. The best is the enemy of the good. We engage, all of us, in an ongoing process, and one generation's perfection turns out to be the next generation's hopelessly flawed inheritance.

I checked my translation against William G. Braude, *Pesikta Rabbati. Discourses for Feasts, Fasts, and Special Sabbaths* (New Haven and London, 1968: Yale University Press) I-II. Where I have cited his rendering, I have so indicated by giving his name and the page number in his translation. I found his translation far superior to his later work on Pesiqta deRab Kahana, and can confidently refer to Braude's quite literal translation the reader who wishes to test my results by applying my methods to *pisqaot* not translated here. The absence of a good analytical reference system is an obstacle, but the basic rendition is sufficiently loyal to the Hebrew that further analytical studies along the lines laid out here are entirely feasible. His philosophy of translation as expressed in Pesiqta deRab Kahana is discussed in my "Translation and Paraphrase," in *Hebrew Studies*, in press for 1987. It suffices to say that his work on Pesiqta Rabbati stands in judgment of his and Kapstein's fanciful and self-indulgent treatment of Pesiqta deRab Kahana. I cannot account for the stunning shift in his approach to translation, but, happily, for the document at hand, he has given us a loyal and faithful account of the words in Hebrew.

My identification system, which makes possible all further analytical effort, rests on the paragraphing in Zeev Wolf, David Luria, and Yeruham Leiner, *Pesiqta Rabbati deRab Kahana*. I did consult the Friedman edition as well, but consistently followed the Menorah one. There each paragraph bears a Hebrew letter. That letter then is represented by the second Roman numeral. Thus I:I is *Pisqa* 1, the first marked paragraph in the cited printed text. The Arabic numeral then marks my estimation of what forms a completed unit of discourse and the letter marks the smallest whole unit of thought, thus I:I.1.A refers to the opening paragraph of *Pisqa* 1, the opening cogent unit of discourse, the initial whole unit of thought.

Since, as I explain in the introduction, this study concludes a long succession of exercises on the description, analysis, and interpretation of Midrash-compilations, involving translations and extensive inquiries on rhetorical, logical, and topical properties of that kind of canonical document of Judaism, I introduce this account with a list of the prior items of mine relevant to the study of midrash-compilations and their traits of literature and intellect. The context for this final work – which now points me in a new direction altogether – will thus be made clear.

Translations and form-analytical studies:

Genesis Rabbah. The Judaic Commentary on Genesis. A New American Translation. Atlanta, 1985: Scholars Press for Brown Judaic Studies.

    I.   *Genesis Rabbah. The Judaic Commentary on Genesis. A New American Translation. Parashiyyot One through Thirty-Three. Genesis 1:1-8:14.*

II. *Genesis Rabbah. The Judaic Commentary on Genesis. A New American Translation. Parashiyyot Thirty-Four through Sixty-Seven. Genesis 8:15-28:9.*

III. *Genesis Rabbah. The Judaic Commentary on Genesis. A New American Translation. Parashiyyot Sixty-Eight through One Hundred. Genesis 28:10-50:26.*

Sifra. The Judaic Commentary on Leviticus. A New Translation. The Leper. Leviticus 13:1-14:57. Chico, 1985: Scholars Press for Brown Judaic Studies. Based on the translation of *Sifra Parashiyyot Negaim* and *Mesora* in *A History of the Mishnaic Law of Purities. VI. Negaim. Sifra.* [With a section by Roger Brooks.]

Sifré to Numbers. An American Translation. I. 1-58. Atlanta, 1986: Scholars Press for Brown Judaic Studies

Sifré to Numbers. An American Translation. II. 59-115. Atlanta, 1986: Scholars Press for Brown Judaic Studies. [III. *116-161*: William Scott Green].

The Fathers According to Rabbi Nathan. An Analytical Translation and Explanation . Atlanta, 1986: Scholars Press for Brown Judaic Studies.

Pesiqta deRab Kahana. An Analytical Translation and Explanation. I. 1-14. Atlanta, 1986: Scholars Press for Brown Judaic Studies.

Pesiqta deRab Kahana. An Analytical Translation and Explanation. II. 15-28. With an Introduction to Pesiqta deRab Kahana. Atlanta, 1987: Scholars Press for Brown Judaic Studies.

Critical studies of literary-historical problems:

History of the Mishnaic Law of Purities. VII. Negaim. Sifra (Leiden, 1975: E.J. Brill)

The Foundations of Judaism. Method, Teleology, Doctrine. Philadelphia, 1983-5: Fortress Press. I-III. I. *Midrash in Context. Exegesis in Formative Judaism.*

The Integrity of Leviticus Rabbah. The Problem of the Autonomy of a Rabbinic Document. Chico, 1985: Scholars Press for Brown Judaic Studies.

Comparative Midrash: The Plan and Program of Genesis Rabbah and Leviticus Rabbah. Atlanta, 1986: Scholars Press for Brown Judaic Studies.

Canon and Connection: Intertextuality in Judaism. Lanham, 1986: University Press of America. *Studies in Judaism* Series.

Midrash as Literature: The Primacy of Documentary Discourse. Atlanta, 1987: Scholars Press for Brown Judaic Studies.

What Is Midrash? Philadelphia,1988: Fortress Press.

Invitation to Midrash: The Working of Rabbinic Bible Interpretation. A Teaching Book. San Francisco, 1988: Harper & Row.

Judaism and Scripture: The Evidence of Leviticus Rabbah . Chicago, 1986: The University of Chicago Press.

As is clear, I have moved through the larger part of the canonical midrash-compilations of late antiquity (and, in the case of Pesiqta Rabbati, perhaps even stumbled into the medieval compilations as well). My findings in literature and history now point me toward a religious-historical *(religionsgeschlichtlich)* problem which, as I said at the outset, is whether and how the rabbinic writings of late antiquity, both the midrash-compilations and the legal writings of the Mishnah, Tosefta, Talmud of the Land of Israel, Talmud of Babylonia, and related writings, on which I have also conducted a sequence of literary and historical studies, form a single statement: a canon, or, in the mythic language of the received tradition, the one whole Torah, formulated in two media, written and oral, of Moses, our rabbi. That problem, while rich in theological implications, remains one of a humanistic character: description, analysis, and interpretation of data, read inductively – if I can figure out how to do so.

It remains to express my cordial thanks to colleagues, beginning with two outside of my University who helped in a very specific way with this book.

Dr. Bernard Mandelbaum, President-emeritus of The Jewish Theological Seminary of America, kindly read my translations of *Pisqaot* One through Five as well as Fifteen and corrected them. He made many important suggestions as well, and I am grateful to him for his generosity in sharing his learning with me. He is remarkably prompt and his detailed comments have proved invariably correct.

Professor William Scott Green, University of Rochester, gave me good advice on planning Parts Two and Three of the work. I always benefit from his critical judgment. He has suffered with me the pangs of framing the next stage in my research – whatever it has been – for more than twenty-one years, from the time he was a junior at Dartmouth College and I an assistant professor of religion at that lovely sanctuary. From then to now we have talked from day to day and struggled through our respective agenda of learning, distinct but related. The reward of teaching is when one's student becomes colleague, critic, and co-worker, with a career and even, as in Professor Green's case, a richly earned reputation of acumen and judgment of his own. Among the twenty-five doctorates I have given, his is the most successful, because, through his own use of things I have taught him, he has made – and is making – for himself very much what is his own statement, his own contribution. The recognition of our field, the academic study of religion, he earned wholly on his own. That is why I take pride in his achievements.

I am grateful, also, to my colleagues and graduate students at Brown University, with whom I was able to discuss aspects of this work as it unfolded.

Professors Wendell S. Dietrich, Ernest S. Frerichs, and Calvin Goldscheider, as well as sometime-visiting Professor Burton Mack, Claremont Graduate School, commented on various ideas I laid before them and offered valuable observations. Professor Goldscheider read Chapters Seven through Eleven and followed the translation of the texts as well. The opportunity for the social sciences and the humanities to meet every day for lunch in the persons of my dear Calvin Goldscheider and myself is not wasted.

My present graduate students, Mr. Paul V. Flesher and Mr. Richard E. Cohen took time out from their own work to think about the problems I took up in mine, and they furthermore eased the everyday burden by helping in countless thoughtful ways. They made no great public display of their devotion, preferring to let their many, remarkably kind and generous actions, speak for themselves. They do, and I am grateful.

JACOB NEUSNER

Thanksgiving Day
November 27, 1986

Program in Judaic Studies
Brown University
Providence, Rhode Island 02912-1826 U.S.A.

Introduction

This book completes the sustained inquiry, which began with my *History of the Mishnaic Law of Purities*. VII. *Negaim. Sifra* (Leiden, 1975: E. J. Brill), into the character of compilations of scriptural exegeses, called *midrashim,* produced in late antiquity by the sages who framed the canon of Judaism. As I shall explain, I now turn toward a different set of problems, which have emerged in the research that now comes to an end. What I have wanted to know is the intent and plan of a rabbinic document of late antiquity, specifically, whether the framers of a document proposed to make a statement through their composition, or whether they wished only to collect and arrange received sayings and stories, without imposing the imprint of their taste and judgment upon the whole. In one composition after another, I have found that the former, rather than the latter, trait predominated. Whatever a group of compositors received they revised and recast in terms of their larger program, even while faithfully honoring the work of their predecessors: a vast labor of tradition in the deepest sense, that is, receiving from the past, handing on to the future. In this final exercise of narrowly-literary analysis, I went in search of what I hoped would be a (mere) scrapbook, thinking that Pesiqta Rabbati, derivative and secondary as it is, would finally provide me with that contrastive case, the null-hypothesis, that would permit me to point in the corpus of rabbinic writings of late antiquity to both documents of integrity and also documents that constituted mere collections and arrangements of essentially miscellaneous materials. That search accounts for the choice of the document at hand, and explains, also, the problematic of this book: the effort to sort out a literary labor of tradition from an exercise in imitation.

As the facts would have it, Pesiqta Rabbati turned out to be neither miscellaneous nor purposive and well crafted. The composite presented its own problems, not the ones I brought to it, and, as I shall explain, made possible the description, in Parts Two and Three of this book, of a kind of historical sequence of literature, that is, a movement from Leviticus Rabbah to Pesiqta deRab Kahana, and from Pesiqta deRab Kahana to Pesiqta Rabbati. That movement does seem to me to exemplify the larger proposition that one transaction can prove traditional, in the sense just now defined, while another may turn out to be imitative, in the same context of meaning. As I shall explain, my fundamental thesis here is that the framers of Pesiqta Rabbati received stunningly effective rhetorical and logical instruments of the expression of thought and used them to slight effect. Epigones and amateurs, they received modes of rhetorical and logical expression of a truly subtle character and made of them little more than conventional forms of a merely syntactical weight and character. But in saying so, I have moved well beyond my story, so let me turn back to the beginning and explain my basic method.

My way in all scholarly inquiry is to start with the document and work inductively. I know no other way than to begin with the text, which is the sole evidence in hand for the Judaism under study, and in a systematic way to work through each of its details, ordinarily by retranslating the whole or a sizable sample thereof. Further, I approach a document from its outer limits and work my way in, trying to allow the document's own characteristic and definitive traits of plan and program, form and doctrine, to guide me. My interest is in three aspects of a document: its rhetorical or formal plan, its traits of logical cogency, which endow the document with general intelligibility, and its topical program. Having defined the formal traits of the document, I investigate the modes of thought that produced, for the framers, intelligible statements: modes of syllogistic discourse and how they work. Then, but only then, I turn to the program of discourse. In that way I propose to describe and analyze a text and work out a program for interpretation as well.

For a number of years this work of rereading the classical texts of the Judaism of the dual Torah has centered on compilations of exegeses of Scripture called *midrash[im]*.

One result is *Judaism and Scripture: The Evidence of Leviticus Rabbah* (Chicago, 1986: University of Chicago Press), which investigates the question of whether this particular Judaism is a scriptural religion, that is, emerges from and restates propositions of the Hebrew Scriptures. It is not. First comes the Judaism – the system at hand, with its concerns and problems – and then comes the canon, beginning with Scripture. So that work argues.

Another is *The Integrity of Leviticus Rabbah. The Problem of the Autonomy of a Rabbinic Document* (Chico, 1985: Scholars Press for Brown Judaic Studies), where I ask about the textuality of a text: what tells me the principles of cogent composition and coherent argument that may or may not characterize a given document. I there inquire into the classifications of writings, from mere scrapbooks of this and that, to collages, and, upward to cogent statements, in this context, texts.

In yet a third, *Comparative Midrash. The Plan and Program of Genesis Rabbah and Leviticus Rabbah* (Atlanta, 1986: Scholars Press for Brown Judaic Studies), I further showed the relationship between the distinctive literary traits of a document and its – I maintain, equally distinctive – theological program, carried out through the exegesis of particular words or phrases to demonstrate large and encompassing propositions. My argument there is that the generative unit of thought is not the verse, which yields its own exegesis (a commonplace apologetic in the modern theological picture of Judaism), but rather the document itself.

This same problem is worked out on a much broader scale than two documents only, in my *Literature and Midrash: The Primacy of Documentary Discourse* (Atlanta 1987: Scholars Press for Brown Judaic Studies), which covers ten documents. There have been other studies on midrash-compilations, e.g., Judaism and Story: The Evidence of The Fathers According to Rabbi Nathan (Chicago, 1987: University of Chicago Press), but these three items mark the principal stages in my inquiry into the midrash-sector of the rabbinic corpus. I now turn in an entirely different direction, to ask how the documents identified as authoritative form not merely a corpus but a canon. So here I complete one line of research and undertake another.

In this consequent and concluding study on tradition and imitation, I want to know how to distinguish from one another texts that share sizable components in common, e.g., complete chapters. Since Pesiqta deRab Kahana and Pesiqta Rabbati intersect, and since Pesiqta deRab Kahana also shares an important corpus of materials with Leviticus Rabbah, it seemed to me important to work out fixed and objective – therefore formal – criteria for comparison and then to undertake a sustained exercise of the comparison of documents – midrash-compilations – that in significant ways cover the same ground. The result, as stated in the title of this book, is to distinguish works of tradition and innovation from those of imitation. Into the category of tradition and innovation fall both Leviticus Rabbah and Pesiqta deRab Kahana.

In my *Judaism and Scripture, Comparative Midrash,* and *Integrity of Leviticus Rabbah,* I have shown how the remarkable authorship of Leviticus Rabbah both received and also revised an important mode of purposefully compiling scriptural exegesis; that authorship took over and richly reworked the approach to midrash-compilation that got underway (within the extant canon) in Genesis Rabbah. In my *Pesiqta deRab Kahana. An Analytical Translation* , and in Chapter Eleven here, I demonstrate how the subsequent authorship improved upon the received approach, now received as traditional, of Leviticus Rabbah. And in the present work I am able to demonstrate the ways in which the authorship of Pesiqta Rabbati has merely imitated, without real understanding, the remarkable mode of cogent discourse fully worked out by the authorship of Pesiqta deRab Kahana – hence *from tradition*, as an ongoing and continuous process of receiving and handing over (in the sense of Avot 1:1: *...qbl...msr...*, that is, receive, hand over) *to* (uncomprehending) *imitation.*

The key to the matter – the fixed and objective criteria to which I made reference – is the use of the received rhetorical forms. The authorship of Leviticus Rabbah received two interesting forms from the authorship of Genesis Rabbah, where, in the unfolding of the literature, they first occur. The authorship of Leviticus Rabbah revised these forms and imposed upon them a stunning discipline, making of them modes of subtle and compelling persuasion in the service of an implicit syllogism. What happened then was that the authorship represented in Pesiqta Rabbati took over these same forms and, not understanding their integrity and vitality, merely aped them without utilizing the potential force for compelling statement of an implicit syllogism that the forms, in the hands of the authorship of the earlier authorships, had made available. They went through motions without real understanding, and even their own innovations proved in my view lifeless and merely interesting. So the midrash-compilation, which had begun its life in Genesis Rabbah and Leviticus Rabbah as a pointed and purposeful act of literature, and had in Pesita deRab Kahana become a mode of argument of remarkable subtlety and force, turned into a collection of information – in places a collage, in places a mere scrapbook of this and that upon a common theme, but no where a text of integrity such as the midrash-compilation had been. That is the point at which we began, the search for a scrapbook in the setting of a variety of documents of compelling integrity. In Chapters Seven through Eleven, I present the literary evidence for these facts and judgments. Since they are offered as a mere initiative in description, analysis, and interpretation, without a broad-ranging survey of the evidence of documents other than those under discussion, I draw no conclusions at this time on the history of the literature of Judaism, therefore on the history of Judaism.

As I said at the outset, my emphasis throughout is on inductive reading of internal evidence. Let me now explain the inductive character of my method, and why I regard the present approach as necessary. Books such as Pesiqta deRab Kahana and Pesiqta Rabbati, which after formulation were accepted as part of the canon of Judaism, that is, of "the one whole Torah of Moses our rabbi revealed by God at Sinai," ordinarily do not contain answers to questions of definition. We have no signed authorship for either compilation; we do not even know, on the basis of internal evidence, when either one of them came to closure, let alone the prior stages of formulation and redaction. All that we can know about these books is contained within their contents, respectively. Comparing the one to the other on the basis of internal evidence therefore requires a sustained inquiry into inductive evidence, that alone. Only in that way shall we gain perspective on both writings. If we hope to interpret the two documents in context – whether the context of history or theology or literature – we shall have to begin with the definition of perspective. And that requires the comparison and contrast of one document with the other. If we wish to describe, analyze, and interpret the midrash-compilations, it is through the analysis of internal evidence, sorted out inductively, that we shall accomplish our purpose.

That inductive inquiry begins with the gross traits of formal rhetoric that characterize the largest cogent units of discourse of a document. I have to prove that the document at hand rests upon clearcut choices of formal preference, so it is, from the viewpoint of form and mode of expression, cogent. That explains why, in my view, I have – as in Chapters Seven and Eight of this book – to demonstrate that formal choices prove uniform and paramount. My next step, for both documents under study here, Pesiqta Rabbati, which I introduce, and Pesiqta deRab Kahana, which serves as our control, is to ask whether the framers of the document have preserved a fixed order in arranging types of units of discourse, differentiated in accord with the rhetorical forms I identified. In the analysis of earlier documents, the Talmud of the Land of Israel, the Tosefta, Genesis Rabbah, and Leviticus Rabbah, I demonstrated that fixed preferences did govern. In both documents I am able to show that, in ordering materials, the framers or redactors paid much attention to the formal traits of their units of discourse. They chose materials of one formal type for beginning their sustained exercises of argument or syllogism, then chose another formal type for the end of their sustained exercises of syllogistic exposition. This seems to me to show that the framers or redactors followed a set of rules which we are able to discern. In this way I answer the question, for the documents under study, of whether or not we deal with texts exhibiting traits of composition, deliberation, proportion, and so delivering a message on their own.

The further step taken here is to ask how cogent the several large units of discourse, called *pisqa/pisqaot,* actually are. In Pesiqta deRab Kahana (as in Leviticus Rabbah), I can show, an implicit syllogism finds sustained proof in one component of a *pisqa* after another. Indeed, the power of Pesiqata deRab Kahana lies in its capacity to say one thing in many ways, and the aesthetic force of the rhetorical program of that document lies in the use of the two formal constructions, the intersecting-verse/base-verse form and the exegetical form, in the same profoundly argumentative way. Is that the case in Pesiqta Rabbati? In the earlier of the two Pesiqtas – Pesiqta deRab Kahana demands a date of ca. A.D. 500, while we have no really clear date for Pesiqta Rabbati at all[1] – the sustained interest in the implicit syllogism imposes its shape upon the principal rhetorical forms at hand, which – for that reason – I call the propositional and the exegetical forms. That does not characterize the use of these same forms for Pesiqta Rabbati. In the later of the two Pesiqtas, I do not find a similar cogency at all. Having compared the formal traits of the two documents, I proceed to bring into juxtaposition their respective topical programs and show they intersect only casually. Each document's authorship evidently wishes to make its own points in its own way.

In Part Three of this book, finally, I undertake three comparative studies. These compare, specifically, the plan and program of Pesiqta deRab Kahana and Pesiqta Rabbati, the treatment of Num. 7:1 by Pesiqta Rabbati, Pesiqta deRab Kahana, and Sifre to Numbers, and, finally, the overall principles of rhetoric and logic that characterize Leviticus Rabbah, Pesiqta deRab Kahana, and Pesiqta Rabbati. The nature and purpose of these three rather substantial exercises of

---

[1] It contains an allusion to the year 1220, but some pericopae state the expectation that after Rome falls, which, for the Middle East, came with the Muslim conquest, Israel will succeed to world domination, and therefore bear a date prior to the year 640. Once we dismiss as possibly pseudepigraphic any number of attributions, we lose all bearings for the document at hand. Since it borrows materials from Leviticus Rabbah, it clearly stands next in line after that document. More than that I cannot say – but, for the purposes of the analysis undertaken here, do not have to say.

comparison become clear in context, and the conclusions I draw, already adumbrated here, are spelled out at the end.

Part One

A SAMPLE OF PESIQTA RABBATI:

Pesiqta Rabbati *Pisqaot* 1 through 5 and 15

Chapter One

Pesiqta Rabbati *Pisqa* 1

Concerning the Prophetic Lection for the Sabbath That Coincides with the New Moon

The verse that recurs throughout derives from the prophetic lection that is read in the synagogue when the New Moon coincides with the Sabbath:

> [*For as the new heavens and the new earth which I am making shall endure in my sight, says the Lord, so shall your race and your name endure;*] *and month by month at the new moon, week by week on the Sabbath, all mankind shall come to bow down before me, says the Lord;* [*and they shall come out and see the dead bodies of those who have rebelled against me; their worm shall not die nor their fire be quenched; and they shall be abhorred by all mankind*] (Is. 66:22-24).

I:I

1. A. May our master instruct us:
    B. In the case of an Israelite who said the blessing for food on the New Moon but forgot and did not make mention of the New Moon [in the recitation of the grace after meals], what does one have to do?
    C. Our masters have taught us:
    D If one has forgotten and not made mention of the New Moon, but, once he has completed reciting the Grace after Meals, remembered on the spot, still having in mind the blessing that he has recited, one does not have to go back to the beginning. But he concludes with a brief blessing at the end, which is as follows: "Blessed are you, Lord, our God, king of the world, who has assigned New Moons to Israel, his people. Blessed are you, Lord, who sanctifies both Israel and the New Moons."

2. A. Simeon b. Abba in the name of R. Yohanan said, "And in reference to the New Moon [in the Grace] one has to say, 'And bestow upon us, Lord our God [the blessing of the festival season].'"
    B. Lo, we learn, the New Moons are equivalent to festivals.
    C. For it is said, *On the day of your rejoicing, and on your festivals, and on your new moons* (Num. 10:10).
    D. And are New Moons equivalent even to the Sabbath?
    E. You may state [the proof of that proposition] as follows:
    F. New Moons are equivalent to festivals and the Sabbath. And how do we know that they are, in fact, equivalent to Sabbaths?

G. It is on the basis of what the complementary reading of the prophetic
    writings [for the New Moon that coincides with the Sabbath] states:
    *...and month by month at the new moon, week by week on the Sabbath,
    all mankind shall come to bow down before me* (Is. 66:23). [The New
    Moon is treated as equivalent in importance to the Sabbath.]

The thematic principle of composition is shown by the simple fact that No.
2 has no bearing upon No. 1. The opening unit is autonomous and presents a
simple legal question. The liturgical reply does not include a proof-text of any
kind. No. 2 then pursues its theological question, on the equivalent importance
of the New Moon to the Sabbath. Since no rule of conduct is adduced, the issue
is theoretical. Then proof derives from the base-text at hand.

I:II

1. A. Thus did R. Tanhuma commence discourse [citing a Psalm that express
        sorrow that one cannot go to the Temple on a pilgrim festival]: *[As a
        hind longs for the running streams, so do I long for you, O God.] With
        my whole being I thirst for God, the living God. When shall I come to
        God and appear in his presence? [Day and night, tears are my food;
        "Where is your God?" they ask me all day long. As I pour out my soul
        in distress, I call to mind how I marched in the ranks of the great to the
        house of God, among exultant shouts of praise, the clamor of the
        pilgrims]* (Ps. 42:1-4).
    B. In respect to this inaugural discourse, [what follows] is the materials that
        occur at the beginning of the discussion of the passage, *After the death
        of the two sons of Aaron* (Lev. 16:1ff).

2. A,. Another matter: *With my whole being I thirst for God,*
    B. specifically [I thirst for the time] when you mete out justice upon the
        nations of the world,
    C. in line with the verse, *You shall not curse God* [meaning, judges] (Ex.
        22:27).

3. A,. Another matter: *With my whole being I thirst for God:*
    B. [I thirst for God specifically, for the time] when you will restore that
        divinity which you formed of me at Sinai:
    C. *I said, You are God* (Ps. 82:6).

4. A.. Another matter: *[With my whole being]I thirst for God:*
    B. [I thirst for God specifically, for the time] [Mandelbaum:] when You will
        be cloaked with the power of divinity as You were cloaked in divinity at
        Sinai]. [Following Braude: I thirst for God specifically for the time when
        you cloak me in divinity as you cloaked me in divinity at Sinai.]
    C. Draw near the end-time and make one alone your divinity in your world:
        The Lord will be king over the entire earth (Zech. 14:9).
    D. That is in line with the exegesis of the statement concerning Jacob: *So
        may God give you dew* (Gen. 27:28), [which may be interpreted, May he
        give you the power of divinity and you take it,] when [therefore] he
        accepts the power of divinity. [This sustains Braude's reading.]

5. A. Another matter: *With my whole being I thirst for God:*
   B. who lives and endures for ever and ever.

6. A. Another matter: *With my whole being I thirst for God:*
   B. who watches over our lives, bringing down rain in its season, and calling up due in its time, for the sake of our lives.

7. A. Another matter: *[With my whole being I thirst for God,] the living God.*
   B. The living God, who lives and endures by his word.
   C. Said R. Phineas the priest, son of Hama, "Even though those who carried the promises among the prophets have died, God, who made the promises, lives and endures."

8. A. *With my whole being I thirst for God, the living God. When shall I come to God and appear in his presence?*
   B. Said Israel to him, "Lord of the world, When will you restore to us the glory that we should go up [to the Temple] on the three pilgrim festivals and see the face of the Presence of God?"
   C. Said R. Isaac, "Just as they came to see, so they came to be seen, for it is said, *'When shall I come to God and appear in his presence?'"*

9. A. **Said R. Joshua b. Levi, "Why did they call it 'the Rejoicing of the Place of the Water Drawing'? Because from there they drink of the Holy Spirit" [Gen. R. LXX:VIII.3.E].**

10. A. They said, "When will you restore us to that glory!
    B. "Lo, how much time has passed since the house of our life [the Temple] was destroyed! Lo, a septennate, lo, a jubilee, lo, seven hundred seventy-seven years [have gone by], and now it is one thousand one hundred and fifty one years [since then]. [Braude, p. 39, n. 19: "The first year referred to is 847, the next, 1221. Both dates I regard as copyists' glosses. Neither date is mentioned in Parma MS, which lacks Section 2 of this Piska."]

11. A. *When shall I come to God and appear in his presence?*
    B. He said to them, "My children, in this age how many times a year did you go up for the pilgrim festivals [in each year]? Was it not merely three times a year? But when the end will come, I shall build it, and you will come up not merely three times a year, but every single month [at the new moon], and every Sabbath you will come up."
    C. That is in line with this verse: *and month by month at the new moon, week by week on the Sabbath, all mankind shall come to bow down before me, says the Lord* (Is. 66:22-24). [That is to say, not only on the festivals but on the New Moon and the Sabbath people will bow down before God, just as, at Nos. 8-9, we have said people do on the pilgrim festivals.]

No. 1 is not articulated, but the important contribution is not to be missed. The intersecting-verse, which will be fully expounded before being drawn into contact with the base-verse, is introduced. The relevance of the intersecting-verse cannot be missed. It speaks of the yearning to go to the Temple on a pilgrim festival, and at the end the promise is made that, when the end comes, Israel will go to the Temple not only for pilgrim festivals, but also for the New Moon and the Sabbath. That eschatological reading of the New Moon, in particular, then is fully articlated in the exposition of the intersecting-verse. Nos. 2, 3, 4 speak of the I, Israel, yearning to gain that union with divinity that it once enjoyed. No. 5, 6 then speak of God, and No. 7 underlines the continuing validity of the promises made to Israel by the prophets. The prophets are no more, but God will keep the promises announced through them. This leads us directly to Nos. 8, 10-11, which come to the point of the compositor of the whole. Specifically, the New Moon will enter the status of a pilgrim festival – and that fundamental proposition certainly has the support of the intersecting-verse as we have already expounded it. So the whole forms a cogent and stunning statement. Only No. 9 is borrowed, verbatim.

I:III

1. A. Another interpretation of the verse ...*and month by month at the new moon, week by week on the Sabbath, all mankind shall come to bow down before me, says the Lord* (Is. 66:22-24):
   B. How is it possible that all mankind will be able to come to Jerusalem every month and every Sabbath?
   C. Said R. Levi, "Jerusalem is going to become equivalent to the Land of Israel, and the Land of Israel equivalent to the entire world."
   D. And how will people come every New Month and Sabbath from the end of the world?
   E. Clouds will come and carry them and bring them to Jerusalem, where they will say their morning prayers.
   D. That is in line with what the prophet says in praise: *Who are those, who fly like a cloud* (Is. 60:8).

2. A. Another interpretation of the verse ...*and month by month at the new moon, week by week on the Sabbath, all mankind shall come to bow down before me, says the Lord* (Is. 66:22-24):
   B. Now lo if the New Moon coincided with the Sabbath, and Scripture has said, Another interpretation of the verse ...*and month by month at the new moon, week by week on the Sabbath,* how [is it possible to do so once on the New Moon and once on the Sabbath, for on the occasion on which the two coincide, they can do it only once, not twice]?
   C. Said R. Phineas, the priest, son of Hama, in the name of R. Reuben, "They will come twice, once for the purposes of the Sabbath, the other time for the purposes of the New Moon. The clouds will carry them early in the morning and bring them to Jerusalem, where they will recite the morning-prayer, and they will then bring them home.
   D. *"Who are those, who fly like a cloud* (Is. 60:8) refers to the trip in the morning.

E. *"And as the doves to the dovecote* (Is. 60:8) refers to the trip in the evening."

3. A. What the verse says is not *Israel,* but rather *all mankind [shall come to bow down before me, says the Lord]* (Is. 66:22-24).

    B. Said R. Phineas, "What is the meaning of *all mankind* [Hebrew: *all flesh* , BSR]?

    C. "Whoever has restrained [BSR] his desire in this age will have the merit of seeing the face of the Presence of God.

    D. "For it is written, *He who closes his eyes from gazing upon evil* (Is. 33:15).

    E. "And what follows? *The king in his beauty will your eyes behold* (Is. 33:17)."

4. A. Another interpretation of the verse *all mankind [shall come to bow down before me, says the Lord]* (Is. 66:22-24):

    B. Does this apply to all the idolators?

    C. Rather, only those who did not subjugate Israel will the Messiah accept.

We proceed to the clause by clause exposition of our base-verse, asking questions that point toward the eschatological theme the compositor wishes to underline. The first question, No. 1, is a practical one. But, we see, the proof-text, Is. 60:8, is then drawn in for further service at No. 2. No. 3 proceeds to the issue of all flesh/mankind, of the base-verse, and No. 4 pursues that same matter – in all, a cogent and well composed discourse.

I:IV.

1. A. On account of what merit will Israel enjoy all of this glory?

    B. It is on account of the merit of dwelling in the Land of Israel.

    C. For the Israelites lived in distress among the nations in this world.

    D. And so you find concerning the patriarchs of the world without end: concerning what did they go to much trouble? Concerning burial in the Land of Israel.

2. A. Said R. Hanina, "All references to shekels that are made in the Torah are to *selas,* in the Prophets are to *litras,* in the Writings are to *centenarii.*"

    B. R. Abba bar Yudan in the name of R. Judah bar Simon: "Except for the shekels that Abraham weighed out for Ephron for the burial ground that he purchased from him, which were centenarii [(Mandelbaum:) the word shekel has the same numerical value as *centenarii*]: *The piece of land cost four hundred silver shekels* (Gen,. 23:15).

    C. "Now take note that he paid for hundred silver centenarii for a burial plot.

    D. "So in the case of Jacob, all the gold that he had ever acquired and all the money that he had been given he handed over to Esau in exchange for his right of burial, so that he should not be buried in it.

    E. "For it is said, *[Joseph spoke to the household of Pharaoh saying, If now I have found favor in your eyes, speak, I pray you, in the ears of Pharaoh, saying, My father made me swearing, saying, I am about to*

die,] in my tomb which I hewed out for myself in the land of Canaan,
there shall you bury me (Gen. 50:4-5).

F. "And so you find that, when he was departing this earth, he imposed on
    Joseph an oath, saying to him, Do not, I pray you, bury me in Egypt
    (Gen. 47:29)."

G. Why so?

H. R. Hanina says, "There is a sound reason."

I. R. Yose says, ""There is a sound reason."

J. Said R. Simeon b. Laqish in the name of R. Eleazar Haqqappar, "It is
    because the dead [of the Land of Israel] will live in the time of the
    Messiah, as David has said, *I shall go before the Lord in the land of the*
    living (Ps. 116:9).

K. "Now [can his meaning be that people do not die there, and] is it really
    the case that in the Land of Israel people live [and do not die]? But do
    people not die there? And is it not the case that outside of the Land of
    Israel is the land where people live?

L. "But as to the Land of Israel, the corpses are commonly found there, and
    when David said, *In the land of the living* , he meant that the dead there
    will live in the days of the Messiah."

The connection to the foregoing is rather tenuous. The compositor simply
introduces the systematic discussion of the value of living in the land by
referring obliquely to what has gone before at 1.A-2, and then proceeding to
collect materials on the importance to the patriarchs and to David and the
Messiah of living in the land. No. 2 is an autonomous entry, parachuted in for
good reasons, and these are spelled out. The dead buried in the Land will live
again. Discourse continues in **I:V**, as we now see.

I:V

1. A. R. Yose asked R. Simeon b. Laqish, "Even will such as Jeroboam son of
            Nabat rise [from the grave when the Messiah comes]?"

        B. He said to him, "Brimstone and salt [will be his fate]."

        C. R. Helbo asked R. Ammi, "Even will such as Jeroboam son of Nabat rise
            [from the grave when the Messiah comes]?"

        D. He said to him, "I asked R. Simeon b. Laqish, and he said to me,
            'Brimstone and salt [will be his fate].'"

        E. R. Berekhiah asked R. Helbo, "Even will such as Jeroboam son of Nabat
            rise [from the grave when the Messiah comes]?"

        F. He said to him, "I asked R. Ammi, and he said to me, 'I asked R. Simeon
            b. Laqish, and he said to me, "Brimstone and salt [will be his fate]."'"

        G. Said R. Berekhiah, "Should we wish to state the mystery, what is the
            sense of his reply to him, 'Brimstone'?

        H. "Is it not the case that the Holy One, blessed be He, is going to exact
            punishment of the wicked in Gehenna only with brimstone and salt! But
            the Temple has been destroyed [with brimstone and salt, which therefore
            have already been inflicted on those buried in the land, inclusive of
            Jeroboam, who, having received his punishment, along with the others,
            therefore will rise from the dead]."

2.   A.   Said R. Judah b. R. Ilai, "For seven years the Land of Israel was burning
          with brimstone and fire, in line with this verse: *The whole land thereof
          is brimstone and salt and a burning* (Deut. 29:22).

3.   A.   Said R. Yose b. Halafta, "For fifty-two years after the destruction of the
          Temple, no one passed through the Land of Israel,
     B.   "in line with this verse, *For the mountains will I take a weeping and a
          wailing...because they are burned up, so that none passes through..both
          the fowl of the heavens and the beast are fled and gone* (Jer. 9:9).
     C.   "Why is this the case?   Because it was burning with the fire that had
          been poured out on it in line with this verse, *From on high has he sent
          fire into my bones* (Lam. 1:13)."

4.   A.   Why was this [done] by God?   It was to exact punishment from Jeroboam
          son of Nabat and his fellows through those seven years during which the
          Land of Israel was burning with fire.
     B.   It follows that even Jeroboam ben Nabat and his fellows will live in the
          time of the Messiah.
     C.   And what was it that saved them from the judgment of Gehenna and to
          live [in the resurrection of the dead]?
     D.   It was the fact that they were buried in the Land of Israel, as it is said,
          His land will make expiation for his people (Dt. 32:43).

The foregoing is concluded here, a distinct essay on Jeroboam, which makes
the point introduced in **I:V** that there is distinct merit in living in the Land of
Israel. Nos. 2, 3 are separates that have been inserted because they contain facts
important for the unfolding argument. No. 4 carries forward the matter begun at
No. 1 and underlines the main point.

I:VI

1.   A.   Said R. Huna the priest, son of Abin, in the name of R. Abba b. Yamina,
          "R. Helbo and R. Hama bar Hanina [differed].
     B.   "R. Helbo said, 'He who dies overseas and is buried overseas is subject to
          distress on two counts, distress because of death, distress because of
          burial.
     C.   "'Why?   For it is written in connection with Pashhur, *And you, Pashhur,
          and all those who well in your house shall go into captivity, and you
          shall to Babylonia and there you shall die and there you shall be buried*
          (Jer. 20:6).'
     D.   "And R. Hama bar Hanina said, 'He who dies overseas, if he comes from
          overseas and is buried in the land, is subject to distress only by reason
          of death alone.'"
     E.   Then how does R. Hama bar Hanina interpret the verse, *...here you shall
          die and there you shall be buried* (Jer. 20:6)?
     G.   Burial in the Land of Israel achieves atonement for him.

2.   A.   R. Beroqia and R. Eleazar b. Pedat were walking in a grove [Braude, p.
          45], and biers came from abroad.   Said R. Beroqia to R. Eleazar, "What

good have these accomplished? When they were alive, they abandoned [the Land] and now in death they have come back!"

B. Said R. Eleazar b. Pedat to him, "No, that is not the case. Since they are buried in the Land of Israel, and a clump of earth of the Land of Israel is given over to them, it effects atonement for them,

C. "as it is said, *And his land shall make expiation for his people* (Deut. 32:43)."

3. A. If that is the case, then have the righteous who are overseas lost out?

B. No. Why not?

C. Said R. Eleazar in the name of R. Simai, "God makes for them tunnels in the earth, and they roll like skins and come to the Land of Israel.

D. "And when they have come to the Land of Israel, God restores their breath to them.

E. "For it is said, *He who gives breath to the people upon it and spirit to them that go through it* (Is. 42:5)."

F. "And there is, furthermore, an explicit verse of Scripture in Ezekiel that makes that point: *You shall know that I am the Lord when I open your graves and bring you to the Land of Israel* (Ez. 37:13).

G. "Then: *I shall put my spirit in you and you shall live* (Ex. 37:14)."

4. A. Thus you have learned that [1] those who die in the Land of Israel live in the days of the Messiah, and [2] the righteous who die overseas come to it and live in it.

B. If that is the case, then will the gentiles who are buried in the Land also live?

C. No, Isaiah has said, *The neighbor shall not say, I too have suffered pain. The people who dwell therein shall be forgiven their sin* (Is. 33:24).

D. The sense is, "My evil neighbors are not going to say, "We have been mixed up [with Israel and will share their fate, so] we too shall live with them."

E. But that one that was the people dwelling therein [is the one that will live,[and what is that people? It is the people that has been forgiven its sin, namely, those concerning whom it is said, *Who is God like you, who forgives sin and passes over transgression for the remnant of his inheritance* (Mic. 7:18) [which can only be Israel].

The established topic continues its course; the compositor has introduced further materials on the theme of living and dying in the Land of Israel. The discourse seems continuous; there is no interest in the base-text and no intersecting-text appears. It is a sustained essay on a topic.

I:VII

1. A. How long are the days of the Messiah?

B. R. Aqiba says, "Forty years, in line with this verse: *And he afflicted you and allowed you to hunger* (Deut. 8:3), and it is written, *Make us glad according to the days in which you afflicted us* (Ps. 90:15). Just as the affliction lasted forty years in the wilderness, so the affliction here is forty years [with the result that the glad time is the same forty years]."

C. Said R. Abin, "What verse of Scripture further supports the position of R. Aqiba? *As in the days of your coming forth from the land of Egypt I will show him marvelous things* (Mic. 7:15)."

D. R. Eliezer says, "Four hundred years, as it is written, *And they shall enslave them and torment them for four hundred years* (Gen. 15:13), and further it is written, *Make us glad according to the days in which you afflicted us* (Ps. 90:15)."

E. R. Berekhiah in the name of R. Dosa the Elder says, "Six hundred years, as it is written, *As the days of a tree shall be the days of my people* (Is. 65:22).

F. "How long are the days of a tree? A sycamore lasts for six hundred years."

G. R. Eliezer b. R. Yose the Galilean says, "A thousand years, as it is written, *For a thousand years in your sight as are but as yesterday when it has passed* (Ps. 90:40), and it is written, *The day of vengeance as in my heart but now my year of redemption is come* (Is. 63:4).

H. "The day of the Holy One, blessed be He, is the same as a thousand years for a mortal."

I. R. Joshua says, "Two thousand years, *according to the days in which you afflicted us* (Ps. 90:15).

J. "For there are no fewer *days* [as in the cited verse] than two, and the day of the Holy One, blessed be He, is the same as a thousand years for a mortal."

K. R. Abbahu says, "Seven thousand years, as it is said, As a bride groom rejoices over his bride will your God rejoice over you (Is. 62:5), and how long does a groom rejoice over his bride? It is seven days,

L. "and the day of the Holy One, blessed be He, is the same as a thousand years for a mortal."

M. Rabbi says, "You cannot count it: *For the day of vengeance that was in my heart and my year of redemption have come* (Is. 63:4)."

N. How long are the days of the Messiah? Three hundred and sixty-five thousand years will be the length of the days of the Messiah.

2. A. Then the dead of the Land of Israel who are Israelites will live and derive benefit from them, and all the righteous who are overseas will come through tunnels.

B. And when they reach the land, the Holy One, blessed be He, will restore their breath, and they will rise and derive benefit from the days of the Messiah along with them [already in the land].

C. For it is said, *He who spread forth the the earth and its offspring gives breath to the people on it* (Is. 42:5).

3. A. When will the royal Messiah come?

B. Said R. Eleazar, "Near to the Messiah's days, ten places will be swallowed up, ten places will be overturned, ten places will be wiped out."

C. And R. Hiyya bar Abba said, "The royal Messiah will come only to a generation the leaders of which are like dogs."

D. R. Eleazar says, "It will be in the time of a generation that is worthy of annihilation that the royal Messiah will come."

E. R. Levi said, "Near the time of the days of the Messiah a great event will
take place in the world."

The final issue in the messianic essay concerns the time that the days of the
Messiah will last. (Braude's translation, p. 46, "How long to the days of the
Messiah," is certainly wrong, as the discussion that follows in No. 3, which
does raise that question, indicates.) The several theories, along with their proof-
texts, are laid out in a clear way. No. 2 then reviews familiar ideas. No. 3 then
goes over another aspect of the matter. None of this composite has been made
up for the purposes of our document.

Chapter Two

Pesiqta Rabbati *Pisqa* 2

Concerning Hanukkah

The verse that recurs throughout derives from a Psalm that refers to the dedication of the Temple and is therefore associated with Hanukkah as the festival commemorating the rededication of the Temple in Maccabean times:

> A Psalm. A song at the dedication of the house of David. *[I will exalt you, O Lord, you have lifted me up and have not let my enemies make merry over me. O Lord, my God, I cried to you and you healed me. O Lord, You brought me up from Sheol and saved my life as I was sinking into the abyss. Sing a psalm to the Lord, all you his loyal servants, and give thanks to his holy name]* (Ps. 30:1-4).

II:I

1. A. May our master instruct us:
   B. As to the lamp kindled in celebration of Hanukkah, at what time does the religious duty pertaining to it [specifically, to light it] apply?
   C. Our rabbis have taught: From the time that the sun sets until most of the shoppers have left the market place.
   D. And where do they light it?
   E. If one was living in an upper story with a window facing the public way, one lights [the lamp there]. But in a time of danger, one lights it within one's house.

2. A. And it is forbidden to perform an act of labor by its light.
   B. R. Assi said, "It is forbidden [even] to use its light for illumination."

3. A. And why does one light lamps on Hanukkah?
   B. When the sons of the Hasmonean, the high priest, conquered the Greek kingdom, as it is said, *When I raised up your sons, O Zion, against your sons, O Ionia [Greece]* (Zech. 9:13), they came into the house of the sanctuary. There they found eight iron rods, which they hollowed out and in which they kindled lights.
   C. And why do people recite the Hallel-Psalms [113-118]?
   D. Because it is written in them, *The Lord is God and has given us light* (Ps. 118:27).
   E. Then why not read them on Purim?

F.   Because it is written [that the Jews gained the power] *to destroy, slay, annihilate all the forces of the people and the province that would assault them* (Est. 8:11).

G.   But Hallel is recited only for the fall of a monarchy, while the monarch of Ahasuerus endured.   On that account the Hallel is not recited [for Purim].

H.   But as to the Greek kingdom, which the Holy One, blessed be He, wiped out, they began to sing hymns and praises, saying, "In the past we were slaves of Pharaoh, slaves of Greece, but now we are the slaves of the Holy One, blessed be He: *Give praise, slaves of the Lord* (Ps. 113:1)."

The legal issue covers the kindling of the Hanukkah lamp, No. 1, use of its light, No. 2, a brief allusion to the reason for the celebration and the liturgy thereof, No. 3. There is, of course, no pretense that the base-verse is subjected to exegesis. The principle of composition is thematic; no particular point is at issue.

II:II

1.   A.   How many Hanukkahs [occasions for rededication through the kindling of lights] are there?

B.   There are seven:

C.   The dedication of heaven and earth, as it is said, *And the heaven and the earth were completed* (Gen. 2:1).   And what dedication [through the kindling of lights] took place? *God placed them in the firmament of the heaven to give light* (Gen. 1:18).

D.   The dedication of the wall: *At the dedication of the wall [of Jerusalem...they sought the Levites ....to bring them to Jerusalem, to obvserve the dedication with joy]* (Neh. 12:27).

E.   The dedication of those who had returned from exile: *The children of Israel...and the children of the exile...offered at the dedication of this house of our God* (Ez. 6:17).

F.   The dedication of the priests, for which we kindle the lamps [under discussion here].

G.   And the dedication of the world to come: *When I free Jerusalem, it will be with lamps* (Zeph. 1:12).

H.   And the dedication of the princes: *This was the dedication[-offering] of the altar...from the princes of Israel* (Num. 7:84).

I.   And the dedication of the sanctuary [the first Temple, by David], the Psalm of which is recited in the present regard: *A Psalm.   A song at the dedication of the house of David* (Ps. 30:1-4).

The climax brings us to the Psalm read for Hanukkah as well as for the stated occasion of the first Temple.   There is no intersecting-verse, and no proposition is argued through the assembly of the facts.   What we have accomplished, however, is important.   We have now placed into its larger context of creation and consecration the Hanukkah celebrated for the Hasmoneans' rededication of the Temple.   That makes a point entirely on its own.   Only the first item points to the kindling of lights, because it is not self-evident; the others take the same for granted. I follow Braude's translation of the Zeph. 1:12.

II:III

1. A. [In connection with the verse, *A Psalm. A song at the dedication of the house of David. I will exalt you, O Lord, you have lifted me up and have not let my enemies make merry over me. O Lord, my God, I cried to you and you healed me. O Lord, You brought me up from Sheol and saved my life as I was sinking into the abyss. Sing a psalm to the Lord, all you his loyal servants, and give thanks to his holy name* (Ps. 30:1-4)], thus did R. Tanhuma bar R. Abba commence discourse: "*Holy men exult in glory, they sing for joy on their beds* (Ps. 149:5).

   B. "In what glory will they exult? It is in the glory that the Holy One, blessed be He, does with the righteous when they take their leave of the world.

   C. "Under ordinary circumstances when someone dies, if he has children, his children attend to him. But with the righteous that is not how it is."

   D. Rather, said R. Isaac, "The Holy One, blessed be He, attends to the righteous. How do we know it? *Your Righteous One [God] will go before you* (Is. 58:8). This refers to the Righteous One of the World, as it is said, *The glory of the Lord will gather you* (Is. 58:9)."

2. A. Said R. Hiyya the Elder, "[When a righteous man takes his leave of the world,] three bands of angels take care of him.

   B. "One says, *Let him come in peace* (Is. 57:2).

   C. "One says, *Let him rest on his bier* (Is. 57:2).

   D. "One walks before him in silence, as it is said, *...walking before him* (Is. 57:2)."

3. A. Said R. Judah bar Simon in the name of R. Josiah, "The Holy One, blessed be He, as it were, says to him, 'Let him come in peace [whole and in one piece] from the wicked.'

   B. "You derive the fact that the Holy One, blessed be He, says to the wicked, 'You [wicked] will have no peace,' from the verse, *There is no peace, says my God to the wicked* (Is. 57:21).

   C. "Now if with his own mouth the Holy One, blessed be He, says to the wicked, 'You will have no peace,' all the more so that to the righteous he will say, 'Let him come in peace.'"

4. A. On that account it is said, *"Holy men exult in glory, they sing for joy on their beds* (Ps. 149:5).

   B. "In what glory will they exult? It is in the glory that the Holy One, blessed be He, does with the righteous when they take their leave of the world."

At this point we have no reason to introduce our base-verse, Ps. 30:1-4, since the entire exposition pertains solely to Ps. 149:5. The point then is well worked out, with the original proposition proposed at No. 1, then secondary illustrations of the same matter at Nos. 2, 3, with a restatement at No. 4. The proof derives from Is. 57:21, as given at No 3.

II:IV

1. A. A further comment on the verse, *Holy men exult in glory, they sing for joy on their beds* (Ps. 149:5):
   B. It is because there [*bed* being understood as bier, we refer to the deceased righteous men] they give praise to the Holy One, blessed be He.

2. A. Said R. Hama bar Yose, "The difference between the living and the deceased righteous is only the power of speech [which the deceased lack].
   B. "For there they give praise to the Holy One, blessed be He, for there their souls are bound up with the living.
   C. "As it is written, *The soul of my lord shall be bound up in the bundle of the living* (1 Sam. 25:29).
   D. "Thus it is written, *they sing for joy on their beds* (Ps. 149:5), and the word for sing for joy refers only to giving praise, as it is written, *The voice of rejoicing and salvation in the tents of the righteous* (Ps. 118:15)."

3. A. A further comment on the verse, *Holy men exult in glory, they sing for joy on their beds* (Ps. 149:5):
   B. [As to the phrase, *they sing for joy on their beds*] said R. Yohanan, "When a sage is in session and expounding, saying, 'This is what R. Aqiba said,' 'This is what R. Simeon b. Yohai said,' their lips stir then, in line with this verse: *gently moving the lips of those that are asleep* (Song 7:10), and, accordingly, *they sing for joy on their beds*."

4. A. Therefore David said, *I shall dwell in your tent forever* (Ps. 61:5).
   B. Now is it possible to think that David imagined that he would live forever? But what is the meaning of this statement, which he made: *I shall dwell in your tent forever* (Ps. 61:5)?
   C. He said, "May it be your will that people should make statements in my name forever in the synagogues and study houses."
   D. Said to him the Holy One, blessed be He, "By your life, even though you have died, your name will never budge from my house forever.
   E. "But in connection with every single offering that they shall make, they will make mention of your name and say your psalms, e.g., *A Psalm of David*.
   F. "And not only so, but since you have given thought to building the house of the sanctuary, even though your son, Solomon, is the one who will build it, I shall inscribe it in your name: *A Psalm. A song at the dedication of the house of David. [I will exalt you, O Lord, you have lifted me up and have not let my enemies make merry over me. O Lord, my God, I cried to you and you healed me. O Lord, You brought me up from Sheol and saved my life as I was sinking into the abyss. Sing a psalm to the Lord, all you his loyal servants, and give thanks to his holy name]* (Ps. 30:1-4)."

Even though Solomon built the Temple, it is credited to David, so states our base-verse, and that is the direction of the entire composition. So the main point, which was neatly inaugurated, is that when deceased, the righteous endure and give praise to God. The examples that end with David are entirely in order. II:IV thus continues II:III unbroken. Nos. 1, 2 therefore work out familiar materials. No. 3 prepares the way for No. 4, though it is, of course, entirely autonomous. Then No. 4 provides the climax and conclusion of the whole – a cogent and powerful statement indeed.

II:V

1. A. Another comment on the verse: *A Psalm. A song at the dedication of the house of David. [I will exalt you, O Lord, you have lifted me up and have not let my enemies make merry over me. O Lord, my God, I cried to you and you healed me. O Lord, You brought me up from Sheol and saved my life as I was sinking into the abyss. Sing a psalm to the Lord, all you his loyal servants, and give thanks to his holy name]* (Ps. 30:1-4):

   B. One verse of Scripture states, *Will you build a house for me* (2 Sam. 7:5) [the implied answer being affirmative], and another verse of Scripture states, *You will not build a house for me* (1 Chr. 17:4).

   C. Now what is the meaning of this? How shall I interpret both verses of Scripture?

   D. The sense of this verse, *You will not build a house for me* (1 Chr. 17:4) is that you are not the one who is going to build it, and the sense of the verse, *Will you build a house for me* (2 Sam. 7:5) is that your son is the one who is going to build it.

2. A. "You gave precedence to the honor owing to yourself over the honor owing to me, for it was only after your saw yourself dwelling in a house made of cedar that you wanted to build the house of the sanctuary,

   B. "while your son, Solomon, gave precedence to the honor owing to me over the honor owing to himself,

   C. "as it is said, *In the eleventh year the house of God was finished* (1 Kgs. 6:37), and afterward *Solomon built his house* (1 Kgs. 7:1)."

3. A. Another explanation [of the fact that one verse of Scripture states, *Will you build a house for me* (2 Sam. 7:5) [the implied answer being affirmative], and another verse of Scripture states, *You will not build a house for me* (1 Chr. 17:4)]:

   B. *Will you build a house for me* (2 Sam. 7:5) means that you will be the one to lay the foundations.

   C. *You will not build a house for me* (1 Chr. 17:4) means that you will not be the one to finish it off.

4. A. Another explanation [of the fact that one verse of Scripture states, *Will you build a house for me* (2 Sam. 7:5) [the implied answer being affirmative], and another verse of Scripture states, *You will not build a house for me* (1 Chr. 17:4)]:

B.   *You will not build a house for me* (1 Chr. 17:4) means that you will in fact not build it.

C.   *Will you build a house for me* (2 Sam. 7:5) means that it will nonetheless bear your name.

D.   For if it were not for you, the fire would not have come down.

E.   How so?

F.   For once the Temple had been built, how many prayers did [Solomon] set forth, but the fire did not come down.

G.   Said R. Helbo in the name of the house of R. Shila, "He went and brought his father, David's bier. He said to him, 'Lord of the ages, if I do not posit sufficient merit by reason of my deeds, do it on account of the acts of loyalty of my father, David.'

H.   "Forthwith the fire came down.

I.   "That is in line with this verse of Scripture: *O Lord God, do not turn away the face of your anointed, remember the acts of loyalty of David your servant* (2 Chr. 6:42).

J.   "And then: *Now when Solomon had finished praying, the fire came down from heaven...and the glory of the Lord filled the house* (2 Chr. 7:1)."

5.   A.   Now if you do not derive from the present passage proof that Solomon brought the bier of David from his grave,

     B.   said R. Berekhiah in the name of R. Helbo in the name of the huse of R. Shila, "There is an explicit verse of Scripture that makes the point:

     C.   "...*I will exalt you, O Lord, you have lifted me up...O Lord, You brought me up from Sheol and saved my life as I was sinking into the abyss* (Ps. 30:2, 4)."

6.   A.   Therefore said Solomon, "Since it is because of the merit of my father, David, that the Holy One, blessed be He, has acted, lo, I shall recite the Psalm for the dedication of the house in his name:

     B.   "*A Psalm. A song at the dedication of the house of David. [I will exalt you, O Lord, you have lifted me up and have not let my enemies make merry over me. O Lord, my God, I cried to you and you healed me. O Lord, You brought my up from Sheol and saved my life as I was sinking into the abyss. Sing a psalm to the Lord, all you his loyal servants, and give thanks to his holy name]* (Ps. 30:1-4).

As we move on to the base-verse, we focus upon the language that has the house of the sanctuary belong to David, that is, not a *Psalm...of David*, but *the house of David*. This then yields the question of 1.B, in which two verses seem to contradict one another, the one assigning the house to David, the other saying David cannot build it. Diverse, completed materials are then assembled to make the point that it was on account of the merit of David that the house of the sanctuary was dedicated properly. No. 1 lays the matter out in general terms. Then No. 2 gives one explanation, No. 3 underlines the question, and No. 4 resolves the matter. No. 5 is appended to No. 4 as a restatement of the same proposition, and No. 6 concludes with an explicit statement concerning the sense of our base-verse.

II:VI

1. A. Another comment on the verse: *A Psalm. A song at the dedication of the house of David. [I will exalt you, O Lord, you have lifted me up and have not let my enemies make merry over me. O Lord, my God, I cried to you and you healed me. O Lord, You brought me up from Sheol and saved my life as I was sinking into the abyss. Sing a psalm to the Lord, all you his loyal servants, and give thanks to his holy name]* (Ps. 30:1-4):

   B. Come and take note of the fact that, while Solomon built the house, it was called in David's name.

   C. David was worthy of building it, but because of a single matter [which will be specified], he did not build it.

   D. And even though he gave thought to building it, Nathan the prophet came and said to him, "You will not build a house for me."

   E. "Why not?"

   F. *For you have spilled a great deal of blood on the ground before me* (1 Chr. 22:8).

   G. When David heard this, he was afraid, saying, "Lo, I have been made unfit to build the house of the sanctuary."

2. A. Said R. Judah b. R. Ilai, "Said to him the Holy One, blessed be He, 'David, do not be afraid. By your life, they [the gentile nations whom you slaughtered] in my view are like a gazelle or a hart [which one may slaughter]. Therefore it is said, *you have spilled a great deal of blood on the ground.*

   B. "For the reference to the ground alludes specifically to the requirement to bury in the ground the blood of the gazelle or hart, as it is said, *The unclean or the clean may eat of the gazelle and of the hart. Only you shall not eat the blood; you shall pour it out upon the earth like water* (Deut. 12:15,16)."

3. A. Another matter: said the Holy One, blessed be He, to him, "By your life, all the blood which you spilled was in my view in the status of an offering."

   B. For so it is written, *For you have spilled a great deal of blood on the ground before me* (1 Chr. 22:8).

   C. Said R. Simeon b. Yohai, "The words, *before me,* refer only to offerings, as it is said, *And he will slaughter the offspring of the herd before the Lord* (Lev. 1:5)."

4. A. Said David to him, "If so, why shall I not build it?"

   B. Said to him the Holy One, blessed be He, "If you build it, it will stand and never be destroyed."

   C. He said to him, "Well and good."

   D. Said to him the Holy One, blessed be He, "It is clearly foreseen before me that [the Israelites[are going to sin, and I shall pour out my wrath against it and destroy it [instead of them], but the Israelites will be saved."

   E. For so it is written, *Upon the tent of the daughter of Zion he has poured out his wrath like fire* (Oam. 2:4).

F. Said to him the Holy One, blessed be He, "Since you have given thought to build it, even though your son, Solomon, actually builds it, it is in your name that I shall inscribe it: *A Psalm. A song at the dedication of the house of David.* (Ps. 30:1)."

The exposition of the opening clause of the base-verse makes the same point as before. No. 1 announces the problem, and the set-piece materials of Nos. 2, 3, provide ample proof. Then No. 4 explains why David did not build the Temple, invoking considerations that are remarkably fresh. The destruction of the Temple itself now is adduced in evidence of the eternity of Israel.

II:VII

1. A. Another comment on the verse: *A Psalm. A song at the dedication of the house of David* (Ps. 30:1):
   B. There were acts of dedication [=II:II]:
   C. The dedication of heaven and earth, as it is written, *And the heaven and the earth were completed* (Gen. 2:1).
   D. The language, *were completed* , refers only to dedication, as it is written, *And all of the work was finished* (Ex. 39:32).
   E. The dedication of Moses, as it is written, *And it came to pass on the day on which Moses finished setting up...* (Num. 7:1) [and the same usage, finished, indicates that it was another occasion for dedication].
   F. The dedication of the house [of the first Temple], as it is written, *A Psalm. A song at the dedication of the house of David* (Ps. 30:1).
   G. And the dedication of the second house [of the Temple], as it is said, *The children of Israel...and the children of the exile...offered at the dedication of this house of our God* (Ez. 6:17).
   H. And the dedication of the wall, as it is said, *At the dedication of the wall of Jerusalem...[they sought the Levites ....to bring them to Jerusalem, to obvserve the dedication with joy]* (Neh. 12:27).
   I. And the one of the present occasion, that is, the dedication of the house of the Hasmoneans.
   J. And the dedication of the world to come, for on that occasion, also, there is the kindling of lights,
   K. as it is written, *Then the light of the moon shall be as the light of the sun, and the light of the sun shall be sevenfold* (Is. 30:26).

The reworking of familiar materials allows us to conclude with a reference to the world to come, so placing the dedication of the Hasmonean house of the sanctuary in its eschatological position.

Chapter Three

Pesiqta Rabbati *Pisqa* 3

Concerning the Eighth Day of Hanukkah

The verse that recurs throughout is associated with Hanukkah because of the reference to the dedication of the tabernacle, and is identified in particular with the eighth day, for obvious reasons:

> On the eighth day the chief of the Manassites, *[Gamaliel son of Pedahzur, came. His offering was one silver dish weighing a hundred and thirty shekels by the sacred standard and one silver tossing-bowl weighing seventy, both full of flour mixed with oil as a grain-offering; one saucer weighing ten gold shekels, full of incense; one young bull, one full-grown ram, and one yearling ram, as a whole-offering; one he-goat as a sin-offering; and two bulls, five full-grown rams, five he-goats, and five yearling rams, as a shared-offering. This was the offering of Gamaliel son of Pedahzur]* (Num. 7:54-59).

III:I

1. A. May our master instruct us:
   B. As to the Hanukkah lamp. oil of which was left over, what does one have to do with it?
   C. We have learned: in the case of a Hanukkah lamp, oil of which was left over on the firest day, one adds oil and kindles it on the second; if oil was left over on the second, one adds oil and kindles it on the third, and so through the rest of the days.
   D. But if oil was left over on the eighth day, one makes a bonfire and burns it up by itself.
   E. Why is that the rule? Because that oil has been designated for performing a particular religious duty, it is prohibited to make use of it [for any other purpose].

2. A. One should not say, "I shall not carry out the religious duty as decreed by the elders since what they say does not derive from the Torah."
   B. Said to him the Holy One, blessed be He, "No, my son. Whatever they decree upon you, carry out, as it is said, *In accord with the Torah which they shall teach you* (Deut. 17:11).
   C. "Even for me they issue decrees: *Whenever you decree something, he shall obey you* (Job 22:28)."

3. A. You may know that that is so for Jacob, for what does Scripture say in that regard?

    B. When he was blessing Ephraim and Manasseh, *He set Ephraim before Manasseh* (Gen. 48:20), so treating the younger as prior to the elder, and his decree was indeed carried out.

    C. When was that the case? In the offerings [of the princes] the tribe of Ephraim brought its offering first, as it is said, *On the seventh day the prince of the children of Ephraim* (Num. 7:48), then *on the eighth day the prince of the children of Manasseh* (Num. 7:54).

The connection to our base-verse is reached only in a circuitous path. First we go over the legal question, No. 1, and then draw from it a conclusion distinct from the law at hand, No. 2, which then yields our inquiry into our base-verse at No. 3. That proves that we listen to what the elders decree, and that even God finds himself bound in the same way.

III:II

1. A. Another teaching concerning *On the eighth day the chief of the Manassites*...(Num. 7:54):

    B. You find that Ephraim offered his offering first, for [he had been designated] first born and elder.

    C. Then Manasseh [brought his].

2. A. Thus did R. Tanhuma bar Abba commence discourse, citing the following verse: *The words of the wise are as goads and as nails well fastened are those that sit together in groups; they are given from one shepherd* (Qoh. 12:11):

    B. "What is the meaning of 'goad'? Just as a goad guides the cow in its furrow, so the words of the Torah guide a person to the ways of the Holy One, blessed be He.

    C. "Well did Solomon say, *The words of the wise are as goads and as nails well fastened are those that sit together in groups; they are given from one shepherd* (Qoh. 12:11)."

3. A. Another matter: the Mishnah refers to the same object as an ox-goad or as a guide, *with an ox-goad* (Judges 3:31), *To set the guides* (1 Sam. 13:21).

    B. Said R. Nathan, "Why is it called a goad? Because it teaches knowledge to a cow. And why is it called a guide? Because it guides the heifer. And why an ox-goad? Because it trains the heifer to plough where it should.

    C. "So the teachings of sages impart understanding among people, give them sense, and teach them the ways of the Holy One, blessed be He.

    D. "Accordingly: *The words of the wise are as goads and as nails well fastened are those that sit together in groups; they are given from one shepherd* (Qoh. 12:11)."

4. A. Another matter: what is the meaning of *goads*?

B. Said R. Berekhiah, "It is a girl's ball, a children's bouncing ball, which one catches and the other throws.

C. "So when sages enter into study-sessions and occupy themselves with Torah, this one gives his position, and that one gives his position, and another gives yet a third position, but the words of each one of them have been given from Moses the shepherd out of what he received from the Unique One of the world.

D. "For *they are given from one shepherd* (Qoh. 12:11).

E. "Might one suppose that, since this one gives one position and that another, do the words just fly in the air?

F. "Scripture says, *And like nails that are planted by masters of assemblies* (Qoh. 12:11).

G. "What is says is not, nails that are set, but rather, *And like nails that are planted by masters of assemblies* (Qoh. 12:11).

H. "Why so? It is because he has made them into nails that are planted.

I. "Now a nail that is a a head is easy to remove. Therefore he said, *And like nails that are planted by masters of assemblies* (Qoh. 12:11).

J. "If the roots of a tree are planted deep, it is hard to uproot the tree, but they are not as strong as iron. But an iron nail is strong.

K. "He has assigned to teachings of the Torah the strength of an iron and compares it to the roots of a tree [that are planted deep]."

5. A. Another matter: just as the roots of a tree spread out in every direction, so teachings of the Torah enter and spread throughout the entire body of a man.

6. A. *The words of the wise are as goads and as nails well fastened are those that sit together in groups; they are given from one shepherd* (Qoh. 12:11):

B. When are they planted in a man like nails?

C. When a master of the Torah comes in for study, and people gather together to listen to him.

7. A. Another matter: just as a goad may be carried, it is possible that the same applies to them?

B. Scripture says, *...as nails well fastened.*

8. A. What is the meaning of the phrase, *...are those that sit together in groups?*

B. When are they [Torah-traditions] planted in a man?

C. When masters of them are gathered together [in death].

D. So long as one's master is alive, one postpones matters. Whenever he needs, [he may think,] "Lo, my master is before me, and I may [just go and] ask him."

E. Once his master dies, lo, he works day and night to preserve his learning.

F. When someone does not have someone to ask, – lo, when are the words of Torah planted in a man? When their masters are gathered together [in death].

9. A. [They are given from one shepherd.] These and those have been given by the Unique One of the world.

   B. *And even more than these, my son, take heed* (Qoh. 12:12):

   C. What is the meaning of the statement, *And even more than these, my son, take heed* (Qoh. 12:12)?

   D. Even more than [you are conscientious] concerning teachings of the Torah, take heed of teachings of the scribes.

   E. Why so? Because if one had come to write down their words, there would have been no end of books.

   F. *Of the making of many books there is no end* (Qoh. 12:12).

10. A. Said R. Abba Sarongela, "If someone [wanted] to write in books the teachings of scribes, *And even more than these, my son, take heed* (Qoh. 12:12).

   B. "What is the sense of that statement?

   C. "It means that confusion [a play on the letters used in the word *more than these*] would come into you.

11. A. *And even more than these, my son, take heed* (Qoh. 12:12):

   B. Said R. Berekhiah the priest, "We read the word for nails as though it were written with an S, but it is spelled with a different sort of Sh, yielding the word for [priestly] watches:

   C. "[The sense then is this:] Just as the priestly watches are twenty-four in all, so there are twenty-four books in the Torah.

   D. "And whoever reads a book other than the twenty four is as if he read in heretical books.

   E. "For the Torah has said, *And even more than these, my son, take heed* (Qoh. 12:12)."

   F. Rabbi says, "Take heed of teaching of scribes more than teachings of the Torah.

   G. "Why? Because they are like goads."

12. A. R. Yohanan would say on the first festival day of the Feast of Tabernacles, "Blessed are you, Lord, our God, king of the world, who has sanctified us by his commandments and commanded us concerning the religious duty of the *lulab*," and on all the other days, he would say, "...and has commanded us the commandments of the elders."

   B. R. Joshua b. Levi wouild concur with R. Yohanan that the first day of the Festival of Tabernacles enjoyed the status of a teaching of the Torah, as it is said, *And you will take for yourself on the first day* (Lev. 23:40), while the other days [were hallowed] by reason of the teachings of the scribes.

   C. Said R. Simeon b. Halafta in the name of R. Ahai, "It is because it is written, *The words of sages are like goads...they are given from one shepherd* (Qoh. 12:11), all the same are words of Torah and words of sages [in status; each derives from its own source, but both enjoy the same authority]."

No. 1 concludes the foregoing. Once we have introduced the theme of the authority of sages, which **III:I** has given us, we pursue that subject. The intersecting-verse, No. 2, then provides us with a rich collection of fairly obvious statements about the authority of "the wise," meaning of course sages. Nos. 3-11 then provide diverse exegeses of the same intersecting-verses, going over the same ground throughout. The conclusion, No. 12, presents no surprises.

III:III

1. A. Another teaching concerning the verse: *The words of the wise are as goods and as nails well fastened are those that sit together in groups; they are given from one shepherd* (Qoh. 12:11):
   B. R. Hiyya bar Abba went into a synagogue and heard the children in session and reciting Scripture there: *From there Abraham journeyed* (Gen. 20:1).
   C. He said, "[Since the word for journey' can also be understood to mean 'split,' as in 'split the fowl in half,'] I said to myself, How great are the words of the sages! For they have said, **Take heed of their burning coals, lest you be burned, for their bite is the bite of a fox, their sting is the sting of the scorpion, and their venom is the venom of a snake [M. Abot 2:10]."**
   D. Why did he say this?
   E. Because it is written earlier, *So the daughters of Lot became pregnant by their father* (Gen. 19:36).

2. A. Now you find that when Abraham came to the land, Lot came along with him, and because he was associated with Abraham, he got rich just as did Abraham,
   B. as it is said, *And Abram went up out of Egypt, he, his wife, and all that he had, and Lot with him, to the south. And Abraham was very rich...and Lot too* (Gen. 13:1, 2, 5).
   C. See how rich they got, so that the land could not bear the two of them together: *And the land could not bear them* (Gen. 13:6).
   D. And if you find it surprising that the land could not bear them, it was not only because of their possessions, which were abundant, but because of the constant bickering among their shepherds.
   E. For so it is written, *And there was strife between the herdsmen of Abram's cattle and the herdsmen of Lot's cattle* (Gen. 13:7).
   F. Why was there bickering between these and those?
   G. But when a person is righteous, his householders are like him and righteous too, as are all those who adhere to him. But when a man is wicked, so too are his householders wicked like him.
   H. The cattle of Abraham would go out muzzled, and those of Lot did not go out muzzled. The herdsmen of Abraham began to argue with those of Lot, and they said to them, Why are you giving Lot a bad name by leaving your cattle unmuzzled]"
   I. The herdsmen of Lot replied, "We are the ones who should protest against you, for you muzzle the cattle. For you know that in the end the cattle of Abraham will end up with Lot, because Abraham has not produced an heir. You are not feeding the herd properly, because you know that Abraham does not have a son, and tomorrow he will die and Lot will inherit him. So you are making yourself righteous at the cost of

the cattle of someone else. Is it the case that whatever his cattle eats it steals? Does it not belong to the beast?

J.   "Has not the Holy One, blessed be He, said to Abraham, *To your seed I will give this land* (Gen. 12:7)? Tomorrow he will die without heirs and Lot, his brother's son, will inherit the land. [Accordingly the cattle are eating what belongs to them.]"

K.   Now who has informed you that it was in regard to these matters that they bickered?

L.   Said R. Judah bar Simon, "Read the end of the cited verse: *And the Canaanites and the Perizzites dwelt in the land* (Gen. 31:7)."

M.   What is the meaning of this matter? But since they were bickering about this matter, as it says, *And there was bickering among the sheperds...*, said the Holy One, blessed be He to them, "This is what I said to Abraham, *To your seed I will give this land* (Gen. 12:7).

N.   "It is to his sons and not to this wicked man, as you imagine. And even as to what I said to Abraham, that I shall give his sons the land, when will that be? When I drive out the Canaanites and Perizzites from it. But I have not yet given it to Abraham, and the Canannites and Perizzites are still in the land. Up to now then owners of the land are yet on it, and yet you say what you have said."

3.   A.   Said R. Azariah, "Just as there was strife between the shepherds of Abraham and the shepherds of Lot, so there was strife between Abraham and Lot. How do we know it?

B.   *"Then Abram said to Lot, Let there be no strife between you and me* (Gen. 13:8)."

C.   *Is not the whole land before you? Separate yourself from me, I pray you* (Gen. 13:9):

D.   Said R. Helbo, "What is written is not 'depart' but 'separate' [which contains the same letters as the word for *mule*].

E.   "Just as the mule does not produce seed, so it is not possible for that man to become associated with the seed of Abraham. [No mixing with the Moabites or Ammonites is possible.]"

4.   A.   *Then Lot lifted up his eyes* (Gen. 13:10):

B.   For he set his eyes on fornication, in line with the usage of the same words in this verse: *The wife of his master lifted up her eyes on Joseph* (Gen. 39:7).

C.   *And saw all the plain of the Jordan* (Gen. 13:10): *For on account of a harlot a man is brought to a loaf of bread* (Prov. 6:26) [the word for "loaf" and that for "plain" being the same]. [Freedman, *Genesis Rabbah* p. 337, n. 4: Translation: "and beheld all the loaf, the immorality, of the Jordan."]

D.   *That it was well watered everywhere* (Gen. 13:10): For all of the women were whores and worthy of being tested as faithless wives.

E.   So did R. Simeon b. Yohai expound matters.

5.   A.   Said R. Eleazar b. Pedat in the name of R. Yose b. Zimra, "See how the wicked Lot deprived Abraham, the righteous, of the capacity of the Word [with God].

B.. "For so long as Lot was associated with him, the Holy One, blessed be He, did not engage in conversation with Abraham. When Lot separated from him, the Word seized hold of Abraham, as it is said, *And the Lord said to Abram after Lot separated from him* (Gen. 13:14).

C. "Therefore when the angels were overturning Sodom and saving Lot because of the merit of Abraham, what did they say to him?

D. *"Escape to the mountain, lest you be swept away* (Gen. 19:17).

E. "The sense was, 'It is on account of the merit of that great mountain, Abraham, that you have been saved. Go to him.'

F. "He said to them, 'I cannot do so, for he has already told me to separate from him. *I cannot flee to the mountain* (Gen. 19:19)."

6. A. A further comment on the same verse, *I cannot escape unto the mountain lest the evil cling to me* (Gen. 19:19):

B. [Lot said,] "All the time that I lived in Sodom, the Holy One, blessed be He, took account of my deeds in comparison to the deeds of the others [in that town], and I could make it. For I was a righteous by comparison to them. But now shall I go to Abraham, the righteous man, so that the Holy One, blessed be He, will weigh out my deeds in comparison to his deeds? I shall not be able to stand, *lest the evil cling to me.*"

C. Said R. Yohanan, "Two people made the same statement, Lot and the woman of Zarephath.

D. "The woman of Zarephath said, *For you have come to me to make mention of my sins and to kill my son* (1 Kgs. 17:18).

E. "She said to him, 'Before you [Elijah] came to me, the Holy One, blessed be He, looked at my [good] deeds and the deeds of the people of my town, and my deeds were more numerous than the deeds of the people of my town. For by comparison to them I was worthy. Now that you have come to me, you have called to mind my sin [since my merit no longer protects me] and so you have killed my son.'"

F. That suffices for what we require to understand the statement, *The words of sages are like goads.*

Once we have introduced the matter of Abraham's journey, No. 1, we follow the story in its own terms, ignoring the point with which we commenced. The matter follows its own course from No. 2 to the end. The reference at the end hardly changes the picture of a compositor who has taken a chunk of materials with no point of relevance to his larger composition and simply inserted it whole.

III:IV

1. A. So too with reference to Jacob: when the time came for him to die, and Joseph got word that he was sick, he began to reflect in his heart.

B. R. Eliezer says, "Joseph reflected in his heart on three matters."

C. R. Samuel bar Nahman said, "Five."

D. [Here are Joseph's reflections:] "My children have been born in Egypt. Perhaps he will bestow a blessing on them.

E. "Perhaps he will turn them into progenitors of tribes.

F. "Perhaps he will treat me as firstborn.

G.   "Perhaps he will remove Reuben from the status of first born.

H.   "And [he further reflected] on why Rachel had not been brought in for burial."

I.   That is why, when he went to him, he took his two sons with him.

J.   The matter may be compared to the case of a priest who went to the threshing floor [to collect the priestly share of the crop] and took his two sons with him, to make known to everyone that they are his sons, that they have a share in the crop as does he.

2.   A.   *And one said to Joseph, lo, your father is ill* (Gen. 48:1):

    B.   Who told him that his father was sick?

    C.   There is he who says, "He perceived it through the Holy Spirit."

    D.   There is he who says, "Bilhah told him, for she was serving Jacob. When he got sick, she came and told Joseph."

    E.   There are they who say, "Benjamin let him know."

    F.   There are they who say, "Joseph had put his own agents in Jacob's house. When they discerned that Jacob was sick, they came and told Joseph."

3.   A.   Lo, the entire praiseworthy trait of Joseph was that he paid remarkable respect for his father and did not come to see him any time he wanted [but only upon ceremony].

    B.   For if others had not come and told him that his father was sick, he would not have known about it.

    C.   This shows you the true righteousness of Joseph, for he did not want to spend time alone with his father,

    D.   so that he would not he would not tell him how his brothers had done what they had done and curse them.

    E.   [Joseph thought,] "I know [the power of] father's righteousness. Whatever he says enjoys the status of a decree. He said to Laban, *With whomever you find your gods, he shall not live* (Gen. 31:32), and my mother died. Now if I were to say to him to curse them, he will curse them, and I shall turn out to destroy the entire world.

    F.   "For the world was created only for the tribes."

    G.   Therefore he did not go to his father whenever he wanted.

4.   A.   *Behold, your son, Joseph, comes to you* (Gen. 48:2):

    B.   *Forthwith: Israel strengthened himself and sat up in the bed* (Gen. 48:2).

    C.   Why did he strengthen himself?

    D.   Said R. Joshua b. Levi, "He showed himself to him sitting up erect. He said, 'The Holy One, blessed be He, has made him ruler of the world, and shall I not pay respect to him? Therefore: *Israel strengthened himself and sat up in the bed*."

5.   A.   Another matter: Why did he strengthen himself?

    B.   "It was so that the tribal progenitors should say how I see Joseph, even while ill, so rising before him, so that they should pay him respect as well."

6. A. Why did he strengthen himself and rise and sit up?

   B. R. Aha said, "'It was so that I should not bestow a blessing on them while seating, and people say that these were the gifts of a dying man, who did not know what he was doing.'"

   C. Therefore he strengthened himself and arose and sat up, so that people would know that these were the gifts of a healthy person [in full command of his senses].

7. A. Another matter: *Israel strengthened himself and sat up in the bed*:

   B. Said R. Phineas b. Hama in the name of R. Aha, "He strengthened himself in prayer.

   C. "He said, 'When I come to bestow a blessing on them, the Holy Spirit will come to rest on me, so that I may bestow a blessing on them in the appropriate way.'

   D. "When he saw Joseph's sons with him, he said to him, 'Lo, for seventeen years you have been asking about my health [in these visits to me], but they did not come. Only now have them come with you. I know what you are thinking. If I bestow a blessing on them, I shall treat as null the word of the Holy One, blessed be He, who said to me, "I shall produce from you twelve tribes," [and these will make it fourteen]. If I do not bestow a blessing on them, lo, you will take offense. I shall bestow a blessing on them. But it will not be on your account, merely because you provided for me, that I give a blessing to them. But [God] instructed me while I was yet in Beth El to bless them: *God almighty appeared to me at Luz...He said to me, Behold, I wll make you fruitful and multiply you and will make of you a company made up of peoples* (Gen. 48:3-4).'"

8. A. Another matter: He misled him here, for [God] did not say, *I shall make you into a nation and a company made up of peoples*.

   B. For lo, we find that when he appeared to him in Beth El when he came from Padan Aram, *He said to me, I am God Almighty. Be fruitful and multiply. A nation and a company of nations will come forth from you* (Gen. 35:9,11).

   C. He should have said to Joseph, "Lo, I shall make you fruitful and multiply you and make you into nations and a company of peoples.' [But that is not the language that he used in reporting to Joseph the earlier vision.]

   D. Why did he say to him only, *a company of peoples*?

   E. Jacob said, "When the Holy One, blessed be He, said this to me, I had eleven tribal progenitors. Now, when Benjamin was born, I thought, 'Lo, this covers what [God] said to me, speaking of a company of nations. But now, [I realize that within the company of nations are included] *the two sons of yours that are born to you in the Land of Egypt before I came to you in Egypt. They in fact are mine* (Gen. 48:5)."

   F. So he said to him, "They are not yours but mine, for [God] said to me, *A nation and a company of nations,* while giving me only Benjamin. Lo, they are not yours but they are mine. Lo, Ephraim and Manasseh are tribal progenitors just like Reuben and Simeon.

   G. "But those that you will beget after them will be called yours. These, however, are called mine."

H. For it is said, *And your issue that you get after them will be yours* (Gen. 48:6).

9. A. Lo, Joseph was informed about two matters, first, that the Word had blessed his two sons: *...the angel who has redeemed me from all evil, bless the lads; [and in them let my name be perpetuated and the name of my fathers Abraham and Isaac; and let them grow into a multitude in the midst of the earth]* (Gen. 48:15-16).

B. And [second, that] he would turn Ephraim and Manasseh into tribes like Reuben and Simeon: *Ephraim and Manassah, even as Reuben and Simeon, shall be mine* (Gen. 48:5).

C. Even though it distressed him, he placed Ephraim before Manasseh.

10. A. As for that statement, *God...appeared to me at Luz* (Gen. 48:3), that is the same as Beth El,

B. for it is written, *So Jacob came to Luz...which is Beth El* (Gen. 35:6).

11. A. Said R. Berekhiah the Priest in the name of R. Berekhiah in the name of R. Levi in the name of R. Samuel bar Nahman, "Jacob explained his making Ephraim and Manasseh into tribes, saying that the Holy One, blessed be He, appeared to me and said to me, *I am God almighty...and kings shall come forth from your loins* (Gen. 35:11).

B. "[Jacob said,] 'Had he said, Kings will come forth from you,' I should have concluded that he referred to the tribal progenitors. But he has said only, *'From your loins,'* referring to the children of my children, thus speaking of Ephraim and Manasseh."

12. A. Said R. Judah the Levite, son of R. Shalom, "If you do not derive the fact from the earlier reference to their forming *a company of nations*, derive it from the present passage:]

B. "He said to me, *Behold I will make you fruitful and multiply you and will make of you a company composed of peoples* (Gen. 48:4).

C. "A further proof derives from the phrase, *a nation and a company of nations*: a nation refers to Benjamin, and a company of nations refers to Ephraim and Manasseh.

D. *"I am God almighty...and kings shall come forth from your loins* (Gen. 35:11): this refers to King Saul, who arose from the tribe of Benjamin, the beginning of Israelite monarchy, concerning whom it is said, *Now there was a man of Benjamin, whose name was Kish, the son of Abiel* (1 Sam. 9:1)."

13. A. Once he had bestowed his blessing on them and treated them as tribal progenitors, he began to speak about the matter of Rachel.

B. [Joseph] said to him, "Why did she not come into the burial ground with you [in the cave of Ephron]," Joseph being greatly distressed about this matter.

C. His father commenced the reply concerning her. What is stated is not, "As for me, when I came from Paddan," but, *I also, when I came from Paddan* (Gen. 48:7).

D. What is the meaning of *I also*?

E. He said to him, "By your life, just as you wanted your mother to come to proper burial, so I wanted the same thing."

F. That is the sense of, *I also, [when I came from Paddan]* (Gen. 48:7).

14. A. *Rachel died to me* (Gen. 48:7):

B. What is the meaning of *to me?*

C. "Mine was the burden of taking care of her."

D. Another interpretation of *Rachel died to me* (Gen. 48:7):

E. "I am the one who bore the loss, for I had pleasure only in her," thus, *"Rachel died to me* (Gen. 48:7), in that I am the one who bore the loss."

15. A. Joseph said to him, "Is it possible that the reason that you did not bring her in for a proper burial was because it was the rainy season?"

B. He said to him, "No, *And there was still some way to come to Ephrath* (Gen. 48:7). [Braude, p. 75: *In coming to Ephrath the earth still looked like a sieve.* The word for a measure of distance may be read to mean, a sieve.]

C. "It was between Passover and Pentecost, when the earth was like a sieve, [Braude, p. 75, n. 52:] [and] seemed to move to and fro with the swaying of the ears of corn from which bread is made."

D. Said Joseph to him, "Make a decree now, and I shall bring her up and bury her."

E. Jacob said to him, "You cannot do so, my son. For I buried her there only at the instruction of the Word. For I too wanted to bring her up and bury her, but the Holy One, blessed be He, did not permit me."

F. For it is said, *And I buried her there* (Gen. 48:7).

G. What is the meaning of *there?*

H. It was on the instruction of the [divine] Word.

I. Why so?

J. For it was entirely clear and foreseen before [God] that the house of the sanctuary would in the end be destroyed, and his children were destined to go forth to exile, and they would pass by the [graves of] the patriarchs and ask them to pray in their behalf, but they would not do them any good.

K. But as they would go on the way, they would come and embrace the grave of Rachel, and she would go and seek mercy from the Holy One, blessed be He, saying before him, "Lord of the age, listen to the sound of my weeping and have mercy on my children, or give me [recompense for] the due-bill that is owing to me [and move my bones to the cave of Machpelah in Hebron]."

L. The Holy One, blessed be He, will forthwith listen to her prayer.

M. How do we know that that is the case?

N. Scripture says, *A voice is heard in Ramah, lamentation and bitter weeping, Rachel is weeping for her children* (Jer. 31:15).

O. And further: *And there is hope for your future, says the Lord, and your children shall return to their border* (Jer. 31:17).

P. Lo, [Jacob] thereby appeased [Joseph] explaining why his mother had not received a proper burial.

16. A. Having seen his sons made into tribal progenitors, Joseph began to bring his sons to his father so that he would bless them,

B. as it is said, *Joseph took both of them, with Ephraim in his right hand [toward Jacob's left hand]* (Gen. 48:13).

C. Why did Joseph do so? When he noted that Jacob mentioned Ephraim first, saying, *Ephraim and Manasseh are like Reuben and Simeon for me,* he feared, lest he disinherit Manasseh from the right of the firstborn. Therefore he brought them near his father, with Manasseh at the father's right hand and Ephraim at the father's left.

17. A. Said the Holy One, blessed be He, "Shall I not let Jacob know who is going to come forth from these: Jeroboam b. Nabat from Ephraim [delete: and Manasseh, who brought an idol into the Temple]."

B. Said R. Hama, "The Holy One, blessed be He, foresaw that Jeroboam b. Nabat would come forth from Ephraim and make two calves."

18. A. What is the meaning of *Who are these* (Gen. 48:13)?

B. *These are your gods, O Israel* (Ex. 32:4).

C. *The king took counsel and made two calves of gold...saying...These are your gods O Israel* (1 Kgs. 12:28).

D. [Since Jacob foresaw what was coming,] the Holy One, blessed be He, took away from him the Holy Spirit:

E. *The eyes of Israel were heavy for age so that he could not see* (Gen. 48:10).

F. Said R. Judah, "The passage means what it says, namely, his eyelids were heavy because of age and would stick together, so when he wanted to see, he would hold them up."

G. Said to him R. Nahman, "God forbid! What is the meaning of *so that he could not see?*

H. "It is that the Holy Spirit was taken away from him."

19. A. *He said to him, "Who are these:"*

B. Lo, for seventeen years they had lived with him, and yet *he said to him, Who are these?*

C. He foresaw the two calves of Jeroboam, who was going to make Israel to sin, saying to them, *"These are your gods, O Israel"* ((1 Kgs. 12:28).

20. A. Another teaching: What is the sense of the word *Who* [which uses Hebrew letters M and Y, that add up to the value of fifty]?

B. He foresaw that fifty myriads of his descendants were destined to fall in battle, with the letter M standing for forty myriads, and Y for ten, lo, fifty myriads.

C. It is to the five hundred thousand when Israel went to do battle [in civil war].

21. A. Joseph began to plead, sayhing to him, "Father, my children are righteous. They are like me."

B. *[They are my sons. They are the ones whom God has given me by this one* (Gen. 48:9):] What is the meaning of *by this one?*

C. He brought their mother, Asenath, before his father and said to him, "Father, by your leave! Even on account of this righteous woman."

22. A. *He said to him, I pray you, bring them to me, and I will bless them* (Gen. 48:9):

B. Jacob began to embrace them, kiss them, and take pleasure in them. He said, "Perhaps through this joy the Holy Spirit will come to rest on him [me], so that I may bless them."

C. But the Holy Spirit did not come back to him.

D. When Joseph saw his distress, he took them and went out and fell on his face and had them prostrate themselves on their faces, and he sought mercy.'

E. Rabbi said, "Forthwith the Holy One, blessed be He, said to the Holy Spirit, 'How long will Joseph be anguished? Reveal yourself quickly and enter into Jacob, so that he may bless them.'

F. "For the Holy One, blessed be He, does not endure seeing a tribal progenitor fall on his face.

G. "Thus when Joshua, son of Joseph's son, fell on his face, forthwith, the Word overtook him, saying to him, *Get up, why have you now fallen on your face* (Josh. 7:10).

H. That is in line with what the prophet says, *I have pampered Ephraim, taking them in my arms, [but they have ignored my healing care. I drew them with human ties, with cords of love; but I seemed to them as one who imposed a yoke on their jaws though I was offering them food]* (Hos. 11:3-4).

I. The word for pampered yields two words, "I the Lord decided the matter," and, "I forced the Holy Spirit to go back to Jacob, so that he could bless Ephraim and take him into his arms.

J. When Jacob said to Joseph, *Bring them please to me that I may bless them*, (Gen. 48:9), on account of what merit was it?

K. It was on this account, *I drew them with human ties*, meaning, on account of the merit of Joseph.

L. *...but they have ignored my healing care.*

23. A. When [Joseph] set Ephraim at his left and Manasseh at his right, Jacob *guided his hands wittingly* (Gen. 48:14).

B. What is the meaning of *guided his hands wittingly*?

C. Said Rabbi, "It means just that."

D. Said R. Judah, "It means that he made his hands [Braude, p. 79:] deal violently with the birthright of Manasseh."

E. And R. Nehemiah said, "The word means that he imparted intelligence to the hands of Jacob through the Holy Spirit, as it is written, *A Psalm in which intelligence was imparted through the Holy Spirit to Ethan the Ezrahite* (Ps. 89:1)."

24. A. When Joseph saw it, he was upset.

B. He took his father's hands to move them from the head of Ephraim and lay them on the head of Manasseh.

C. So it is said, *When Joseph saw that his father was laying his right hand upon the head of Ephraim, it displeased him and he held up his father's hand* (Gen. 48:17).

D. Jacob said to Joseph, "Do you want to move my hand not at my own will and volition? The [strength of that hand is such that it overcame] angel that is third in the world."

E. Said R. Berekhiah b. Rabbi, "This hand has grappled with the prince of the host above, and you imagine that you can move it against my will?"

F. And his father refused, saying, "What do you say? This is the one? I know it. But were you thinking that because I would always ask you what your brothers did to you, and you would not tell me, do you then think that I did not know? I knew, my son, I knew."

G. He began to bestow his blessing:

H. *He blessed them that day, saying, By you shall Israel bless, saying, God make you as Ephraim and as Manasseh. And he set Ephraim before Manasseh* (Gen. 48:20).

25. A. The Holy One, blessed be He, said, "Since Jacob has made a decree that Ephraim should be first, so too the offerings of the princes, when they come to make an offering, will find that ephraim makes his offering first, before Manasseh.

B. *On the seventh day...the..prince of the children of Ephraim* (Num. 7:48), and then, *On the eighth day the chief of the Manassites, Gamaliel son of Pedahzur, came* (Num. 7:54).

Until No. 25, the entire composition focuses upon Jacob and Joseph. Only the final item explains the linkage to our larger context.

III:V

1. A. Another matter concerning the verse *On the eighth day the chief of the Manassites* (Num. 7:54-59):

B. You find that in every matter Ephraim came before Manasseh, as to judges, standards, kings, and offerings.

C. Joshua, then Gideon b. Joash of the tribe of Manasseh.

D. As to the standard: *The standard of the camp of Ephraim* (Num. 2:18), and then: *And next to him shall be the tribe of Manasseh* (Num. 2:20).

E. As to kings: Jeroboam b. Nabat of Ephraim, then came Jehu b. Manasseh from Manasseh.

F. And why did Ephraim enjoy that merit? Because he diminished himself.

G. For the Holy One, blessed be He, loves whoever humbles himself:

H. *For though the Lord is high, he regards the humble* (Ps. 138:6).

2. A. And who let you know that he humbled himself? As it is said, *And Israel stretched out his right hand and put it on Ephraim's head, and he was the lesser one* (Gen. 48:14), that is to say, Ephraim made himself small.

B. But Manasseh would go forth and engage with his father in great affairs.

3. A. Said the Holy One, blessed be He, since he has diminished himself, he has gained the merit of having this honor.

B. And now, if one who is small and diminishes himself gains merit for such honor, a great person who diminishes himself all the more so.

C. *On the eighth day the chief of the Manassites, [Gamaliel son of Pedahzur, came. His offering was one silver dish weighing a hundred and thirty shekels by the sacred standard and one silver tossing-bowl weighing seventy, both full of flour mixed with oil as a grain-offering; one saucer weighing ten gold shekels, full of incense; one young bull, one full-grown ram, and one yearling ram, as a whole-offering; one he-goat as a sin-offering; and two bulls, five full-grown rams, five he-goats, and five yearling rams, as a shared-offering. This was the offering of Gamaliel son of Pedahzur]* (Num. 7:54-59).

Only at the end, by a circuitous route, to we revert to our base-verse. Viewed as a whole, the sequence of topics is hardly coherent, and I cannot imagine a less cogent composition, even though long stretches of the parts, e.g., the whole of **III:IV**, flow smoothly.

Chapter Four

Pesiqta Rabbati *Pisqa* 4

Concerning the Sabbath of Hanukkah

The verse that recurs throughout derives from the prophetic lection that is read in the synagogue on the first Sabbath that coincides with the festival of Hanukkah:

> [*Then Elijah said to all the people, Come here to me. They all came, and he repaired the altar of the Lord which had been torn down.*] He took twelve stones, one for each tribe of the sons of Jacob, the man named Israel, by the word of the Lord. [*With these stones he built an altar in the name of the Lord*] (1 Kgs. 18:30-32).

IV:I

1. A. May our master instruct us:
    B. Since the Prayer-service covering the Additional Offerings is not recited on the weekdays of Hanukkah, if one is reciting the Prayer-service covering the Additional Offerings in connection with the New Moon [should that fall on Hanukkah or for the Sabbath, for that matter], should he make mention of Hanukkah in the Prayer-service covering the Additional Offerings?
    C. Our masters have taught us:
    D. Said R. Simon in the name of R. Joshua, "In the case of the New Moon that coincided with Hanukkah, even though there is no recitation of the Prayer-service covering the Additional Offerings so far as Hanukkah is concerned, in the case of the New Moon he has to make mention of Hanukkah in the Prayer-service covering the Additional Offerings. As to a Sabbath which coincides with Hanukkah, even though there is no recitation of the Prayer-service covering the Additional Offerings so far as Hanukkah is concerned but only so far as the Sabbath is concerned, nonetheless he has to make mention of Hanukkah in the Prayer-service covering the Additional Offerings."

2. A. And where, in the liturgy, does one make mention of Hanukkah [under the stated circumstances]?
    B. In the prayer of thanksgiving.

3. A. You find that all of the wonders which the Holy One, blessed be He, has done for Israel and is destined to do for them are on account of the merit owing to the tribal progenitors.

B.   Even the house of the sanctuary is destined to be rebuilt on account of the merit owing to the tribal progenitors,

C.   for it is written, *Jerusalem that will be rebuilt* (Ps. 122:3), which is followed by, *Because there the tribes are to go up* (Ps. 122:4).

D.   So too everything that the Holy One, blessed be He, created was on account of the merit of the [twelve] tribal progenitors:

E.   *In the beginning* (Gen. 1:1) you find twelve months in the year, twelve Zodiacal stars in the firmament, twelve hours in the day, twelve hours in the night.

F.   Said the Holy One, blessed be He, "Even the creatures of the heights and those of the lower regions I have created only on account of the merit of the tribal progenitors."

G.   For so it is written, *For the sake of all these has my hand made* (Is. 66:2).

H.   It is on account of the merit of *all these, the twelve tribal progenitors of Israel* (Gen. 49:28),

I.   on that account there are   the twelve Zodiacal stars in the firmament, twelve hours [in the day, twelve hours in the night].

J.   Therefore, when Elijah came to bring Israel under the wings of the Presence of God, he took twelve stones in accord with the number of the tribal progenitors and built them into an altar.

K.   How do we know? It is on the basis of the prophetic lesson at hand: *[Then Elijah said to all the people, Come here to me. They all came, and he repaired the altar of the Lord which had been torn down.]* He took twelve stones, one for each tribe of the sons of Jacob, the man named Israel, by the word of the Lord. *[With these stones he built an altar in the name of the Lord]* (1 Kgs. 18:30-32).

Nos. 1, 2 go over the legal question, which is a thoughtful one. Since no arrangement for a liturgy for the Additional Service covers the Hanukkah festival, if and when on Hanukkah such a liturgy for the Additional Offiering is conducted, do we include a reference to Hanukkah? The answer is that we do. The topic shifts abruptly at No. 3 to a very general observation that all miracles – thus including the one of Hanukkah – are done on account of the merit of the twelve tribes. Since the matter of Hanukkah is not mentioned at all, it follows that the compositor has a ready-made item which he has included essentially because of the relevance of his prophetic lection to Hanukkah.

IV:II

1.   A.   And so did R. Tanhuma be R. Abba commence discourse: *"And by a prophet the Lord brought Israel out of Egypt and by a prophet was he preserved* (Hos. 12:14).

B.   *"And by a prophet the Lord brought Israel out of Egypt* – this refers to Moses.

C.   *"...and by a prophet was he preserved* – this refers to Elijah.

D.   "You find that two prophets arose for Israel out of the tribe of Levi, Moses was first, Elijah the last, both of them on a mission to serve as the redeemer of Israel.

E. "Moses redeemed them from Egypt on a mission [of God]: *Come now, therefore, and I shall send you to Pharaoh* (Ex. 3:10).

F. "Elijah will redeem them in the age to come on a mission: *Behold, I shall send you Elijah the prophet* (Mal. 3:23).

G. "In the case of Moses, who redeemed them from Egypt in the beginning, they never again returned to slavery in Egypt, so in the case of Elijah, when he redeems them from the fourth monarchy, namely, Edom, they will never again revert to slavery, but will have eternal salvation."

2. A. And you find that Moses and Elijah were alike in all regards:

B. Moses was a prophet, and so was Elijah.

C. Moses was called *man of God* (Deut. 33:12), and Elijah was called *man of God* God (1 Kgs. 17:18).

D. Moses went up, and so did Elijah, as it is said, *And Moses went up to God* (Ex. 19:3), *And it came to pass when Elijah went up to heaven* (2 Kgs. 2:1).

E. Moses killed the Egyptian, and Elijah killed Hiel: *But when Hiel became guilt through Baal, he died* (Hos. 13:1).

F. Moses was sustained (KLKL) by a woman, the daughter of Jethro, *Call him that he may eat bread* (Ex. 2:20), and Elijah was too: *Bring me I pray you a piece of bread* (1 Kgs. 17:11).

G. Moses fled from Pharaoh, and Elijah fled from Jezebel.

H. Moses fled and came to a well, and so did Elijah: *He arose and went...and came to Beer Sheba* (1 Kgs. 19:3).

I. In the case of Moses, *And the cloud covered him six days* (Ex. 14:16), and Elijah went up in a whirlwind: *And it came to pass, when the Lord would take up Elijah by a whirlwind* (2 Kgs. 2:1).

J. In the case of Moses, it is said, *If these men die the common death of all men* (Num. 16:29), and in the case of Elijah: *As the Lord, the God of Israel, lives, before whom I stand, there shall not be dew nor rain these years except according to my word* (1 Kgs. 17:1).

K. In the case of Moses: *And the Lord passed by before him* (Ex. 34:16), and in the case of Elijah: *And behold the Lord passed by* (12 Kgs. 19:11).

L. In the case of Moses: *Then he heard the voice* (Num. 7:89), and in the case of Elijah: *And behold there came a voice* (1 Kgs. 19:13).

M. Moses gathered all Israel to mount Sinai, and Elijah gathered them to Mount Karmel.

N. Moses wiped out idolatry, *Put every man his sword upon his thigh* (Ex. 32:27), and Elijah wiped out idolatry, seizing the prophets of Baal and killing them.'

O. Moses was a zealot: *Whoever is on the Lord's side, let him come to me* (Ex. 32:26),and so was Elijah: *Elijah said to all the people, Come near, I ask, to me...and he repaired the altar of the Lord that had been thrown down* (1 Kgs. 18:30).

P. Moses was hidden in a cave, *I will put you in a cleft of the rock* (Ex. 33:22), and so was Elijah, who stayed there: *And he came to a cave and lodged there* (1 Kgs. 19:9).

Q. In the case of Moses: *He came to the mountain of God* (ex. 3:12), and in the case of Elijah: *And he came to the mount of God* (1 Kgs. 19:8).

R. Moses came to the wilderness, *He led the flock to the farthest end of the wilderness* (Ex. 3:1), and so did Elijah: *But he himself went into the wilderness* (1 Kgs. 19:4).

S. With Moses God communicated through an angel: *And the angel of the Lord appeared to him* (Ex. 3:2), so too with Elijah: *And behold an angel* (1 Kgs. 19:5).

T. Moses remained for forty days and forty nights without eating or drinking, and so Elijah: *Elijah went on the strength of that meal forty days* (1 Kgs. 19:8).

U. Moses stopped the orb of the sun, *This day will I being to put the dread of you upon the peoples that are under the heaven* (Deut. 12:25), and so did Elijah: *This day let it be known that you are God in Israel* (1 Kgs. 18:36).

V. Moses prayed in behalf of Israel, *Destroy not your people and your inheritance* (Deut. 9:26), and so did Elijah: *Hear me, O Lord, hear me, for you turned their heart backward* (1 Kgs. 18:367).

W. When Moses prayed in behalf of Israel, he relied upon the merit of the patriarchs, *Remember Abraham, Isaac, and Israel* (Ex. 32:13), and so did Elijah: *O Lord, God of Abraham, Isaac, and Israel* (1 Kgs. 18:36).

X. It was through Moses that Israel undertook love for God, *All that the Lord has spoken we will do and listen to* (Ex. 24:7), and so too through Elijah: *The Lord he is God* (1 Kgs. 18:39).

Y. Moses made a tabernacle over an area measuring two seahs of seed, and Elijah made a trench in an area of the same size.

Z. In one respect we find that Moses was greater than Elijah, for to Moses [God] said, *But as for you, stand you here by me* (Deut. 5:28), while to Elijah: *What do you do here, Elijah* (1 Kgs. 19:9).

AA. Moses brought fire down, and so did Elijah. When Moses brought fire down, all of Israel stood and saw it: *There came a fire from before the Lord, and when all the people saw it, they shouted* (Lev. 9:24). So too in the case of Elijah: *When all the people saw it they fell on their faces* (1 Kgs. 18:39).

BB. Moses built an altar and Elijah built an altar. Moses called the altar that he built by the name of the Lord: *Moses called it by the name, 'The Lord is my standard'* (Ex. 17:15), and Elijah: *And with the stone he built an altar in the name of the Lord* (1 Kgs. 18:32).

CC. When Moses built the altar, he built it out of twelve stones, corresponding to the number of the children of Israel, and when Elijah built the altar, he too built it out of twelve stones, corresponding to the number of the children of Israel, as it is said, *He took twelve stones, one for each tribe of the sons of Jacob, the man named Israel, by the word of the Lord. With these stones he built an altar in the name of the Lord* (1 Kgs. 18:30-32).

The intersecting-verse invites attention to the comparison of Moses and Elijah, No. 1, and No. 2 beautifully articulates that matter. This leads us directly to our base-verse. I cannot imagine a more perfect execution of the form – or a more tedious and pointless one.

IV:III

1. A. *[Then Elijah said to all the people, Come here to me. They all came, and he repaired the altar of the Lord which had been torn down. He took twelve stones, one for each tribe of the sons of Jacob, the man named Israel, by the word of the Lord. With these stones he built an altar in the name of the Lord* (1 Kgs. 18:30-32)]: that is in line with what he said to Israel: *Thus says the Lord, The heaven is my throne and the earth is my footstool; [where could you build a house for me, what place could serve as my abode? All this was made by my hand, and thus it all came into being, declares the Lord]* (Is. 66:1-2).

   B. It was at the end of his period of prophecy that Isaiah made the prophecy contained in this verse.

   C. When was it that he so prophesied? It was in the time of Manasseh.

   D. When Manasseh brought the idol into the Temple, Isaiah began to prophesy to Israel, saying to them, "How can you take pride? Is it because of this house that you have built for me? The upper regions and the lower regions cannot contain my glory, and do I need this house, which you have built for me?

   E. *"Where could you build a house for me?*

   F. "Lo, Nebuchadnezzar is going to come up and destroy it and send you into exile."

   G. Forthwith Manasseh grew wrathful at him and said to them, "Seize him."

   H. They ran after him to arrest him. He fled from them.

   I. A carob-tree opened itself up and swallowed him.

   J. Said R. Isaac bar Hanina bar Papa bar Isaac, "So [the king] brought carpenters who sawed the carob-tree, and the blood dripped down.

   K. "That is in line with this verse of Scripture: *Moreover, Manasseh shed innocent blood in great quantity, until he had filled Jerusalem from side to side* [Hebrew: *mouth to mouth*] (1 Kgs. 21:16)."

   L. Is such a thing possible? The point is that he killed Isaiah, with whom God spoke, in line with this verse of Scripture: *Mouth to mouth I spoke to him* (Num. 12:8).

   M. Isaiah began to rebuke the Israelites: *"The heaven is my throne and the earth is my footstool.* As to this house which has been built, do not think that it will be rebuilt on your account, but it will be on the account of the merit of others altogether."

   N. On what account will it be rebuilt?

   O. R. Judah the Levite b. R. Shalom says, "It is on account of the Torah.

   P. "And that is the reference when God says, *where could you build a house for me, what place could serve as my abode?*

   Q. "And on what account will it be rebuilt? On this count: *All this was made by my hand,* and the word *this* refers to the Torah, as in the following verse, *This is the statutes, ordinances, and Torahs* (Lev. 26:46)."

   R. And R. Joshua the Priest b. R. Nehemiah said, "It was on account of the tribal progenitors: *All these are the twelve tribes of Israel* (Gen. 49:28)."

   S. When Elijah the power of the merit of the tribal progenitors, that it was even in the rebuilding of the house of the sanctuary that the Israelites derived sufficient merit only through the tribal progenitors, when he came to Mount Karmel to bring Israel under the wings of the Presence of God, he collected twelve stones, corresponding to the number of the tribes, and with them built the altar: *Then Elijah said to all the people, Come here to me. They all came, and he repaired the altar of the Lord which had been torn down. He took twelve stones, one for each tribe of the sons of Jacob, the man named Israel, by the word of the Lord. With these stones he built an altar in the name of the Lord* (1 Kgs. 18:30-32).

The concluding composition goes over the ground of CC above, making precisely the same point, but in a different way. The long exercise on the intersecting-verse serves to bring us back to our base-verse, and the whole is cogent and well presented – a far superior statement of the matter than the foregoing.

Chapter Five

Pesiqta Rabbati *Pisqa* 5

Concerning the Sabbath of Hanukkah

The verse that recurs throughout derives from the lection that is read in the synagogue when Hanukkah coincides with a second Sabbath, e.g., starting and ending on the Sabbath day:

> And it came to pass on the day that Moses completed setting up the Tabernacle, *[he anointed and consecrated it; he also anointed and consecrated its equipment, and the altar and its vessels. The chief men of Israel, heads of families, that is, the chiefs of the tribes who had assisted in preparing the detailed lists, came forward and brought their offering before the Lord]* (Num. 7:1-2).

V:I.

1. A. May our master instruct us [concerning the correct procedure when one person reads aloud from the Hebrew of Scripture and another translates the passage into Aramaic for the community? Specifically may the same person both read the text and also translate it? May the one who translates the text do so by reading from a written document, thus giving the impression of reading aloud from an Aramaic, rather than Hebrew, original?]:

   B. What is the law as to having the one who translates the Torah-lection actually read aloud the Torah-lection itself?

   C. What is the law as to permitting the one who translates the Torah-lection to read aloud from a written text?

   D. Our rabbis have taught:

   E. It is forbidden [for the one who pronounces the translation] to glance at a written text, and it also is forbidden for the one who reads the Hebrew text of the Torah aloud to raise his eyes from the Torah.

   F. For the Torah has been given only in writing, as it is said, *I shall write on the tablets...* (Ex. 34:1).

   G. And it also is forbidden for the one who pronouces the translation to set his eyes upon the Torah-text [so that he does not give the wrong impression that he is reading an Aramaic original].

   H. Said R. Judah b. Pazzi, "There is a verse of Scripture that makes this point explicitly: *The Lord said to Moses, Write these words* (Ex. 34:27), lo, this refers to Scripture, which was given in writing.

I. *"For these words are given orally* [and not in writing] (Ex. 34:27, lo, [this refers] to the translation into Aramaic, which is to be stated orally."

2. A. Said R. Judah b. R. Shalom, "Moses wanted the Mishnah to be handed on in writing. The Holy One, blessed be He, foresaw that the nations were going to translate the Torah, proclaiming it in Greek, saying that they are Israel.

    B. "Said the Holy One, blessed be He, to Moses, "Now Moses, the nations of the world are destined to claim, 'We are Israel, we are the true children of the Omnipresent,' while Israel will say, 'We are the children of the Omnipresent.' And then the scales will be evenly balanced.'

    C. "Said the Holy One, blessed be He, to the nations, 'Now if you say that you are my children, I shall know the truth only by reference to who has my mysteries in his position. They are the ones who are my children.'

    D. "Then the nations will say to him, 'And what are these mysteries of yours?'

    E. "He will say to them, 'These mysteries are the Mishnah.'"

    F. Now how is all of this to be derived from exegesis?

    G. Said R. Judah the Levite, son of R. Shalom, "Said the Holy One, blessed be He, to Moses, 'How can you want the Mishnah to be written down? How are we to tell the difference between Israel and the nations of the world?

    H. "It is written, *"If I should write for him the larger part of my Torah, then he would have been seen as a stranger* (Hos. 8:12) – if so, they would have been held to be strangers [being unable to point to their knowledge of the Mishnah as evidence of their unique calling]."

No. 1 and No. 2 of course do not relate, since what is oral for No. 1 is the translation of Scripture from Hebrew to Aramaic, while what is at issue at No. 2 is the Mishnah as a document to be memorized and not written down. The point of No. 1 is that the law requires preserving a clear distinction between what is written, which is Scripture in Hebrew, and what is presented orally and not as though read, which is the translation of Scripture into the vernacular. No. 2 makes the quite separate point that, while the nations of the world have possession, in Greek, of Scripture, only Israel has possession of God's *gnosis*, the Mishnah, which is learned by memory.

V:II.

1. A. Another interpretation of the verse, *If I should write for him the larger part of my Torah, then he would have been seen as a stranger* (Hos. 8:12):

    B. This is one of the three matters for which Moses was prepared to give his life, on account of which the Holy One, blessed be He, gave them in his name [in line with the sense of the verse, I should write *for him*, meaning, *in his name*].

    C. The three are the rule of justice, the Torah, and the building of the tabernacle in the wilderness.

D.   How do we know that that is so of the Torah: *Remember the Torah of Moses, my servant* (Mal. 3:22).

E.   The rule of justice: *Moses the lawgiver...maintained the righteous judgments of the Lord and his ordinances among Israel* (Deut. 33:21).

F.   How do we know that Moses was prepared to give his life for the sake of the tabernacle:

G.   R. Hiyya b. Joseph said, "On each of the seven days of the consecration of the tabernacle, Moses would dismantle the tabernacle twice a day and then set it up again [thus, morning and evening, for the obligatory daily whole-offering done twice a day]."

H.   R. Hanina the Elder said, "Three times a day he would dismantle it and then erect it."

I.   And should you suppose that someone of the tribe of Levi would give him a hand, our masters have said, "He by himself would dismantle it, and no person of Israel helped him in any way.

J.   "How [do we know that Moses did it by himself]? As it is said, *And it came to pass on the day that Moses completed setting up the Tabernacle, [he anointed and consecrated it; he also anointed and consecrated its equipment, and the altar and its vessels. The chief men of Israel, heads of families, that is, the chiefs of the tribes who had assisted in preparing the detailed lists, came forward and brought their offering before the Lord]* (Num. 7:1-2). [All that the others did was make the lists and then give their own offering. Moses did the rest.]"

The insertion of this entire composition, covering **V:I.3** and **V:II,** is now clearly to lead us to the conclusion of J. The relevant point then is that Moses did the work by himself, sacrificially, and therefore Scripture credits to him the making of the tabernacle. Braude reads the proof-text, *And it came to pass on the day that Moses' strength had all but given out because of the settings up of the tabernacle,* which has the merit of translating the proof-text, with its use of the letters KLH, which can mean, *be completed,* and, by extension, *exhaust,* within the context of the sense intended here: self-sacrifice.

V:III.

1.   A.   Thus did R. Tanhuma b. R. Abba commence discourse:*Who has ascended heaven and come down? [Who has gathered up the wind in the hollow of his hand? Who has wrapped the waters in his garment? Who has established all the extremities of the earth? What is his name or his son's name, if you know it? Every word of God is pure, a shield to those who take refuge in him. Do not add to his words, lest he indict you and you be proved a liar]* (Prov. 30:4):

     B.   "This verse of Scripture is to be expounded with reference to God and Moses.

     C.   "How so?

     D.   *"Who has ascended heaven and come down?*

     E.   "This refers to the Holy One, blessed be He: *God has gone up amid acclamation* (Ps. 47:6).

     F.   "The matter may be compared to the case of a mortal king who was going from one place to another. They bring trumpets and sound them before him. So did they do before the Holy One, blessed be He, as in the following verse: *With trumpets at the blast of the horn raise a shout before the Lord King* (Ps. 98:6).

G. *"...and come down:* this refers to the Holy One, blessed be He: *And the Lord came down on Mount Sinai* (Ex. 19:20).

H. *"Who has gathered up the wind in the hollow of his hand?*

I. "This refers to the Holy One, blessed be He: *In whose hand is the soul of every liiving thing, and the breath of all mankind* (Job 12:10).

J. *"Who has wrapped the waters in his garment?*

K. "This refers to the Holy One, blessed be He: *He binds up the waters in his thick clouds* (Job 26:8).

L. *"Who has established all the extremities of the earth?* [Braude: Who has raised up all those who have come to their end upon the earth]

M. "This refers to the Holy One, blessed be He, who revives the dead: *Your dead shall live, my dead bodies shall arise* (Is. 26:19), also: *The Lord kills and brings alive* (1 Sam. 2:6).

N. *"What is his name?*

O. "It is God, the Almighty, Hosts, the Lord. What is his name? It is the Lord: *I am the Lord, that is my name* (Is. 42:8).

P. *"...or his son's name, if you know it:*

Q. "This refers to Israel: *Thus says the Lord, Israel is my son, my first born* (Ex. 4:22)."

2. A. *Who has ascended heaven and come down?*

B. Who is this one, whose prayer goes up to heaven and brings down rain?

C. This is one who shares out the tithes that he owes [not by exact calculation] but merely by fistfuls.

D. *Who has gathered up the wind in the hollow of his hand?*

E. This is one who does not divide up the tithes that he owes in the proper manner. He holds back rain.

3. A. Another interpretation: *Who has ascended heaven and come down?*

B. This refers to Elijah: *Elijah went up by a whirlwind into heaven* (2 Kgs. 2:11).

C. *...and come down?*

D. *Go down with him, do not be afraid* (2 Kgs. 1:15).

E. *Who has gathered up the wind in the hollow of his hand?*

F. *As the Lord, God of Israel, lives, before whom I stand, there shall not be dew nor rain these years* (1 Kgs. 17:1).

G. *Who has wrapped the waters in his garment?*

H. *Elijah took his cloak and wrapped it together and smote the waters and they were divided* (1 Kgs. 2:8).

I. *Who has established all the extremities of the earth?*

J. *And Elijah said, See, your son lives* (1 Kgs. 17:23).

4. A. Another interpretation: *Who has ascended heaven and come down?*

B. This refers to Moses: *And Moses went up to God* (Ex. 19:3).

C. *and come down?*

D. *And the Lord spoke to Moses, Go, get down* (Ex. 32:7).

E. *Who has gathered up the wind in the hollow of his hand?*

F. This refers to Moses: *As soon as I have gone out of the city, I shall spread forth my hands to the Lord* (Ex. 9:29).

G. *Who has wrapped the waters in his garment?*

H. *With the blast of your nostrils the waters were piled up* (Ex. 15:8).

I. *Who has established all the extremities of the earth?*

J. This is Moses: Said R. Abba bar Kahana, "This refers to the standards that Moses set up: *Each man with his own standard, according to the signs* (Num. 2:2)."

K. R. Simeon in the name of R. Joshua b. Levi, "This refers to the tabernacle: *And it came to pass on the day that Moses completed setting up the Tabernacle, [he anointed and consecrated it; he also anointed and consecrated its equipment, and the altar and its vessels. The chief men of Israel, heads of families, that is, the chiefs of the tribes who had assisted in preparing the detailed lists, came forward and brought their offering before the Lord]* (Num. 7:1-2)."

5. A. Our rabbis have taught: **On three things the world stands: the Torah, the Temple service [cult], and acts of lovingkindness [M. Abot 1:2].**

B. And you find that twenty-six generations arose from when the world was made until the Torah was given.

C. The Holy One, blessed be He, guided them in his mercy.

D. As a counterpart to those generations, David said twenty-six times: *For his mercy endures forever* (Ps. 136).

6. A. Said R. Huna the Priest, son of Abin, in the name of R. Aha, "Moses made a veiled allusion to them at the sea: *You have led them in your mercies* (Ex. 15:13).

B. "This refers to the twenty-six generations that arose from the creation of the world until the Torah was given.

C. *"You guided them by your strength* (Ex. 15:13): this refers to the Torah, which is called strength: *The Lord will give strength to his people* (Ps. 29:11).

D. "What was the world like at that time? It was like a three-legged chair, which had only two legs and could not stand. [Thus there were the people and the Torah, but no cult.] When the tabernacle – *to your holy habitation* (Ex. 15:13) – was set up, the universe was firmly established.

E. *"And it came to pass on the day that Moses completed setting up the Tabernacle"*

F. "What is written is only *the* tabernacle [and the *the* adds something, namely], with the sense, [setting up] thje world, like the creation of heaven and earth: *He who spreads them out as a tabernacle for habitation* (Is. 40:22)."

The point of No. 1 is realized at the end. Moses is the one who established the tabernacle as God's residence, as the base-verse indicates. So the force of the intersecting-verse is to identify Moses with the Holy One, in that Moses established the tabernacle for God (*established all the extremities of the earth*).

No. 1 then accomplishes the first of the two points, with interpolated materials, following the excellent pattern of No. 1, at Nos. 2, 3. Then No. 1 resumes at No. 4, and the point for point correspondence between God and Moses is worked out, reaching our climax at K. No. 5 then prepares the way for No. 6, with which it is continuous.

V:IV.

1. A. Another interpretation of the verse, *And it came to pass on the day that Moses completed [setting up the Tabernacle, [he anointed and consecrated it; he also anointed and consecrated its equipment, and the altar and its vessels. The chief men of Israel, heads of families, that is, the chiefs of the tribes who had assisted in preparing the detailed lists, came forward and brought their offering before the Lord]* (Num. 7:1-2).

   B. This is pertinent to the following verse: *Awake O north, and come O south* (Song 4:16).

   C. *Awake O north* refers to whole-offerings, which are slaughtered at the north side of the altar.

2. A. R. Eliezer b. Pedat said, "The children of Noah offered peace-offerings [and not whole-offerings]."

   B. "What is the basis for that statement?

   C. *"And Abel brought of the firstlings of his flock and of their fat portions* (Gen. 4:4).

   D. "What is the sense of the phrase, *and of their fat portions* (Gen. 4:4)?

   E. "The fat of the beast was offered on the altar [and not eaten by the one who brought the beast, but the pertinent portions of the beast were eaten by the one who brought it, hence it was a peace offering that Abel brought]."

   F. And R. Yose bar Hanina said, "They prepared them in the status of whole-offerings [burning up the entire animal and not keeping any portions for the sacrificer (who does the rite) and *sacrifier* (who benefits from the rite)]."

   G. How does R. Yose bar Hanina treat this passage: *and of their fat portions* (Gen. 4:4)? He interprets it to refer to the fat animals [and not to the portions of those that were offered up, but only referring to "the best of the flock"].

   H. R. Eleazar objected to R. Yose bar Hanina, "And is it not written, *And Jethro, Moses' father-in-law, took a burnt-offering and sacrifices* (Ex. 18:12)? [The reference to a burnt-offering would suffice, so the inclusion of the further reference to "sacrifices" indicates that there was an offering made in a different classification, hence, peace-offerings.]"

   I. [How does R. Yose bar Hanina deal with this verse?] He accords with the view of him who said that Jethro came to Moses *after* the giving of the Torah, [at which point Jethro was in the status of an Israelite. Hence the type of offering Jethro gave would indicate only what Israelites did when they made their sacrifices and would not testify to how children of Noah, prior to the giving of the Torah, in general offered up their animals.]

   J. R. Yannai said, "It was after the giving of the Torah that he came."

   K. R. Hiyya the Elder said, "It was prior to the giving of the Torah that he came."

L. R. Eleazar [objected to the view of R. Yose bar Hanina], "And lo, it is written: *And he sent the young men of the children of Israel, who offered burnt-offerings and sacrificed peace-offerings of oxen unto the Lord* (Ex. 24:5)? [This was before revelation, and hence would indicate that the children of Noah, belonging to the category of the Israelites at that time, prior to the Torah, in fact offered not only whole offerings but also peace offerings, just as Eleazar maintains.]"

M. He said to him, "Indeed, we have learned from the Torah that that was an innovation for the occasion."

N. Hezekiah b. R. Hiyya interpreted the reference to *peace-offerings* to mean that they offered up the beasts with their hides, without flaying them and cutting them into pieces. [That constituted an innovation. So even though the verse refers to peace-offerings, in fact the animals were offered up as whole-offerings, hide and all.]

O. Said R. Joshua of Sikhnin in the name of R. Levi, "Scripture supports the view of R. Yose bar Hanina. Note what is written:

P. R. Joshua of Sikhnin in the name of R. Levi: "Also the following verse supports the view of R. Yose bar Hanina: When Scripture refers to the meal-offering, what is stated is not, that is the meal-offering,' and when it says, *This is the Torah of the guilt-offering* (Lev. 7:1), it does not say, 'That is the guilt-offering.' But when Scripture comes to the matter of the whole-offering, what does Scripture say? *This is the Torah governing the preparation of the whole-offering, that is the whole-offering [of which people already are informed]* (Lev. 6:2) meaning, that whole-offering that the children of Noah used to offer up.

Q. "When Scripture speaks of peace-offerings, it states, *And this is the law of the sacrifice of peace-offering* (Lev. 7:11), but it is not written, *'which they offered up,'* but rather, 'which they *will* offer up' (Lev. 7:11), meaning, only in the future. [Hence peace-offerings' rules, allowing the sacrificer and *sacrifier* a share in the animal that is offered up, represented an innovation, not formerly applicable, in support of the view of R. Yose bar Hanina that such offerings' rules constituted an innovation.]"

R. The following verse of Scripture also supports the view of R. Yose bar Hanina: *Awake, O north wind* (Song 4:16) refers to the whole offering, which was slaughtered at the north side of the altar. What is the sense of "awake"? It speaks of something that was asleep and now wakes up.

S. *And come, you south* (Song 4:16) speaks of peace-offerings, which were slaughtered [even] at the south side of the altar. [And what is the sense of "come"? It speaks of a new and unprecedented practice. Hence the rules governing peace-offerings constituted an innovation. Freedman, *Genesis Rabbah*, p. 184, n. 1: Thus it was only now, after the giving of the Torah, that the practice of sacrificing peace-offerings was introduced.]

3. A. Said R. Simon in the name of R. Samuel b. R. Nahman, "Scripture says, *An altar of dirt you will make for me, and you will make an offering on it of your whole-offerings and peace offerings* (Ex. 20:21)."

    B. R. Reuben says, "In a place that is suitable for whole offerings and suitable for peace-offerings [is where these offerings will be made]. From the midddle of the altar and to the northern side it is suitable for whole-offerings, and from the middle of the altar and southward is the area suitable for peace-offerings."

4 . A. *Blow on my garden that the spices thereof may flow out* (Song. 4:16):
   B. This refers to the incense-offering.

5 . A. *Let my beloved come into his garden* (Song 4:16):
   B. Said R. Nehunia, "Torah teaches proper conduct. A husband should not come in until the bride gives him permission."

6 . A. *And eat his precious fruits* (Song 4:16):
   B. This refers to the offerings.

The intersecting-verse becomes relevant only at the very end, at which point we refer to the altar. No. 6 is the one point at which we regain the base-verse. No. 2 raises its own question, a debate parachuted down with no bearing upon our passage at all. The reason, of course, is that our intersecting-verse enters in at 2.S. Otherwise there is no point of contact. 2.T then accounts for the inclusion of No. 3, 4, and 5 – that is, a hodgepodge of comments on the intersecting-verse. In no way is the base-verse illuminated. That is not what is at issue in the compositors' program. The model, rather, is one of a scrapbook in which one collects materials on a given topic: a file that is topical and not purposeful and composed with a proposition in mind. But in the unfolding of the whole, as we see, the composition becomes somewhat more successful.

V:V.

1 . A. *I have come into my garden, my sister, my bride* (Song 5:1):
   B. To what is the matter compared? To the case of a king who said to the citizens of a state to build him a palace. They built it and assembled at the gate of the palace crying out, "Let the king come into the palace."
   C. What did the king do? He went in through a side door and sent an announcement saying to them, "Do not cry out! I have already come into the palace."
   D. So too, when the tabernacle had been erected, the Israelites said, *"Let my beloved come into his garden* (Song 4:16)."
   E. The Holy One, blessed be He, sent to them and said, "Why are you concerned? *I have come into my garden, my sister, my bride* (Song 5:1)."

2 . A. Another matter concerning the verse, *I have come into my garden, my sister, my bride* (Song 5:1):
   B. Said R. Simeon bar Yosni, "What is written is not, I have come into a garden, but *I have come into my garden, [my sister, my bride]* (Song 5:1).
   C. "What is the explanation of 'my garden'? 'I have returned to the garden from which I had departed.'
   D. "That is in line with this verse: *The Lord God was moving about in the garden* (Gen. 3:8) [Braude, p. 102: 'The Lord God hastened and went up from the garden.'"

3. A. *I have gathered my myrrh with my spice, I have eaten my liquid honey as well as my honeycomb* (Song 5:1): this refers to the Most Holy Things and the Lesser Holy Things.

   B. *I have drunk my wine with my fat* (Song 5:1): this refers to the drink offerings and the fats.

4. A. Another interpretation of the verse *I have gathered my myrrh with my spice, I have eaten my liquid honey as well as my honeycomb, I have drunk my wine with my fat* (Song 5:1): this refers to three things which the princes did improperly, but which, nonetheless, the Holy One, blessed be He, accepted.

   B. The first is that an individual may not present as a voluntary offering an incense-offering, but every prince brought an incense-offering, in line with this verse of Scripture: *One tolden pan of ten shekels full of incense* (Num. 7:14).

   C. An individual may not offer a sin-offering unless he knows precisely what sin he has commited inadvertently: *If his sin...become known to him, he shall bring for his offering a goat* (Lev. 4:23), but the princes made a sin-offering for a sin of which none was aware: *His offering was...a male of the goats for a sin-offering* (Num. 7:16).

   D. An individual's offering does not override the restrictions of the Sabbath, but the offering of one prince did override the restrictions of the Sabbath: *On the seventh day...the prince...of the children of Ephraim* (Num. 7:48).

5. A. *Eat O friends drink, yes, drink abundantly O beloved* (Song 5:1):

   B. This refers to Israel, who are called friends: *For my brethren and friends' sakes* (Ps. 12:8).

6. A. Another interpretation of the verse *Let my beloved come into his garden* (Song 4:16):

   B. Do not read the letters for garden as they are given, but rather, to mean, "to the marriage canopy."

   C. When was this the case? *And it came to pass on the day that Moses completed setting up the Tabernacle* for the word for *completed* is written so that it may be read as *nuptial*, [hence, this was the day that Israel as bride entered the marriage canopy].

Now the selection of the intersecting-verse makes sense within the framework of the compositor, who wishes to dwell on the notion that the day on which the tabernacle was completed marked the marriage of Israel to God. Then the base-verse, with its possibility of a play on the word for complete and nuptial, has guided us to Song 4:16, 5:1, and the rest follows. But then the miscellaneous character of the rest is clear, since the treatment of Song 5:1, with its reference to liquid honey and so forth, is wholly autonomous of the purpose and direction of exegesis. So once an intersecting-verse is chosen, then its interests will guide the whole, and no proposition joining each of the parts will account for the inner cogency of the composition as a whole – for there is none.

V : VI.

1. A. Another interpretation of the verse *And it came to pass on the day that Moses completed setting up the Tabernacle, [he anointed and consecrated it; he also anointed and consecrated its equipment, and the altar and its vessels. The chief men of Israel, heads of families, that is, the chiefs of the tribes who had assisted in preparing the detailed lists, came forward and brought their offering before the Lord]* (Num. 7:1-2):

   B. This is relevant to the following verse: *For there is a man whose labor is with wisdom and with knowledge and with skill* (Qoh. 2:21).

   C. This refers to Bezalel, who made the tabernacle with wisdom and knowledge, in line with this verse of Scripture: *I have filled him with the spirit of God, in wisdom and understanding and knowledge* (Ex. 31:3).

   D. *Yet to a man who has not labored therein shall he leave of his portion* (Qoh. 2:21):

   E. This refers to Moses, who did not labor to create the tabernacle, yet it is called by his name, as it is said: *And it came to pass on the day that Moses completed setting up the Tabernacle.*

   F. What is written is not, *And it came to pass on the day that* Bezalel *completed setting up the Tabernacle,*

   G. but rather, *And it came to pass on the day that Moses completed setting up the Tabernacle.*

   H. Thus we see the meaning of the verse: *Yet to a man who has not labored therein shall he leave of his portion.*

The focus now is upon the curious fact that Scripture assigns the making of the tabernacle to Bezalel and also credits it to Moses. The rest follows, and the intersecting-verse here provides an observation upon the fact.

V : VII.

1. A. *And it came to pass on the day that Moses completed setting up the Tabernacle, [he anointed and consecrated it; he also anointed and consecrated its equipment, and the altar and its vessels. The chief men of Israel, heads of families, that is, the chiefs of the tribes who had assisted in preparing the detailed lists, came forward and brought their offering before the Lord]* (Num. 7:1-2):

   B. What he said he would do, he did.

2. A. Said R. Joshua b. Levi, "The Holy One, blessed be He, stipulated with Israel while they were yet in Egypt that he would bring them out of Egypt only on condition that they make a tabernacle, in which he would bring his Presence to rest among them, as it is said, *And they shall know that I am the Lord their God, who has brought them forth out of the land of Egypt, that I may dwell among them* (Ex. 29:46)..

   B. "When the tabernacle was set up, the Presence of God descended and dwelt in it. At that moment was carried out the entire stipulation.

   C. "Therefore it is said, *And it came to pass* (Num. 7:1).

   D. "What he said he would do, he did."

3. A. Another matter concerning the verse: *And it came to pass* (Num. 7:1):

B. Said Rab, "[What came to pass] is something that had never been created in the world before this time.

C. "For from the time that the world was created, the Presence of God had never come to rest among the lower creatures. But once Moses had set up the tabernacle, the Presence of God came to rest among the lower creatures."

D. And R. Simeon b. Yohai says, "What is the sense of *And it came to pass* (Num. 7:1)? It had been in being and ceased and then come into being once again.

E. "For so you find that from the beginning of the credation of the world, the Presence of God was among the creatures of the lower world, in line with this verse of Scripture:

F. *"And they heard the voice of the Lord God walking in the garden* (Gen. 3:8).

G. "When the first man sinned, the Presence of God rose up to the first firmament. When Cain went and murdered his brother, the Presence of God went up to the second firmament. When the generation of Enosh went and sinned – *then the practice of calling on the name of the Lord [in vain] began* (Gen. 4:26) – it went up to the third firmament. When the generation of the Flood went and sinned, in line with this verse, *And the Lord saw that the wickedness of man was great* (Gen. 6:5), it went up to the fourth firmament. When the generation of the dispersion went and sinned – *Come, let us build a city with its top in heaven* (Gen. 11:4) – the Presence of God went up to the fifth firmament. When the people of Sodom went and sinned, it went up to the sixth: *The men of Sodom were wicked and sinners* (Gen. 13:13). When the Philistines came and sinned – *and Abimelech, king of Gerar, sent and took Sarah* (Gen. 20:2) – it went up to the sevnth.

H. "Abraham came along and laid up a treasure of good deeds, and the Presence of God came down from the seventh firmament to the sixth. Isaac came along and stretched out his neck on the altar, and the Presence of God went down from the sixth to the fifth. Jacob came along and planted a tent for the Torah-study, in line with this verse, *And Jacob was a perfect man, living in tents* (Gen. 25:27), and the Presence of God came down from the fifth to the fourth firmament. Levi came along and brought it down from the fourth to the third, Kehath came along and brought it from the third to the second, Amram came along and brought it from the second to the first.

I. "Fortunate are the righteous who create on earth a dwelling place for the Presence of God.

J. "For so it is written: *Truly the upright will make a dwelling place on the earth* (Prov. 2:21).

K. "Moses came along and brought the Presence down, in line with this verse: *The cloud covered the tent, and the glory of the Lord filled the tabernacle* (Ex. 40:34)."

4. A. It is written, *Behold heaven and the heaven of heavens cannot hold you* (1 Kgs. 8:27).

B. And it is written, *And the glory of the Lord filled the tabernacle* (Ex. 40:34).

C. Said R. Joshua of Sikhnin in the name of R. Levi, "To what may the matter be compared? To a cave open at the edge of the sea. The sea floods upward and fills the cave, but the sea is not diminished.

D. "So even though it is written, *And the glory of the Lord filled the tabernacle* (Ex. 40:34), nonetheless the upper worlds and the lower worlds did not lose any of the splendor of the glory of the Holy One, blessed be He, in line with this verse: *Do I not fill the heaven and the earth, says the Lord* (Jer. 23:24)."

5. A. [Resuming Simeon's statement, where 3:J left off:] "Therefore it is written here, *And it came to pass* (Num. 7:1), indicating that just as the Presence of God at the beginning of the creation of the world had been below, but had arisen upward by stages and then returned now to dwell below,

B. "so now it would remain: *And it came to pass on the day that Moses completed setting up the Tabernacle.*"

What is subject to interpretation is the phrase, *And it came to pass on the day that Moses completed setting up the Tabernacle.* No. 1 offers a simple statement. Then No. 2 clarifies No. 1. Nos. 3, 5 work on the sense of the language, and it came to pass, with the two positions – something new, something renewed – fully spelled out, with an interpolation at No. 4.

V:VIII.

1. A. Another interpretation concerning the same phrase, namely, *And it came to pass [on the day that Moses completed setting up the Tabernacle, he anointed and consecrated it; he also anointed and consecrated its equipment, and the altar and its vessels. The chief men of Israel, heads of families, that is, the chiefs of the tribes who had assisted in preparing the detailed lists, came forward and brought their offering before the Lord]* (Num. 7:1-2).

B. Said R. Hiyya b. R. Abba in the name of R. Yohanan, "The following exegetical principle we brought up from the exile of Babylonia.

C. "Any passage in which the words, *And it came to pass* appear is a passage that relates unparalleled misfortune."

D. Along these same lines said R. Simeon b. R. Abba in the name of R. Yohanan: "It may serve this meaning but also the opposite. Specifically, in any passage in which it says, *It came to pass in the days of*, speaks of distress without parallel, e.g.,

E. "*And it came to pass in the days of Ahasuerus* (Est. 1:1) [cf. also: *Haman undertook to destroy, to slay, and to annihilate all the Jews, young and old, women and children, in one day* (Est. 3:13)] – can there be a greater misfortune?

F. "*And it came to pass in the days in which the judges ruled, there was a famine in the land* (Ruth 1:1) – can there be a greater misfortune?

G. "And any passage in which it says, *And it came to pass*, speaks of joy without parallel:

H. "*Let there be light and there was light* (Gen. 1:3) – is there greater joy than that!

I.   *"And it came to pass on the eighth day* (Lev. 9:1) – is there greater joy than that!

J.   "So too here: *And it came to pass [on the day that Moses completed setting up the Tabernacle* – is there greater joy than that!"

2. A.   Said R. Samuel b. Nahman, "In any passage in which it is written, *And it came to pass* , there is no distress that can compare to that, and in any passage in which it is written, *And it was*, there is no greater joy than that."

   B.   They said to R. Samuel b. Nahman, "Lo, it is written, *And light came to pass.* What distress came about on that occasion?"

   C.   He said to them, "It was that its light was destined to be stored away on account of the lights [of the sun and the moon]."

   D.   They said to him, "And lo, it is written, *And it came to pass on the eighth day* (Lev. 9:1). What distress came about on that occasion?"

   E.   He said to them, "Nadab and Abihu were going to die."

   F.   They said to him, "And lo, it is written, *And it came to pass [on the day that Moses completed setting up the Tabernacle.* What distress came about on that occasion?"

   G.   He said to them, "It is because the tabernacle was destined to be stored away on account of the house of the sanctuary."

   H.   They said to him, "And lo, it is written, *And it was when Jerusalem was taken* (Jer. 38:28). [What joy can be involved here?]"

   I.   He said to them, "There is no joy like it, for [had the city not been taken,] the prophet would not have had the right to say so to Israel, *The punishment of your sin has been accomplished, daughter of Zion* (Lam. 5:22)."

The inquiry into the sense of *And it came to pass* unfolds at Nos. 1, 2. No. 1 deals with our passage, but No. 2 does not., which means that the composite was complete before insertion here. Samuel b. Nahman's exercise is in any case irrelevant.

V:IX.

1. A.   *And it came to pass on the day that Moses completed setting up the Tabernacle, [he anointed and consecrated it; he also anointed and consecrated its equipment, and the altar and its vessels. The chief men of Israel, heads of families, that is, the chiefs of the tribes who had assisted in preparing the detailed lists, came forward and brought their offering before the Lord]* (Num. 7:1-2).

   B.   [Since the letters of the word for and *it came to pass* may also be read, Woe, we ask:] who said, "Woe"?

   C.   Said R. Abba, "It is as if the Holy One, blessed be He, said woe.

   D.   "To what may the matter be compared? To the case of a king who had a shrewish wife. The king said to her, 'Make a purple cloak for me.'

   E.   "All the time that she was busy making the cloak, she kept her peace. But after a while she finished the cloak and gave it to the launderer who completed the work, and she brought it to the king.

F. "When the king saw it, he began to cry, 'Woe.' She said to him, 'My lord, O King, your purple cloak is finished and you say, 'Woe'?

G. "He said to her, 'It is because I am worried that you will go back to your complaining.'

H. "So you find that the Israelites were always complaining, in line with this verse: *And the people murmured against Moses and against Aaron* (Ex. 15:24).

I. "So too: *And the whole congregation of the children of Israel murmured* (Ex. 16:23).

J. *"You have killed the people of the Lord* (Num. 17:6).

K. "The Holy One, blessed be He, asked them to make a tabernacle: *And let them make me a sanctuary* (Ex. 25:8).

L. "So you find that all the time that the Israelites were occupied with the making of the tabernacle, they did not have occasion to complain. But once they had finished the tabernacle, the Holy One, blessed be He, cried, 'Woe.'

M. *"And it came to pass on the day that Moses ended* (Num. 7:1).

N. "They said, 'Lord of the age, the tabernacle is finished, and yet you cry, 'Woe.'

O. "He said to them, 'I shall tell you why I cry woe. It is because I am afraid that you are going to go and starting grumbling against me as you have been in the past.'"

2. A. *And it came to pass on the day that Moses completed setting up the Tabernacle, [he anointed and consecrated it; he also anointed and consecrated its equipment, and the altar and its vessels. The chief men of Israel, heads of families, that is, the chiefs of the tribes who had assisted in preparing the detailed lists, came forward and brought their offering before the Lord]* (Num. 7:1-2).

B. [Since the letters of the word for and *it came to pass* may also be read, Woe, we ask:] who said, "Woe"?

C. The firstborn said, "Woe," for the right of the priesthood was taken away from them.

D. Our rabbis have taught: **Before the tabernacle was set up, sacrifices on the high places was permitted, and the work of the sacrifice was carried on by the firstborn [M. Zeb. 14:4],**

E. and so it is written, *Let not the priests and the people break through to come up to the Lord* (Ex. 19:24), for up to that time the Torah had not been given, and the priesthood had not been assigned to Aaron.

F. And so it is written, *Let not the priests and the people break through to come up to the Lord* (Ex. 19:24).

3. A. [As to the verse, *Let not the priests and the people break through to come up to the Lord* (Ex. 19:24),] R. Joshua b. Qorhah and Rabbi:

B. One of them says, "The reference to the priests in fact speaks of the first born."

C. And his colleagues say, "The reference to the priests applies to Nadab and Abihu."

4. A. *The golden thing has ceased, the Lord has broken the staff of the wicked*
        (Is. 14:4-5):
    B. Said R. Abba bar Mamal, "This refers to the firstborn."

5. A. Therefore when the tabernacle was set up, they cried out, "Woe."
    B. *And it came to pass on the day* (Num. 7:1).

6. A. Another matter: *And it came to pass on the day that Moses completed
        setting up the Tabernacle, [he anointed and consecrated it; he also
        anointed and consecrated its equipment, and the altar and its vessels. The
        chief men of Israel, heads of families, that is, the chiefs of the tribes
        who had assisted in preparing the detailed lists, came forward and brought
        their offering before the Lord]* (Num. 7:1-2).
    B. [Since the letters of the word for and *it came to pass* may also be read,
        Woe, we ask:] who said, "Woe"?
    C. The angels said, "Woe."
    D. They said, "Now the Holy One, blessed be He, will leave the upper
        regions and go down and dwell in the lower regions."
    E. Nonetheless, the Holy One, blessed be He, conciliated them, saying to
        the creatures of the upper world, "By your lives! The Principal [of God's
        presence] is above, in line with this verse: *His glory covers the heavens,
        and the earth is full of his praise* (Hab. 3:3)."
    F. Said R. Simon in the name of R. Simeon in the name of R. Joshua, "The
        Holy One, blessed be He, in fact was kidding with them when he said,
        'The Principal is above,' for lo, it is written, *His glory is upon earth and
        heaven, for he has raised up the horn of his people* (Ps. 148:13-14).
        That is, first on the earth, then in heaven.
    G. "Therefore they said, 'Woe.' *And it came to pass on the day that Moses
        completed setting up the Tabernacle.*"

7. A. Another matter: *And it came to pass on the day that Moses completed
        setting up the Tabernacle, [he anointed and consecrated it; he also
        anointed and consecrated its equipment, and the altar and its vessels. The
        chief men of Israel, heads of families, that is, the chiefs of the tribes
        who had assisted in preparing the detailed lists, came forward and brought
        their offering before the Lord]* (Num. 7:1-2).
    B. [Since the letters of the word for and *it came to pass* may also be read,
        Woe, we ask:] who said, "Woe"?
    C. The nations of the world said, "Woe."
    D. Why did they say woe? Because they said, "Before the Holy One, blessed
        be He, was living with them, he would watch over them and do their
        battles for them, and now that they have made a tabernacle for them and
        he dwells with them, all the more so.
    E. Therefore they said, "Woe:" *And it came to pass on the day that Moses
        completed setting up the Tabernacle.*"

The exercise of interpreting the language, *And it came to pass,* leads us
through a number of possibilities, all the while making a single point, which is

that the Israelites' building of the tabernacle had important consequences for the entire world.

V:X.

1. A.   Another matter concerning the issue at hand: *And it came to pass on the day that Moses completed setting up the Tabernacle, [he anointed and consecrated it; he also anointed and consecrated its equipment, and the altar and its vessels. The chief men of Israel, heads of families, that is, the chiefs of the tribes who had assisted in preparing the detailed lists, came forward and brought their offering before the Lord]* (Num. 7:1-2).

   B.   What passage occurs just prior to this one? It is the blessing of the priests: *May the Lord bless you and keep you* (Num. 6:24).

   C.   Said R. Joshua of Sikhnin, "To what may the matter be compared? To the case of a king who betrothed his daughter and was making a banquet of betrothal for her, over which the evil eye had effect.

   D.   "The king went on to marry her off. What did he do [in consequence of the earlier experience]?

   E.   "He gave her an amulet. He said to her, "Keep this amulet on you, so that the evil eye will not affect you any more.'

   F.   "So too when the Holy One, blessed be He, came to give the Torah to Israel at Sinai, he made for them a great public celebration, in line with this verse: *And all the people perceived the thunderings* (Ex. 20:15).

   G.   "This event was only the betrothal, in line with the following: *Go to the people and sanctify them to me* (Ex. 19:10).

   H.   "But the evil eye had effect, so the tablets were broken, as it is said, *Moses broke them beneath the mountain* (Ex. 32:19).

   I.   "When they came some time later and made the tabernacle, the Holy One, blessed be He, first handed over to them the priestly blessings, so that the evil eye should not have effect on them.

   J.   "Therefore Scripture first wrote, *May the Lord bless you and keep you,* and then, *And it came to pass on the day that Moses completed setting up the Tabernacle.*"

2. A.   Another matter concerning the issue at hand: Why does Scripture say first, *May the Lord bless you and keep you* (Num. 6:24), followed by *And it came to pass on the day that Moses completed setting up the Tabernacle?*

   B.   Said R. Abbahu, "The traits of the Holy One, blessed be He, are not the same as the traits of mortals.

   C.   "When a mortal king enters a town, the townspeople praise him and exult him and honor him, and then he carries out all of their needs. He builds them public buildings and does other deeds to please them.

   D.   "But the Holy One, blessed be He, is not that way. Rather, before the Israelites made the tabernacle, he gave them the blessings first, as it is written, *May the Lord bless you and keep you,* and then, *And it came to pass on the day that Moses completed setting up the Tabernacle.*"

3. A.   Another interpretation of the verse *And it came to pass on the day that Moses completed setting up the Tabernacle* [now explaining the word-choice for completed, which means also, bring to an end]:

B. Said R. Judah b. R. Shalom in the name of R. Levi, "There is not a quarter-*qab*'s sewing space of ground in the earth which does not contain nine *qabs* of demons." [This will now be applied to the present case.]

C. Said R. Yohanan, "When the tabernacle was set up, the demons were brought to an end in the world, for it is written, *There shall no evil thing befall you, nor shall any plague come near your tent* (Ps. 91:10) — once the tabernacle was set up."

D. Said R. Simeon b. Laqish, "Why do I require proof merely from the book of Psalms? It is a matter deriving from the Torah: *May the Lord bless you and keep you* — from demons.

E. "When will this take place? *And it came to pass on the day that Moses completed setting up the Tabernacle.*"

F. A further statement of the same matter: *And it came to pass on the day that Moses completed setting up the Tabernacle.*

G. What is written is not that "Moses set up," but Moses *completed setting up*. What then came to an end on that day were the demons, which were removed from the world.

The word finish bears the meaning, bring to an end, with the result that we wish to know what ended. It is the evil eye or demonic rule, which the cult counteracts. Hence when the cult was set up, demons were driven out of the world. No. 1 makes that point in terms of the misadventure involved in giving the Torah. No. 2 has its own message, not pertinent to the larger setting, and then No. 3 repeats the point of No. 1.

V:XI.

1. A. Another interpretation of the verse, *And it came to pass on the day that Moses completed setting up the Tabernacle, [he anointed and consecrated it; he also anointed and consecrated its equipment, and the altar and its vessels. The chief men of Israel, heads of families, that is, the chiefs of the tribes who had assisted in preparing the detailed lists, came forward and brought their offering before the Lord]* (Num. 7:1-2):

   B. One may commence discourse by citing this verse: *Go forth, you daughters of Zion, and gaze upon King Solomon* (Song 3:11).

   C. This may then be worked out as indicated in discourse on the Song of Songs.

2. A. Another interpretation of the verse, *And it came to pass on the day that Moses completed setting up the Tabernacle, [he anointed and consecrated it; he also anointed and consecrated its equipment, and the altar and its vessels. The chief men of Israel, heads of families, that is, the chiefs of the tribes who had assisted in preparing the detailed lists, came forward and brought their offering before the Lord]* (Num. 7:1-2):

   B. One may commence discourse by citing this verse: *I shall hear what the Lord God will speak, for he will speak peace to his people and to his saints [but let them not turn back to folly]* (Ps. 85:9):

   C. You find that, when the Israelites did that deed, the Holy One, blessed be He, was angry with them, in line with this verse: *I have seen this people and lo, it is a stiff-necked people* (Ex. 32:9).

D.   Moses forthwith went and sought mercy before the Holy One, blessed be He, so that he might be conciliated with Israel, as it is written, *And Moses besought the Lord his God and said, Lord, why do you get so angry? Turn from your fierce wrath and repent of this evil against your people* (Ex. 32:11).

E.   Forthwith the Holy One, blessed be He, was conciliated with them, as it is written, *And the Lord repented of the evil which he said he would to to his people* Ex. 32:14).

F.   Moses went and [following Braude, p. 113] inclined his ear in the tabernacle, [thinking to himself,] "It is possible that the Holy One, blessed be He, harbors a grudge against Israel?" So it is written, *I shall hear what the Lord God will speak, for he will speak peace to his people and to his saints but let them not turn back to folly* (Ps. 85:9).

G.   "Is it possible that he is still bearing anger against them? But when [as in the cited verse] the name of *the Lord* appears, it is an indication that he deals mercifully with them."

H.   Forthwith the Holy One, blessed be He, reassured him that he bore no grudge against Israel, in line with this verse: *And the Lord passed by before him and proclaimed, The Lord, the Lord, God, merciful and gracious* (Ex. 34:6).

I.   Said R. Simon, "Why is it written in the verse *The Lord, the Lord, God,* (Ex. 34:6), that is, two times?

J.   "It indicates that God reassured him."

K.   He said to him, "Moses, up to this time I treated them in accord with the attribute of mercy, that is, until they had done that deed. So too, even now I shall deal with them in accord with the attribute of mercy."

L.   Now Moses was standing there, and the word came into his ear as through a pipe so that none of the Israelites could hear. But when Moses's face got red, the people knew that the word was with him."

3. A.   Said R. Berekiah the Priest in the name of R. Judah bar R. Simon, "Said the Holy One, blessed be He, to him, 'Moses, in the past there was hatred between me and my children, enmity between me and my children, competition between me and my children.

B.   "But now there will be love between me and my children, fraternity between me and my children, comradeship between me and my children, in line with this verse: *I shall hear what the Lord God will speak, for he will speak peace to his people and to his saints but let them not turn back to folly* (Ps. 85:9).

4. A.   Another interpretation of the verse *I shall hear what the Lord God will speak, for he will speak peace to his people and to his saints but let them not turn back to folly* (Ps. 85:9):

B.   Said R. Joshua the Priest b. R. Nehemiah, "This is what R. Eleazar said, 'Before the tabernacle was set up, there was strife in the world, but once the tabernacle was set up, peace was made in the world.

C.   "'How do we know that fact? *I shall hear what the Lord God will speak, for he will speak peace to his people and to his saints but let them not turn back to folly* (Ps. 85:9):

D. "'When is that the case? *When glory is made to dwell in our land* [because of the setting up of the tabernacle], *surely his salvation will be near those who bear him* (Ps. 85:10).'"

E. Said R. Simeon b. Laqish, "Why do I have to draw evidence from the book of Psalms? It is a teaching of the Torah: *The Lord lift up his countenance upon you and give you peace* (Num. 6:26).

F. "When [is this the case]? *On the day that Moses finished setting up the tabernacle.*"

5. A. Another comment on: *On the day that Moses finished setting up the tabernacle:*

B. Said R. Joshua b. Levi, "By a hint said the Holy One, blessed be He, to Israel, that when they should set up the tabernacle, he would bestow the blessings on them.

C. "How do we know [that he gave such an indication in advance]? It is written, *An altar of earth you shall make for me...in every place where I cause my name to be mentioned I shall come to you and bless you* (Ex. 30:32).

D. "Therefore when they made the tabernacle, the Holy One, blessed be He, bestowed the blessings upon them:

E. *The Lord bless you and keep you.*

F. "When was this? *On the day that Moses finished setting up the tabernacle.*"

6. A. Said R. Simon, "When the Holy One, blessed be He, said to Israel to put up the tabernacle, he hinted to them that when the tabernacle was set up below, a tabernacle would be set up above.

B. *"On the day that Moses finished setting up the tabernacle:*

C. What is written is *the* tabernacle, bearing the sense that it was that very tabernacle that had been above."

7. A. *On the day that Moses finished setting up the tabernacle:*

B. Said the Holy One, blessed be He, "In this world, when the tabernacle was set up, I commanded Aaron and his sons to bless you.

C. "But in the coming age I in my own person shall bless you, for so it is written, *The Lord bless you out of Zion, even he who made heaven and earth* (Ps. 134:3)."

No. 1 presents a note on an unrealized discourse. No. 2 introduces an intersecting-verse which allows us to make the point that when the tabernacle was constructed, it represented an assurance of God's love for Israel. No. 3 makes the same point, using the same verse, but states matters more smoothly. No. 4 goes over the matter yet a third time. No. 5 then makes the same point but does so in line with the prior interest in the juxtaposition of the Priestly Blessing with the account of Moses's setting up of the tabernacle.

Chapter Six

Pesiqta Rabbati *Pisqa* 15 Which is Pesiqta deRab Kahana *Pisqa* 5

The verse that recurs throughout derives from the synagogue lection for the fourth of four designated Sabbaths in preparation for the spring season, HaHodesh, the New Month, announcing the advent of Nisan, in which Passover falls.

> *[The Lord said to Moses and Aaron in the land of Egypt,]* "This month *[shall be for you the beginning of months; it shall be the first month of the year for you]*" (Ex. 12:1-2)

Since the present *pisqa* occurs also at Pesiqta deRab Kahana, our principal interest is to determine the relationship between our Pesiqta's version and that of the other. What I have done is reproduce my translation of the *pisqa* as it occurs at Pesiqta deRab Kahana. Then I have inserted in **bold face type** materials that occur only in the version of Pesiqta Rabbati. In ***italicized bold face type*** I signify materials that occur only in Pesiqta deRab Kahana. Where there are variations in wording that seem noteworthy, I give the Pesiqta Rabbati's version in **bold face type,** and Pesiqta deRab Kahana's version in ***italicized bold face type***. This permits us to see the extent to which the present document contains alternative readings of importance. I have not signified minor variations in wording, which do not seem to me to tell us much about the taste, judgment, or even literary interests, of the authorship or editorship of our document. My sole question is whether Pesiqta Rabbati's authorship substantially revises or leaves pretty much in their received condition the materials it has taken over from Pesiqta deRab Kahana.

Pesiqta Rabbati XV [=Pesiqta deRab Kahana V]:I

1. A. *[The Lord said to Moses and Aaron in the land of Egypt,]* "This month *[shall be for you the beginning of months; it shall be the first month of the year for you]*" (Ex. 12:1-2):
   B. *He appointed the moon for [lunar] seasons, yet the sun knows its coming* (Ps. 104:19): Said R. Yohanan, "Only the orb of the sun was created for the purpose of giving light.
   C. *"Let there be light* (Gen. 1:14):
   D. "What is written is *light* [in the singular].

E. "If so, why was the moon created? It was for the signification of the seasons, specifically so that, through [regular sightings of the moon, Israelites would] sanctify new months and years."

F. R. Shila of Kefar Tamarata in the name of R. Yohanan: "Nonetheless: *The sun knows its coming* (Ps. 104:19). On the basis of that statement, we have the following rule: people count the advent of the new moon only once the sun has set."

G. [Proving the foregoing proposition,] *Yusta,* an associate, in the name of R. Berekhiah: "As it is said, *And they traveled from Raamses in the first month on the fifteenth day of the month* (Num. 33:3). Now if one counts only by the month, up to this point there had been only fourteen [Genesis Rabbah 6:1: thirteen] sunsets. [Freedman, *Genesis Rabbah*, p. 41, n. 4: This is based on the tradition that the Nisan – the first month – in which the Exodus took place fell on a Thursday, while the actual new moon occurred after midday on the preceding Wednesday. It is further assumed that, when this happens, the moon is not visible until the second evening following, i.e., the evening of Friday. Hence if we counted time solely from when the new moon is visible, then by the Thursday on which they left, a fortnight after, there would only have been thirteen sunsets. Since, however, it is called the *fifteenth* of the month, we see that the month was calculated from the first sunset after the new moon.]

H. "One must therefore conclude that one counts the beginning of the month only from sunset."

2. A. R. *Azariah* /Zeira in the name of R. Hanina: "Only the orb of the sun was created for the purpose of giving light.

B. *"Let there be light* (Gen. 1:14):

C. "What is written is *light* [in the singular].

D. "If so, why was the moon created at all?

E. "The Holy One, blessed be He, foresaw that the nations of the world were going to make [the heavenly bodies] into gods. Said the Holy One, blessed be He, 'Now if they are two and contradict one another, and nonetheless, the nations of the world treat them as gods, if they are only one, how much the more so [will the nations of the world find reason to worship the heavenly body]!'"

F. R. Berekhiah in the name of R. Simon: "Both of them were created in order to give light, as it is said, *And* they *shall serve for light* (Gen. 1:14)."

3. A. *And they shall serve as lights* (Gen. 1:15). *And God put them in the firmament of the heaven* (Gen. 1:17). *And they shall serve as signs and for seasons* (Gen. 1:14).

B. *And they shall serve as signs* (Gen. 1:14) refers to Sabbaths, for it is written, *For it is a sign for between me and you* (Ex. 31:13)..

C. *And for seasons* refers to the three pilgrim festivals.

D. *And for days* refers to new months.

E. *And years* refers to the sanctification of years.

F. Indicating in all that the nations of the world will follow a solar calendar, and Israel, a lunar one:

G. *The Lord said to Moses and Aaron in the land of Egypt, "This month shall be for you the beginning of months; it shall be the first month of the year for you"* (Ex. 12:1-2)

What captures interest in the base-verse is the reference to month, that is, new moon, and the stress that it is the new moon that marks the beginning of the months and the years. The further theme, to appear shortly, joins the new moon's appearance to the coming redemption, and further identifies the month of the original redemption, the Exodus, as the month of the final redemption. That of course is Nisan, the month in which Passover falls. Accordingly, the first of the two themes at hand – the importance of the lunar calendar – makes its appearance now, and the second, the association of redemption with the new moon of Nisan, will shortly make its appearance. This composition serves at Genesis Rabbah 6:1 and only at the end makes its contribution to the exegesis of Ex. 12:1-2. The intersection is merely thematic; there is no interest in the base-verses, which at Genesis Rabbah 6:1 do not occur anyhow. Nos. 1, 2 work out the implications of the intersecting-verse, which introduces the view that, while the sun is meant to give light, the moon serves some other purpose. That other purpose is for Israel's calendar, as we see at the end. We see the view, which is Yohanan's, is contradicted at the end by Berekhiah. The force of the intersecting-verse is not merely to illuminate the base-verse but to propose a syllogism in connection with the theme at hand, which, autonomous of the exegetical task, is subject to discussion and dispute on its own. So the syllogism has been (re)cast in exegetical form. But it remains a syllogistic argument. No. 3 is a narrowly exegetical exercise and the contrast then is probative. The differences between the versions of Pesiqta Rabbati and Pesiqta deRab Kahana are negligible.

Pesiqta Rabbati XV [=Pesiqta deRab Kahana V]:II

1. A. *Great things have you done, O Lord my God; your wonderful purposes and plans are all for our good; [none can compare with you; I would proclaim them and speak of them, but they are more than I can tell]* (Prov. 40:5):
   B. R. Hinenah bar Papa says two [teachings in respect to the cited verse]: "All those wonders and plans which you made so that our father, Abraham, would accept the subjugation of Israel to the nations were *for our good*, for our sake, so that we might endure in the world."
   C. Simeon bar Abba in the name of R. Yohanan: "Four things did the Holy One, blessed be He, show to our father, Abraham: the Torah, the sacrifices, Gehenna, and the rule of the kingdoms.
   D. "The Torah: *...and a flaming torch passed between these pieces* (Gen. 15:17).
   E. "Sacrifices: *And he said to him, Take for me a heifer divided into three parts* (Gen. 15:9).
   F. "Gehenna: *behold a smoking fire pot.*
   G. "The rule of the kingdoms: *Lo, dread, a great darkness* (Gen. 15:12)."
   H. "The Holy One, blessed be He, said to our father, Abraham, 'So long as your descendants are occupied with the former two, they will be saved

from the latter two. If they abandon the former two of them, they will be judged by the other two.

I. "'So long as they are occupied with study of the Torah and performance of the sacrifices, they will be saved from Gehenna and from the rule of the kingdoms.

J. "'But [God says to Abraham] in the future the house of the sanctuary is destined to be destroyed and the sacrifices nullified. What is your preference? Do you want your children to go down into Gehenna or to be subjugated to the four kingdoms?'"

K. R. Hinena bar Pappa said, "Abraham himself chose the subjugation to the four kingdoms.

L. "What is the scriptural basis for that view? *How should one chase a thousand and two put ten thousand to flight, except their rock had given them over* (Deut. 32:30). That statement concerning the rock refers only to Abraham, as it is said, *Look at the rock from which you were hewn* (Is. 51:1)..

M. *"But the Lord delivered them up* (Deut. 32:30) teaches that God then approved what he had chosen."

2. A. R. Berekhiah in the name of R. Levi: "Now Abraham sat and puzzled all that day, saying, 'Which should I choose, *Gehenna or subjugation to the kingdoms*? The one is worse than the other.?'

B. "Said the Holy One, blessed be He, to him, 'Abraham, how long are you going to sit in puzzlement? Choose without delay.' That is in line with this verse: *On* that day *the Lord made a covenant with Abram saying* (Gen. 15:18)."

C. What is the meaning of, *saying*?

D. R. Hinena bar Pappa said, "Abraham chose for himself the subjugation to the four kingdoms."

E. We have reached the dispute of R. Yudan and R. Idi and R. Hama bar Haninah said in the name of a certain sage in the name of Rabbi: "The Holy One, blessed be He, [not Abraham] chose the subjugation to the four kingdoms for him, in line with the following verse of Scripture: *You have caused men to ride over our heads, we have been overcome by fire and water* (Ps. 66:12). That is to say, *you have made ride over our heads various nations, and it is as though we went through fire and through water* (Ps. 66:21)."

3. A. R. Hinena bar Papa said a further teaching.

B. R. Hinenah bar Papa says: "All those wonders and plans which you made were so that a man might desire his wife.

C. "What is the Scripture basis for that view? *And Adam knew his wife again* (Gen. 4:25).

D. "What is the meaning of *again*? The lust for sexual relations that he had had was now augmented [so explaining the meaning of the word *again*].

E. "In the past, if he did not see her, he did not lust after her. Now, whether or not he saw her, he desired her."

F. R. Abba bar Yudan in the name of R. Aha: "This is an indication for commercial travelers and for sailors to remember their wives and come home as quickly as they can."

4. A. **R. Hiyya bar Pappa said a further matter. R. Hanina bar Papa said**/*R. Simon said*, "'All those wonders and plans which you made were so that the nations of the world would *not* accept your Torah.

   B. "'Now was it not perfectly obvious to you that the nations of the world were not going to accept your Torah?'

   C. "Why did it appear as though he were making the circuit of the nations? It was so as to double the reward that was coming to us."

5. A. For R. Simeon said, "...*your wonderful purposes are all for our good:* for all those two thousand four hundred forty-eight years before the Israelites had gone forth from Egypt, the Holy One, blessed be He, was sitting and making calculations, intercalating the years, sanctifying the years, celebrating the new months. When the Israelites went forth from Egypt, he handed the task over to them.

   B. "That is in line with this verse of Scripture: *The Lord said to Moses and Aaron in the land of Egypt, saying, ["This month shall be for you the beginning of months; it shall be the first month of the year for you"]* (Ex. 12:1-2).

   C. "What is the meaning of *saying*? He said to them, From now on, lo, these are given over to you: *this month shall be* for you *the beginning of months; it shall be the first month of the year for you.*""

The intersecting-verse raises the issue of how God's purposes are all for our good. The possibilities are worked out in such a way that, in the end, Israel's command of the calendar becomes a marked of exceptional favor. No. 1 introduces the matter of the subjugation to the nations, which now is *for our good*. Abraham and God chose precisely the situation in which Israel now found itself. No. 2 carries forward that same topic, now moving away from the intersecting-verse but making the established point. No. 3 then deals with the first Man. No. 4 addresses the distinguishing mark of Israel, its possession of the Torah. It is difficult to make sense of No. 4 as we now have it; it seems to lack a referent. What wonders and plans Simeon has in mind are not at all clear. But No. 5 leads us back to our base-verse, and now we have a clear route to Abraham's choice of subjugation to the nations, first Egypt, now Edom. Israel is in charge of the movement of the seasons, sanctifying the new moon and recognizing the course of the planets in the heavens. That dominion endures even now. The sun and moon travel their circuits in the heaven under the supervision of Israel, a considerable consolation in the present circumstance. Once more the differences between the two Pesiqtas are neglible.

Pesiqta Rabbati XV [=Pesiqta deRab Kahana V]:III

1. A. *Hope deferred makes the heart sick, [but a desire fulfilled is a tree of life. He who despises the word brings destruction on himself, but he who respects the commandments will be rewarded. The teaching of the wise is a fountain of life, that one may avoid the snares of death]* (Prov. 13:12-14):

B. R. Hiyya bar Ba opened discourse by citing the verse: *"Hope deferred makes the heart sick* – this refers to one who betrothes a woman and takes her as his wife only after delay.

C. *"...but a desire fulfilled is a tree of life* – this refers to one who betrothes a woman and takes her as his wife right away."

2. A. Another interpretation: *"Hope deferred makes the heart sick* – this refers to David, who was anointed and then ruled only after **a few years/*two years*** had passed.

B. *"...but a desire fulfilled is a tree of life* – this refers to Saul, who was anointed and then ruled right away.

C. On account of what merit [did Saul have that good fortune]?

D. On account of the merit accruing for the good deeds which were to his credit, for he was humble and modest.

E. For he ate his ordinary food [not deriving from his share of an animal sacrificed in the Temple, for example] in a state of cultic cleanness [as if he were eating holy food deriving from his share of an offering made in the Temple].

F. And, further, he would spend his own funds so as to protect the funds of Israel.

G. And he treated as equal the honor owing to his servant with the honor owing to himself.

H. R. Judah bar Nahman in the name of R. Simeon b. Laqish: "For he was one who was subject to study of the Torah: *By me [the Torah speaks] princes rule* (Prov. 18:16). *By me kings rule* [and Saul ruled through his study of the Torah] (Prov. 8:15)."

3. A. R. Ishmael taught on Tannaite authority, "Before a man has sinned, people pay him reverence and awe. Once he has sinned, they impose on him reverence and awe.

B. "Thus, before the first man had sinned, he would hear [God's] voice in a workaday way. After he had sinned, he heard the same voice as something strange. Before he had sinned, the first man heard God's voice and would stand on his feet: *And they heard the sound of God walking in the garden in the heat of the day* (Gen. 3:8). **Said R. Abba bar Kahana, "What is written is not merely, 'going along,' but 'walked on,' in the sense of leaving, for he lept upward [toward heaven] and departed."** After he had sinned, he heard the voice of God and hid: *And man and his wife hid* (Gen. 3:8)."

C. Said R. Aibu, "At that moment the height of the first Man was cut down and he became a hundred cubits high."

D. [Ishmael continues:] "Before the Israelites sinned, what is written in their regard? *And the appearance of the glory of the Lord was like a consuming fire on the top of the mountain before the eyes of the children of Israel* (Ex. 24:17)."

E. Said R. Abba bar Kahana, "There were seven veils of fire, one covering the next, and the Israelites gazed and did not fear or take fright."

F. "But when they had sinned, even on the face of the intercessor [Moses] they could not look: *And Aaron and all the children of Israel feared...to come near* (Ex. 34:40)."

4. A. R. **Isaac/*Phineas*** bar Abun in the name of R. Hanin: "Also the intercessor felt the sin: *Kings of hosts do flee, do flee* (Ps. 68:13)." [This is now explained.]

   B. R. Yudan in the name of R. Aibu says, "'Angels of hosts' is not what is written here, but what is written is *Kings of hosts,* the kings of the angels, even Michael, even Gabriel, were not able to look upon the face of Moses.

   C. "But after the Israelites had sinned, Moses could not gaze even on the faces of lesser angels: *For I was in dread of anger and hot wrath* (Deut. 9:19)."

5. A. Before the deed of David [with Bath Sheba] took place, what is written? *For David: The Lord is my light and my salvation, of whom shall I be afraid?* (Ps. 27:1).

   B. But after that deed took place, what is written? *I will come upon him while he is weary and weak-handed* (2 Sam. 17:2).

6. A. Before Solomon sinned, he could rule over demons and demonesses: *I got for myself...Adam's progeny, demons and demonesses* (Qoh. 2:8).

   B. What is the sense of *demons and demonesses*? For he ruled over demons and demonesses.

   C. But after he had sinned, he brought sixty mighty men to guard his bed: *Lo, the bed of Solomon, with sixty mighty men around it, all of them holding a sword and veterans of war* (Song 3:7-8).

7. A. Before Saul had sinned, what is written concerning him? *And when Saul had taken dominion over Israel, he fought against all his enemies on every side, against Moab, against the Ammonites, against Edom, against the kings of Zobah, and against the Philistines; wherever he turned he put them to the worse* (1 Sam. 14:47).

   B. After he had sinned what is written concerning him? *And Saul saw the camp of the Philistines and was afraid* (1 Sam. 28:5).

8. A. Another interpretation of the verse *Hope deferred makes the heart sick*:

   B. Said R. Hiyya bar Abba, "This refers to the Israelites before they were redeemed.

   C. "You find that when Moses came to the Israelites and said to them, 'The Holy One, blessed be He, has said to me, *Go, say to Israel, I have surely remembered you,* (Ex. 3:16), they said to him, 'Moses, our lord, it is still a mere remembering! *What is my strength, that I should wait? And what is my end, that I should be patient? Is my strength the strength of stones, or is my flesh bronze? [In truth I have no help in me, and any resources is driven from me]* (Job 6:11-13).

   D. "'Is our strength the strength of stones? is our flesh made of bronze?'

   E. "But when he said to him, '*This month you will be redeemed,*' they said, 'That is a good sign.'

   F. "...but a desire fulfilled is a tree of life: *This month shall be for you the beginning of months; it shall be the first month of the year for you*" (Ex. 12:1-2)

The extensive treatment of the intersecting-verse does not prepare us for the final clarification of the base-verse at No. 8, and that is because the composite bears a heavy and inappropriate accretion of useless material. The point is that when Moses made his announcement that in the cited month of Nisan, the Israelites would be redeemed, that marked the end of hope deferred and the beginning of the desire fulfilled. But nothing has prepared us for that excellent conclusion. No. 1 gives a straightforward application of the verse. No. 2 brings us to David and Saul. The intrusion of Nos. 3-7 is not easy to explain, except as a secondary amplification on the theme of Saul. The first Man, the Israelites, Moses, David, Saul all are examples of the effect of sin, which takes a proud person and humbles him. We see, therefore, a vast insertion of irrelevant materials. No,. 8 then brings us back to the point at issue, and we have to regard the rest of the composite as a rather mindless amplification of a minor point – the mere mention of Saul! The basic intent, however, in introducing the intersecting-verse is striking and well executed at the end.

Pesiqta Rabbati XV [=Pesiqta deRab Kahana V]:IV

1. A. *[The Lord said to Moses and Aaron in the land of Egypt,]* "This month *[shall be for you the beginning of months; it shall be the first month of the year for you]"* (Ex. 12:1-2): Judah bar Nahman in the name of R. Simeon b. Laqish opened discourse by citing the following verse of Scripture: *"Oh send out your light and your truth; let them lead me, let them bring me to your holy hill and to your dwelling. [Then I will go to the altar of God, to God my exceeding joy; and I will praise you with the lyre, O God, my God]* (Ps. 43:3-4).

   B. *"...send out your light* refers to Moses: *And Moses did not know that his face was glistening with beams of light* (Ex. 34:29).

   C. *"...and your truth* refers to Aaron, **Your truth and light be with your holy one (Deut. 33:8).** [PRK:] *The Torah of truth was in his mouth* (Malachi 2:7).

   D. *"Your truth and light be with your holy one* (Deut. 33:8)."

   E. And there are those who reverse matters:'

   F. *"...send out your light* refers to Aaron: *Your truth and light be with your holy one* (Deut. 33:8).

   G. *"...and your truth* refers to Moses, *Not so is my servant Moses, in all my household the most trustworthy* (Num. 12:7)."

2. A. Said R. Isaac, "Even at the sea Moses foresaw that he was not going to enter the Land of Israel: *She keeps her eye on the doings of her household* (Prov. 31:27).

   B. "What is written in the pertinent passage is not, 'you will bring it and plant it,' but rather, *You brought them in and planted them* (Ex. 15:17).

   C. "Yet it is written: *...let them lead me, let them bring me to your holy hill and to your dwelling.*

   D. "This refers to the **frontier-area/***scribes* of the Land of Israel, who are as holy as the Land of Israel itself."

3. A. Another comment on the verse: *Oh send out your light and your truth; [let them lead me, let them bring me to your holy hill and to your dwelling. Then I will go to the altar of God, to God my exceeding joy; and I will praise you with the lyre, O God, my God]* (Ps. 43:3-4).

   B. *...send out your light* refers to Moses and Aaron, through whom the Holy One, blessed be He, sent light to Israel to redeem them from Egypt.

   C. When did this take place?

   D. In this month: *This month for you is the first of the months* (Ex. 12:2).

A long sequence of wide-ranging passages about redemption, each ending, "When did this take place? In this month: *This month for you is the first of the months* (Ex. 12:2), now begins. A particular point of contact between the "illustrative" passage and the topic at hand, Ex. 12:2, never is specified. The general theme of redemption in Nisan than accounts for pretty much everything that follows; in no way can we regard the exercise as mainly exegetical. In fact it is a syllogistic exposition, through innumerable examples, of the single fact that redemption takes place "in this month." No. 1 sets the stage for No. 3, with No. 2 a secondary expansion of No. 1. Specifically, we apply the intersecting-verse to Moses, then to Aaron, then to both. But how the intersecting-verse opens the base-verse to a deeper meaning is not self-evident, since, as I said, the reversion to the base-verse seems artificial and mechanical. On the basis of this case one could revert to the any base-verse one wished. The theme, however, is clearly conventional – that is to say, syllogistic: redemption on the first of the months. And that is I believe what has guided the authorship at hand which wishes to read each of the base-verses as another instance in the unfolding of Israel's redemption.

Pesiqta Rabbati XV [=Pesiqta deRab Kahana V]:V

1. A. R. Levi opened discourse by citing the following verse: *And you shall be holy to me [because I the Lord am holy. I have made a clear separation between you and the heathen, that you may belong to me]* (Lev. 20:26).

   B. R. Yudan in the name of R. Hama bar Hanina, R. Berekhiah in the name of R. Abbahu: "Had it been stated, 'And I shall separate the nations of the world from you,' the nations of the world could not have survived. But what it says is, *I have made a clear separation between you and the heathen.*

   C. "It is like someone who sorts out the good grain from the bad, choosing and coming back and choosing again [because there is still good left to be chosen (Mandelbaum)].

   D. "If, however, he were to choses the bad from the good, he makes a choice and does not go back and make a further selection."

2. A. [Reverting to 1.A:] said R. Levi, "In all their deeds the Israelites are different from the nations of the world, in their manner of ploughing, sowing, reaping, making sheaves, threshing, working at the threshing floor and at the wine press, counting and reckoning the calendar:

   B. "As to ploughing: *You will not plough with an ox and and ass together* (Deut. 22:10).

C. "sowing: *You will not sow your vineyard with mixed seeds* (Lev. 22:9).

D,. "reaping: *You will not gather the gleaning of your harvest* (Lev. 19:9).

E. "making sheaves: *And the forgotten sheaf in the field you will not recover* (Deut. 24:12).

F. "threshing: *You will not muzzle an ox in its threshing* (Deut. 25:4).

G. "working at the threshing floor and at the wine press: *You will provide liberally [for the Hebrew servant] out of your threshing floor and wine press* (Deut. 15:14).

H. "counting and reckoning the calendar: The nations of the world reckon by the sun, and Israel by the moon: *This month will be for you the first of the months* (Ex. 12:2)."

The inclusion of our base-verse is in a syllogism that on its own makes its main point. The base-verse simply supplies another fact for the larger proposition at hand. Mandelbaum (private communication) comments, "This is a key insight, that God can come back and pick other nations for different purposes."

Pesiqta Rabbati XV [=Pesiqta deRab Kahana V]:VI

1. A. *I sleep [but my heart is awake. Listen! My beloved is knocking: "Open to me, my sister, my dearest, my dove, my perfect one, for my head is drenched with dew, my locks with the moisture of the night]* (Song 5:2):

    B. Said the community of Israel before the Holy One, blessed be He, "Master of the age, While *I am asleep* at the house of the sanctuary [because it is destroyed], but *my heart is awake* in the houses of assembly and study.

    C. "*I am asleep* as to the offerings, but *my heart is awake* as to the religious duties and acts of righteousness.

    D. "*I am asleep* as to religious duties, but *my heart is nonetheless awake* to carry them out.

    E. "*I am asleep* as to the end, but *my heart is awake* as to redemption.

    F. "*I am asleep* as to redemption, but *the heart* of the Holy One, blessed be He, *is awake* to redeem **me/us**."

2. A. Said R. Hiyya bar Abba, "How do we know that the Holy One is called 'the heart of Israel'?

    B. "On the basis of this verse: *Rock of my heart and my portion is God forever* (Ps. 73:26)."

3. A. ...*My beloved is knocking* refers to Moses: *And Moses said, Thus said the Lord, At about midnight I shall go out in the midst of Egypt* (Ex. 11:4).

    B. *Open to me:* said R. Yose, "Said the Holy One, blessed be He, '*Open to me* [a hole] as small as the eye of a needle, and I shall open to you a gate so large that troops and siege-engines can go through it.'"

    C. ...*my sister:* [God speaks:] "*My sister* in Egypt, for they became my kin through two religious duties, the blood of the Passover-offering and the blood of circumcision."

D. ...*my dearest* at the sea, for they showed their love for me at the sea, *And they said, the Lord will reign forever and ever* (Ex. 15:19).

E. ...*my dove* at Marah, where through receiving commandments they become distinguished for me like a dove.

F. ...*my perfect one: My perfect one* at Sinai, for they became pure **perfect for me** at Sinai: *And they said, all that the Lord has spoken we shall do and we shall hear* (Ex. 24:7)."

G. R. Yannai said, "*My perfect one: my twin*, for I am not greater than they, nor they than I."

H. R. Joshua of Sikhnin said in the name of R. Levi, "Just as in the case of twins, if one of them gets a headache, the other one feels it, so said the Holy One, blessed be He, '*I am with him in trouble* (Ps. 91:15)."

I. ...*for my head is drenched with dew. The heavens dropped dew* (Judges 5:4).

J. ...*my locks with the moisture of the night: Yes, the clouds dropped water* (Judges 5:4).

K. When is this the case? In this month: *This month is for you the first of the months* (Ex. 12:2).

The pattern is the same as before: an extended disquisition on a theme remote from our base-verse, ending with an artificial and unprepared for introduction of the base-verse. The sole relevant point is that the beginning of God's relationship to Israel is with the first of the months. Nothing else pertains. But the proposition, that God and Israel share one and the same destiny, on its own is stunning.

Pesiqta Rabbati XV [=Pesiqta deRab Kahana V]:VII

1. A. *Hark! My beloved! Here he comes, bounding over the mountains, leaping over the hills. [My beloved is like a gazelle, or a young wild goat: there he stands outside our wall, peeking in at the windows, glancing through the lattice. My beloved answered, he said to me, Rise up, my darling; my fairest, come away. For now the winter is past, the rains are over and gone; the flowers appear in the countryside; the time is coming when the birds will sing, and the turtle-dove's cooing will be heard in our land; when the green figs will ripen on the fig-trees and the vines give forth their fragrance. Rise up my darling, my fairest, come away]* (Song 2:8-10):

    B. R. Judah, R. Nehemiah [below, No. 2], and rabbis [below, No. 3]:

    C. R. Judah says, "*Hark! My beloved! Here he comes* refers to Moses.

    D. "When Moses came and said to Israel, 'In this month you will be redeemed,' they said to him, 'Moses, our lord, how are we going to be redeemed? Did not the Holy One, blessed be He, say to our father, Abraham, *"Your descendants will be sojourners in a land that is not theirs and they will be slaves there, and they will be oppressed for four hundred years"* (Gen. 15:13)? And is it not the case that we have to our account only two hundred and ten years [of slavery in Egypt]?'

    E. "He said to them, 'Since he wants to redeem you, he does not pay attention to your reckoning of accounts. But *bounding over the mountains, leaping over the hills* means that he is skipping over foreordained calculations of the end and over all reckonings and times.

F. "'In this month you will be redeemed: *This month is for you the beginning of months* (Ex. 12:2).'"

2. A. R. Nehemiah says, *"Hark! My beloved! Here he comes* refers to Moses.
   B. "When Moses came and said to Israel, 'In this month you will be redeemed,' they said to him, 'Moses, our lord, how are we going to be redeemed? And the land of Egypt is filled with the filth of idolatry that belongs to us.'
   C. "He said to them, 'Since he wants to redeem you, he does not pay attention to your idolatry. But he goes *bounding over the mountains, leaping over the hills,* and hills refers to idolatry, in line with this verse: *On the tops of mountains they make sacrifices and in hills they offer incense* (Hos. 4:12).'"

3. A. Rabbis say, *"Hark! My beloved! Here he comes* refers to Moses.
   B. "When Moses came and said to Israel, 'In this month you will be redeemed,' they said to him, 'Moses, our lord, how are we going to be redeemed? And we have no good deeds to our credit.'
   C. "He said to them, 'Since he wants to redeem you, he does not pay attention to your wicked deeds. But to whom does he pay attention? To the righteous who are among you, for example, Amram and his court.
   D. "For *hills and mountains* refers only to courts, in line with this verse: *That I may go and seek out upon the mountains* (Judges 11:37)."

4. A. Said R. Yudan, "As to slavery and sojourning in a land that is not theirs, *...that your descendants will be sojourners in a land that is not theirs and they will be slaves there, and they will be oppressed for four hundred years,*
   B. "including even the years that they were at ease [cf. Braude and Kapstein, p. 101]."

5. A. R. Yudan in the name of R. Eliezer son of R. Yose the Galilean, R. Hunah in the name of R. Eliezer b. Jacob: *"Hark! My beloved! Here he comes* refers to the messiah-king.
   B. "When he came and said to Israel, 'In this month you will be redeemed,' they said to him, 'Messiah-king, our lord, how are we going to be redeemed? Did not the Holy One, blessed be He, say that he would make us slaves among the seventy nations?'
   C. "And he answered them with two replies, saying to them, 'If one of you has gone into exile to Barbaria and one to Sarmatia/**Britannia**, it is as if all of you had gone into exile.'
   D, "'Furthermore, this wicked government drafts soldiers from each nation. If one Samaritan comes and is drafted, it is as if the whole of his nation has been subjugated. *If one Ethiopian comes and is drafted, it is as if the whole of his nation has been subjugated.*
   E. "'In this month you will be redeemed,' *This month is for you the beginning of months* (Ex. 12:2)."

The mélange of themes – Israel's love-affair with God, expressed in the Song of Songs, Israel's redemption from Egypt, Israel's redemption in the near future, the subjugation to the wicked kingdom, and the importance of the month of Nisan – is worked out as before. But the choice of the intersecting-verse is fully vindicated at No. 1. God can choose the time of redemption, skipping over all obstacles. As we shall see, the exposition of the intersecting-verse runs on and on, since we take full account of the entire pericope of Scripture, beginning to end. But the choice is fully validated. The return to the base-verse is natural and appropriate. The stress now is that God is not bound by prior calculations, but can do as he likes, God can overlook Israel's failings, and God finds in Israel's righteous ample reason for redeeming the whole nation (No. 1, 2, 3). No. 4 is a brief appendix to No. 1. Then No. 5 resumes the discussion, now with a powerful application to the present. We now continue with the exposition of the intersecting-verse. The reversion to the base-verse will not again prove so natural and compelling. I see no substantial variations in the two versions.

Pesiqta Rabbati XV [=Pesiqta deRab Kahana V]:VIII

1. A. *My beloved is like a gazelle, or a young wild goat: [there he stands outside our wall, peeking in at the windows, glancing through the lattice. My beloved answered, he said to me, Rise up, my darling; my fairest, come away]* (Song 2:8-10):

   B. *My beloved is like a gazelle:* said R. Isaac, "You say to us, 'Come hither.' Come hither to us, for you come to us first.'" [Braude and Kapstein, p. 101 (following Mandelbaum, who cites Lieberman, but who is not cited by them): The word for beloved, when separated into two parts, makes two Greek words, standing for *come hither* and *God*, so in the first part, 'You O God say to us, Come hither,' and in the second part, Israel replies, 'God, you come to us before we stir.']"

2. A. *[My beloved is like a gazelle:]* Said R. Isaac,"Just as a gazelle skips and jumps from tree to tree, hut to hut, fence to fence, so the Holy One, blessed be He, skipped from Egypt to the Sea, from the sea to Sinai.

   B. "In Egypt they saw him: *And I shall pass through through the land of Egypt on that night* (Ex. 12:12)

   C. "At the sea they saw him: *And Israel saw the great hand* (Ex. 14:32).

   D. "At Sinai they saw him: *And the Lord spoke from Sinai, he came and shown from Seir to him* (Deut. 32:2)."

3. A. *...or a young wild goat:*

   B. R. Yose b. R. Haninah said, "Like the young of a gazelle."

4. A. *...there he stands outside our wall:*

   B. *For on the third day the Lord came down before the eyes of the entire people* (Ex. 19:11

   C. *...peeking in at the windows:*

   D. *And the Lord came down* (Ex. 19:20).

   E. *...glancing through the lattice:*

   F. When he said, *I am the Lord your God* (Ex. 20:23),

   G. *My beloved answered, he said to me:*

I.   What did he say to me? *I am the Lord your God* (Ex. 20:23).

Pesiqta Rabbati XV:IX:1=Pesiqta deRab Kahana V:VIII.5.

5. A.   *[My beloved is like a gazelle:]* Said R. Isaac,"Just as a gazelle skips and jumps from tree to tree, hut to hut, fence to fence, so the Holy One, blessed be He, skips from one synagogue to another, one study-house to another.

    B.   "On what account? So as to bless Israel.

    C.   "On account of whose merit? On account of the merit of Abraham, who remained seated at the oak of Mamre [where he was praying and studying].

    D.   "That is in line with this verse of Scripture: *And the Lord appeared to him at the oak of Mamre, when he was sitting down at the door of the tent* (Gen. 18:1)."

6. A.   *[As he sat at the door of his tent in the heat of the day* (Gen. 18:1)]:

    B.   R. Berekhiah in the name of R. Levi: "What is written is *he sat* [and not in the progressive tense, while he *was sitting*]. When the Holy One, blessed be He, appeared to him, our father Abraham tried to stand.

    C.   "Said the Holy One, blessed be He, to him, 'Remain seated.' Our father Abraham sat down.

    D.   "Said the Holy One, blessed be He, to him, '[You thereby serve as a model for your children.] Abraham, whenever your children enter synagogues and school houses, they may sit while my Glory remains standing.

    D.   "'What text of Scripture so indicates? *God stands in the congregation of God* (Ps. 82:1).'"

7. A.   R. Haggai in the name of R. Isaac: "What is written is not standing but 'stationed at his post' [Freedman, *Genesis Rabbah ad loc.*:], which is to say, 'ready,'

    B.   "[Genesis Rabbah adds:] in line with this verse: *You shall be stationed on the rock* (Ex. 33:21)."

8. A.   R. Samuel b. R. Hiyya b. R. Yudan in the name of R. Haninah: "In response to each and every statement of praise with which Israel praises the Holy One, blessed be He, he brings his Presence to rest on them.

    B.   "**What is the text that makes that point?** *You are holy, O you who are enthroned upon the praises of Israel* (Ps. 22:4)."

9. A.   *...or a young wild goat:*

    B.   R. Yose b. R. Haninah said, "Like the young of a gazelle."

10. A.   *...there he stands outside our wall:* outside the walls of synagogues and school houses.

    B.   *...peeking in at the windows:* from among the shoulders of the priests.

    C.. *...glancing through the lattice:* from among the entwined fingers of the priests.

    D.   *...My beloved answered, he said:* What did he say to me? *May the Lord bless you and keep you* (Num. 24:6).

Pesiqta Rabbati XV:X:1=Pesiqta deRab Kahana V:VIII.11.

11. A. Another interpretation of the verse: *My beloved is like a gazelle:*
    B. Said R. Isaac, "Just as a gazelle appears and goes and disappears, so the first messiah [Moses] appeared to them and then went and disappeared from their sight."
    C. How long did he disappear from sight?
    D. Judah b. Rabbi says, "Three months, in line with this verse of Scripture: *They met Moses and Aaron standing to meet them* (Ex. 5:20)."

12. A. *...or a young wild goat:*
    B. R. Yose b. R. Haninah said, "Like the young of a gazelle."

13. A. *...there he stands outside our wall:* outside the walls of the Western wall of the house of the sanctuary, which will never be destroyed.
    B. *...peeking in at the windows:* through the merit of the patriarchs.
    C.. *...glancing through the lattice:* through the merit of the matriarchs.
    D. This serves to teach you that just as there is a difference between a window and a lattice, so there is a difference between the merit of the patriarchs and the merit of the matriarchs.

14. A. R. Berekhiah in the name of R. Levi, "Like the first redeemer, so will the final redeemer be:
    B. "Just as the first redeemer appeared to them and then went and disappeared from them, so the final redeemer will appear to them and then go and disappear from them."
    C. And how long will he disappear from them?
    D. R. Tanhumah in the name of R. Hama bar Hoshaia, R. Menahema in the name of R. Hama bar Hanina: "Forty-five days, in line with this verse of Scripture: *From the time when the regular offering is abolished and 'the abomination of desolation' is set up, there shall be an interval of one thousand two hundred and ninety days. Happy the man who waits and lives to see the completion of one thousand three hundred and thirty-five days* [a difference of forty-five days] (Dan. 12:11-12)."
    E. "As to the forty-five days that remain over the figure given in the earlier verse, what are they? They are the forty-five days on which the Messiah, having appeared to them, will go and disappear from them."
    F. Where will he lead them?'
    G. Some say, "To the wilderness of Judea," and some, "To the wilderness of Sihon and Og."
    H. That is in line with this verse of Scripture: *Therefore I will seduce Israel and bring her into the wilderness* (Hos. 2:16).
    I. He who believes in him will eat saltwort and the roots of the broom and live, for *in the wilderness they pick saltwort with wormwood and the roots of the broom are their food* (Job 30:4).
    J. And he who does not believe in him will go to the nations of the world, who will kill him.
    K. Said R. Isaac bar Marian, "At the end of forty-five days the Holy One, blessed be He, will appear to them and bring down manna.

L. "Why? *For there is nothing new under the sun* (Qoh. 1:9).

M. "What is the pertinent scriptural verse? *I am the Lord your God from the land of Egypt; I will make you dwell in tents again as in the days of the festival* (Hos. 12:10)."

The systematic exegesis of the intersecting-verse continues, now without the slightest pretense of interest in the base-verse. The messianic focus of the present composition is all that joins the passage to our context. And much that is given seems miscellaneous, a set of diverse materials on a single theme. We review the redemption of Israel from Egypt, No. 2, for the reason made explicit at the end: the first redemption is the model for the second redemption. The form for the whole is shown at Nos. 2-4, a form repeated with minor variations later on. The obvious insertions, Nos. 6-8, provide the necessary appendix as indicated. Nos. 9-10 move from the redemption of Israel from Egypt to Israel today, in the synagogues and school houses. Then, at Nos. 11-13, we complete the matter. No. 14 then adds its appendix of episodic information. As we see now, Pesiqta Rabbati continues this pericope without a break.

Pesiqta Rabbati XV:X.15 [=Pesiqta deRab Kahana V:IX.1]

1. A. *My beloved answered, he said to me, [Rise up, my darling; my fairest, come away. For now the winter is past, the rains are over and gone; the flowers appear in the countryside; the time is coming when the birds will sing, and the turtle-dove's cooing will be heart in our land; when the green figs will ripen on the fig-trees and the vines give forth their fragrance. Rise up my darling, my fairest, come away]* (Song 2:8-10):

   B. Said R. Azariah, "Is not 'answering' the same thing as 'saying'?

   C. *"He answered me* through Moses, *and said to me,* through Aaron."

   D. What did he say to me?

   E. *Rise up:* bestir yourself.

   F. *...my darling:* daughter of Abraham, [the congregation of Israel] who made me beloved in my world.

   G. *...my fairest:* daughter of Isaac, who made me beautiful in my world, when his father bound him on the altar.

   H. *...come away:* daughter of Jacob, who listened to his father and his mother: *And Jacob listened to his father and his mother* (Gen. 28:17).

   I. *For now the winter is past:* this refers to the four hundred years that were decreed for our fathers to spend in Egypt.

   J. *...the rains are over and gone:* this refers to the two hundred and ten years.

Pesiqta Rabbati XV:XI:1=Pesiqta deRab Kahana V:X.2.

2. A. Another interpretation: *For now the winter is past:* this refers to the two hundred ten years.

   B. *...the rains are over and gone:* this refers to the subjugation.

3. A. Are not the rain and the winter the same thing?

   B Said R. Tanhuma, "The principal trouble of the winter is the rain [which lasts eighty-six days], the principal [and truly difficult] part of the subjugation of Israel [in Egypt] was only the eighty-six years from the time that Miriam was born."

C. And why was she called Miriam?

D. Said R. Isaac, "It is a name that contains the meaning of bitterness, in line with this verse: *And they embittered their lives with hard work and with mortar* (Ex. 1:14)."

4. A. *...the flowers appear in the countryside:* this refers to Moses and Aaron.

B. *...the time is coming when the birds will sing:* the time for the foreskin [to be properly cut off] has come,

C. The time for the Egyptians to be cut off has come.

D. The time for the idolatry to be removed from the world has come: *And against all the gods of Egypt I shall execute judgment, I am the Lord* (Ex. 12:2).

E. The time for the sea to be split has come: *And the waters split open* (Ex. 14:21).

F. The time for the recitation of the Song at the Sea has come: *Then Moses sang* (Ex. 15:1).

G. The time for the Torah to be given has come: *The Lord is my strength and my song* (Ex. 15:2).

H. Said R. Bibi: "[The appropriate text is this one:] *Your statutes have become my songs* (Ps. 119:54)."

I. Said R. Tanhuma, "The time for the Israelites to make a song for the Holy One, blessed be He, has come: *The Lord is my strength and my song* (Ex. 15:2)."

5. A. *...and the turtle-dove's cooing will be heart in our land:*

B. Said R. Yohanan, "[Since the word for turtle-dove uses letters that may yield *guide*, we read:] 'the voice of the good guide is heard in our land.' This refers to Moses: And Moses said, *Thus said the Lord, At about midnight I shall go forth into the midst of Egypt* (Ex. 11:4)."

6. A. *...when the green figs will ripen on the fig-trees:*

B. This refers to the three days of darkness, on which the wicked of Israel perished.

7. A. *...and the vines give forth their fragrance:*

B. This refers to those who remained, who repented and were accepted.

C. Moses said to them, "All this wonderful fragrance is coming from you, and you are sitting here! *Rise up my darling, my fairest, come away.*"

Pesiqta Rabbati XV:XII:1=Pesiqta deRab Kahana V:X.8.

8. A. Another interpretation: *My beloved answered, he said to me, [Rise up, my darling; my fairest, come away. For now the winter is past, the rains are over and gone; the flowers appear in the countryside; the time is coming when the birds will sing, and the turtle-dove's cooing will be heart in our land; when the green figs will ripen on the fig-trees and the vines give forth their fragrance. Rise up my darling, my fairest, come away]* (Song 2:8-10):

B. Said R. Azariah, "Is not 'answering' the same thing as 'saying'?

C.   *"He answered me* through Joshua, *and said to me*, through Eleazar."

D.   What did he say to me? *Rise up, my darling; my fairest, come away'*

E.   *For now the winter is past:* this refers to the forty   years that the Israelites spent in the wilderness..

J.   *...the rains are over and gone:* this refers to the thirty-eight years [after the rejection of the Land], in which anger was poured out on Israel [[and the generation of the wilderness was left to die out].

K.   *...the flowers appear in the countryside:* this refers to the spies: *One representative, one representative for each tribe* ((Num. 34:18)..

L.   *...the time is coming when the birds will sing:* the time for the foreskin [to be properly cut off] has come,

M.   The time for the Canaanites to be cut off has come.

N.   The time for the Land of Israel to be cut up has come: *Among these you will cut up the land* (Num. 26:53).

O.   *...and the turtle-dove's cooing will be heart in our land:*

P.   Said R. Yohanan, "[Since the word for turtle-dove uses letters that may yield *guide,* we read:] 'the voice of the good guide is heard in our land.' This refers to Joshua: *And Joshua commanded the officers of the people, saying* (Josh. 1:10)."

Q.   *...when the green figs will ripen on the fig-trees:*

R.   This refers to the baskets of first fruits.

S.   *...and the vines give forth their fragrance:*

T.   This refers to the drink-offerings.

Pesiqta Rabbati XV:XIII:1=Pesiqta deRab Kahana V:X.9.

9. A.   Another interpretation: *My beloved answered, he said to me, [Rise up, my darling; my fairest, come away. For now the winter is past, the rains are over and gone; the flowers appear in the countryside; the time is coming when the birds will sing, and the turtle-dove's cooing will be heart in our land; when the green figs will ripen on the fig-trees and the vines give forth their fragrance. Rise up my darling, my fairest, come away]* (Song 2:8-10):

B.   Said R. Azariah, "Is not 'answering' the same thing as 'saying'?

C.   *"He answered me* through Daniel, *and said to me*, through Ezra."

D.   What did he say to me? *Rise up, my darling; my fairest, come away.*

E.   *For now the winter is past:* this refers to the seventy years of the dominion of Babylonia.

F.   **But were they not only fifty-two years?**

G.   **Said R. Levi, "Deduct the eighteen years in which the echo was going forth and chirping in the palace of Nebuchadnezzar, saying to him, 'Bad servant!   Go forth and destroy the house of your lord, for the children of your lord do not obey him.'"**

H.   *...the rains are over and gone:* this refers to the fifty-two years of the dominion of Media.

10. A.   *Another interpretation: For now the winter is past: this refers to the seventy years that the Israelites spent in exile.*

B.   *But were they not merely fifty-two years?*

C. *Said R. Levi, "Eighteen years were taken off the total, for every eighteen years an echo would go forth and resound in the palace of Nebuchadnezzar, saying to him, Wicked servant, go forth with the sword against the house of your master, for the children of your master do not obey him."* [The only difference between the two documents is in the placing of this pericope.]

11. A.   *...the rains are over and gone:* this refers to the subjugation.

B.   *...the flowers appear in the countryside:* for instance, Daniel and his colleagues, Mordecai and his colleagues, Ezra and his colleagues.

C.   *...the time is coming when the birds will sing:* the time for the foreskin [to be properly cut off] has come,

D.   The time for the wicked to be broken has come: *The Lord has broken the staff of the wicked* (Is. 14:5).

E.   The time for Babylonians to be removed has come.

F.   The time for the house of the sanctuary to be rebuilt has come: *Greater will be the glory of the second house* (Haggai 2:9).

G.   *...and the turtle-dove's cooing will be heart in our land:*

H.   Said R. Yohanan, "[Since the word for turtle-dove uses letters that may yield guide, we read:] 'the voice of the good guide is heard in our land.' This refers to Cyrus: *Thus said Cyrus, king of Persia, All the nations of the world...(Ezra 1:2)."*

I.   *...when the green figs will ripen on the fig-trees:*

J.   This speaks of the baskets of first fruits.

K.   *...and the vines give forth their fragrance:*

L.   This refers to the drink-offerings.

M.   *Moses said to them, "All this wonderful fragrance is coming from you, and you are sitting here! Rise up my darling, my fairest, come away."*

Pesiqta Rabbati XV:XIV:1=Pesiqta deRab Kahana V:X.12.

12. A.   Another interpretation: *My beloved answered, he said to me, [Rise up, my darling; my fairest, come away. For now the winter is past, the rains are over and gone; the flowers appear in the countryside; the time is coming when the birds will sing, and the turtle-dove's cooing will be heart in our land; when the green figs will ripen on the fig-trees and the vines give forth their fragrance. Rise up my darling, my fairest, come away]* (Song 2:8-10):

B.   Said R. Azariah, "Is not 'answering' the same thing as 'saying'?

C.   *"He answered me* through Elijah, *and said to me,* through the messiah-king."

D.   What did he say to me? *Rise up, my darling; my fairest, come away.*

E.   *For now the winter is past:*

F.   Said R. Azariah, "This refers to the wicked kingdom, which misled people.

G.   "That is in line with the following: *When your brother, son of your mother, misleads you* (Deut. 13:7)."

H.   *...the rains are over and gone:* this refers to the subjugation [to Rome].

I.   *...the flowers appear in the countryside:*

J. Said R. Isaac, "It is written, *The Lord showed me four craftsmen* (Zech. 2:3). These are they: Elijah, the messiah-king, Melchisedek, and the priest anointed for war."

K. *...the time is coming when the birds will sing:* the time for the foreskin [to be properly cut off] has come,

L. *The time for the Egyptians to be cut off has come.*

M. The time for the wicked to be broken has come: *The Lord has broken the staff of the wicked* (Is. 14:5).

N. The time for the wicked kingdom to be uprooted from the world has come.

O. The time for the revelation of the kingdom of heaven has come: *The Lord shall be king over all the earth* (Zech. 14:9).

P. *...and the turtle-dove's cooing will be heart in our land:*

Q. Said R. Yohanan, "[Since the word for turtle-dove uses letters that may yield *guide*, we read:] 'the voice of the good guide is heard in our land.' This refers to the messiah king: *How beautiful on the hills are the feet of the bringer of glad tidings* (Is. 52:7)."

S. *...when the green figs will ripen on the fig-trees:*

T. Said R. Hiyya bar Abba, "Close to the days of the messiah a great thing will happen, and the wicked will perish in it.

U. *"...and the vines give forth their fragrance:*

V. "This refers to those who remained: *And those who remained in Zion, and the remnant in Jerusalem, will be holy* (Is. 4:3)."

Pesiqta Rabbati XV:XV:1=Pesiqta deRab Kahana V:X.13.

13. A. And rabbis say, "In the septennate in which the son of David comes, in the first of the seven year spell, *I shall cause it to rain on one town and not on another* (Amos 4:7).

B. "In the second, the arrows of famine will be sent forth.

C. "In the third there will be a great famine, and men, women, and children will die in it, and the Torah will be forgotten in Israel.

D. "In the fourth, there will be a famine which is not really a famine, and plenty which is not plentiful.

E. "In the fifth year, there will be great plenty, and people will eat and drink and rejoice, and the Torah will again be renewed.

F. "In the sixth there will be great thunders.

G. "In the seventh there will be wars.

H. "And at the end of the seventh year of that septennate, the son of David will come."

I. Said R. **Abbuha/Abbaye**, "How many septennates have there been like this one, and yet he has not come."

J. But matters accord with what R. Yohanan said, "In the generation in which the son of David comes, disciples of sages will perish, and those that remain will have faint vision, with suffering and sighing, and terrible troubles will come on the people, and harsh decrees will be renewed. Before the first such decree is carried out, another will be brought along and joined to it."

K. Said R. Abun, "In the generation in which the son of David comes, the meeting place will be turned over to prostitution, the Galilee will be destroyed, Gablan will be desolate, and the Galileans will make the rounds from town to town and find no comfort.

L. "Truthful men will be gathered up, and the truth will be fenced in and go its way."

M. Where will it go?

N. A member of the household of R. Yannai said, "It will go and dwell in small flocks in the wilderness, in line with this verse of Scripture: *Truth shall be among bands* (Is. 59:15)."

O. Said R. Nehorai, "In the generation in which the son of David comes, youths will humiliate old men, sages will rise before youths, a slave girl will abuse her mistress, a daughter-in-law her mother-in-law, a man's enemies will be his own householders, a son will not be ashamed for his father, the wisdom of scribes will turn rotten, the vine will give its fruit but wine will be expensive."

P. Said R. Abba bar Kahana, "The son of David will come only to a generation which is liable for total extermination."

Q. Said R. Yannai, "The son of David will come only to a generation the principal leaders of which are like dogs."

R. Said R. Levi, "If you see one generation after another blaspheming, look for the footsteps of the messiah-king.

S. "What verse of Scripture indicates it? *Remember Lord the taunts hurled at your servant, how I have borne in my heart the calumnies of the nations; so have your enemies taunted us, O Lord, taunted the successors of your anointed king* (Ps. 89:51).

T. "What follows? *Blessed is the Lord for ever, amen, amen* (Ps. 89:52)."

The systematic work on Song 2:8-10 is completed in a highly formalized exercise. We apply the verse to the following messianic figures in succession: Moses and Aaron and the redemption from Egypt, Nos. 1-7, Joshua and Eleazar, No. 8, thus the conquest of the Land; Ezra and Daniel, Nos. 9-11, thus the return to the Land; Elijah and the messiah-king, No. 12+13, an appendix of familiar materials (cf. B. San. 97a). The message is clear from the topics chosen to illuminate the transaction described by the verse between God and Israel: a love affair brought to its fulfilment in the messianic rule. Our "base-verse" has long since been forgotten. The only important points of variation between the two versions lie in the printers' differences as to paragraphing.

Pesiqta Rabbati XV:XV=Pesiqta deRab Kahana V:X:

1. A. R. Jonah opened discourse by citing this verse of Scripture: *So I got her back for fifteen pieces of silver, a homer of barley, [and a measure of wine; and I said to her, Many a long day you shall live in my house and not play the wanton and have no intercourse with a man, nor I with you. For the Israelites shall live many a long day without king or prince, without sacrifice or sacred pillar, without image or household gods, but after that they will again seek the Lord their God and David their king and turn anxiously to the Lord for his bounty in days to come]* (Hos. 3:2-5).

B.   Said R. Yohanan, "*So I got her back* for me, *for fifteen pieces of silver*, lo, fifteen; *and for a homer of barley*, lo, thirty, and *a half-homer of barley*, lo, sixty.

C.   "This refers to the sixty religious duties that Moses inscribed for us in the Torah."

D.   For R. Yohanan said in the name of R. Simeon b. Yohai, "There were three passages that Moses wrote for us in the Torah, in each one of which there are sixty religious duties, and these are they:

E.   "the passage concerning the Passover offering, that concerning torts, and that concerning *'you shall be holy.'*"

F.   R. Levi in the name of R. Shilah of Kefar Tamratah, "There are seventy in each."

G.   Said R. Tanhumah, "They really do not differ. One who treats the passage concerning the Passover-offering as containing seventy religious duties treats it as encompassing the passage on the phylacteries. One who treats the passage on torts as containing seventy religious duties maintains that it encompasses the passage covering the year of release. One who treats the passage of Holy Things as including seventy religious duties encompasses with it the passage on *orlah*-fruit."

2. A.   Another interpretation of the verse, *so I got her back for fifteen pieces of silver:*

B.   Lo, the reference to fifteen pieces of silver brings us to the fifteenth day of Nisan.

C.   When is this? It is in this month: *This month is for you the beginning of months* (Ex. 12:2).

The intersecting-verse is drawn to the base-verse by an artificial means familiar from earlier passage and in no way illuminates the base-verse. The deeper pertinence, of course, derives from Israel's redemption in the stated month, which is coherent with the theme of the exegesis of the verses in Song as God's love for Israel. Israel is like Hosea's wife, hence the passage at hand completes the foregoing. We cannot doubt that the final composition – meaning the selection and arrangement of diverse materials into a single syllogism – derives from a single authorship, which wishes to make its own cogent statement and has succeeded in doing so.

Pesiqta Rabbati XV:XVII=Pesiqta deRab Kahana V:XI:

1. A.   *This month is for you [the first of months, you shall make it the first month of the year]* (Ex. 12:2):

B.   [Reading the letters for *month* to sound like the word, *innovation*:] R. Berekhiah in the name of R. Yudan b. R. Simeon: "Said the Holy One, blessed be He, to Israel, 'There will be an innovation as to redemption for you in the age to come.

C.   "'In the past I never redeemed one nation from the midst of another nation, but now I am going to redeem one nation from the midst of another nation.'

D.   "That is in line with this verse of Scripture: *Has God tried to go and take for himself a nation from the midst of another nation* (Deut. 4:34)."

2. A. R. Joshua bar Nehemiah in the name of R. Yohanan bar Pazzi: "'A nation from the midst of a people' is not written here, nor do we find, 'a people from the midst of a nation,' but *a nation from the midst of a nation* [like itself, that is, in precisely the same classification].

   B. "For the Egyptians were uncircumcised and the Israelites also were uncircumcised. The Egyptians grew ceremonial locks, and so did the Israelites.

   C. "Therefore by the rule of strict justice, the Israelites ought not to have been redeemed from Egypt."

   D. Said R. Samuel bar Nahmani, "If the Holy One, blessed be He, had not bound himself by an oath, the Israelites in fact would never have been redeemed from Egypt.

   E. *"Therefore say to the children of Israel, I am the Lord, and I shall take you out of the burdens of Egypt* (Ex. 6:6).

   F. "The language, *[I am the Lord]* therefore, refers only to an oath, as it is said, *Therefore I take an oath concerning the house of Eli* (1 Sam. 3:4)."

3. A. Said R. Berekhiah, "*You have redeemed your people with your arm* (Ps. 77:16) — with naked power.

   B. Said R. Yudan, "From the phrase, *To go and take a nation from the midst of another nation*, to the phrase *great terrors* (Deut. 4:34) are seventy-two letters.

   C. "Should you claim there are more, you should deduct from the count the last reference to *nation* [Egypt], which does not count."

   D. R. Abin said, "It was for the sake of his name that he redeemed them, and the name of the Holy One, blessed be He, consists of seventy-two letters."

4. A. [*"This month is for you the first of months, you shall make it the first month of the year]* (Ex. 12:2)]: Said R. Joshua b. Levi, "The matter may be compared to the case of a king whose son was taken captive, and he put on [the garb of] vengeance and went and redeemed his son, and he said, 'Count the years of my reign as beginning from the time of the redemption of my son.'

   B. "So said the Holy One, blessed be He, 'Count the years of my reign as beginning from the time of the Exodus from Egypt.'"

5. A. *"This month is for you [the first of months, you shall make it the first month of the year]* (Ex. 12:2)]: R. Levi in the name of R. Hama bar Hanina said, "The matter may be compared to the case of a king who married many wives, but he did not write for them either a marriage-license or the dates of the marriage.

   B. "But when he married a woman of good family and the daughter of noble parents, he wrote for her a marriage license and wrote the date of the marriage.

   C. "So too of all the women whom Ahasuerus married, he did not write for any one of them either a marriage-license or the date of the marriage. But when he married Esther, the daughter of a good family and of noble lineage, he wrote for her both a marriage-license and the date of the marriage.

D. "He wrote for her a marriage-license: *On the tenth month, the month of Tebeth* (Est. 2:16).

E. "And he wrote for her the date of the marriage: *In the seventh year of his reign* (Est. 2:16)."

We move on to the exegesis of the base-verse, now essentially in its own terms as to word-choice and contents. No. 1 takes up the word *month,* which can be read as new, with the result that is given. Nos. 2 and 3 carry forward the exegesis of the proof-text of No. 1 and so form an extended appendix. Nos. 4, 5 then explain why the month has been chosen as the first of the months, a very persuasive explanation at that. It is the month in which Israel is redeemed, and the two parables, No. 4 and No. 5, then explain the rest. But No. 5 clearly serves another setting entirely, and it does not fit into this context so well as No. 4.

Pesiqta Rabbati XV:XVII.6=Pesiqta deRab Kahana V:XII.1:

1. A. Said R. Berekhiah, *"This month is for you [the first of months, you shall make it the first month of the year]* (Ex. 12:2):

   B. "[The waxing and waning of the moon serve] as an omen for you.

   C. *"The seed of David...shall be established for ever as the moon* (Ps. 89:38):

   D. "Like the moon, which is full and then obscured.

   E. "If you have merit, lo, you will count days like the moon's waxing, but if you do not have merit, then you will count days like the moon's waning.

   F. "Abraham, Isaac, Jacob, Judah, Perez, Hezron, Ram, Aminadab, Nachshon, Salman, Boaz, Obed, Jesse, David, Solomon:

   G. *"Then Solomon sat on the throne of the Lord as king* (1 Chr. 29:23) − [all provide cases of counting days as] the moon when it is waxing.

   H. "Lo, in these cases the count was like the waning moon: Rehoboam, Abijah, Assa, Jehoshaphat, Jehoram, Ahaziah, Joash, Amaziah, Uzziah, Jotham, Ahaz, Hezekiah, Manasseh, Ammon, Josiah, and Zedekiah: *He blinded the eyes of Zedekiah* (2 Kgs. 25:7) − lo, [all these give us cases of] counting the days like the moon in its waning.

The exegesis of the word for month, identifying it with the moon, then joins the moon's waxing and waning to Israel's history and explains the whole by reference to merit. This is a strikingly cogent exegesis of the base-verse in terms of its own word-choices.

Pesiqta Rabbati XV:XVIII=Pesiqta deRab Kahana V:XIII:

1. A. *This month is for you [the first of months, you shall make it the first month of the year]* (Ex. 12:2):

   B. *...for you* means that it is handed over to you.

   C. Said R. Joshua b. Levi, "The matter may be compared to the case of a king who had a clock. When his son grew up, he handed over to him his clock."

D. Said R. Yose bar Haninah, "The matter may be compared to the case of a king who had a watchtower. When his son grew up, he handed over to him his watchtower."

E. Said R. Aha, "The matter may be compared to the case of a king who had a ring. When his son grew up, he handed over to him his ring."

F. Said R. Isaac, "It may be compared to the case of a king who had many treasuries, and there was a key for each one of them. When his son grew up, he handed over to him all the keys."

G. Said R. Hiyya bar Abba, "The matter may be compared to a carpenter who had tools. When his son grew up, he handed over to him the tools of his trade."

H. And rabbis say, "The matter may be compared to the case of a physician who had a case of medicines. When his son grew up, he handed over to him his medicine case."

Pesiqta Rabbati XV:XIX.1=Pesiqta deRab Kahana V:XIII.2:

2. A. R. Hoshaiah taught on Tannaite authority, "The court below made a decree saying, 'Today is the new year.'

B. "Said the Holy One, blessed be He, to the ministering angels: 'Set up a platform, let the attorneys go up, let the clerks go up, for the court below has made a decree, saying, "Today is the New Year."'

C. "If the witnesses [to the appearance of the new moon of Tishre] delayed in coming, or the court decided to intercalate the year on the next day [so that that day would not be the new year], the Holy One, blessed be He, says to the ministering angels, 'Take away the platform, take away the advocates and take away the clerks, for the court below has made a decree saying, "Tomorrow [not today] is the New Year."'

D. "What verse of Scripture proves this point? *For it is a statute for Israel, a judgment of the God of Jacob* (Ps. 81:5).

E. "If it is not *a statute for Israel*, it is – as it were – also not *a judgment of the God of Jacob*."

3. A. R. Phineas, R. Hezekiah in the name of R. Simon: "All the ministering angels assemble with the Holy One, blessed be He, saying to him, 'Lord of the ages, when will it be the New Year?'

B. "And he says to them, 'Me do you ask? You and I should ask the court down below.'

C. "What verse of Scripture proves this point? *For the Lord our God is near whenever* we *call to him* (Deut. 4:7).

D. "And *we* call to him only on the set feasts, in line with this verse of Scripture: *These are the set feasts of the Lord, the holy convocations [which* you *shall proclaim]* (Lev. 23:4)."

E. R. Qerispa in the name of R. Yohanan, "In the past: *These are the set feasts of the Lord.* But from now on: *which* you *shall proclaim:*

F. "He said to them, 'If *you* proclaim them, they are my set feasts, and if not, they are not my set feasts.'"

We move on to the possessive: *for you.* The main point is announced at No. 1, presented in an implicit way at No. 2, and then given full articulation at No. 3. The declaration of the new moon – and the calendar that depends on it –

is in the hands of Israel. God has handed the matter over to Israel at the beginning of redemption. The basic idea is well expressed and assuredly rests on the base-verse.

Pesiqta Rabbati XV:XX=Pesiqta deRab Kahana V:XIV:

1. A. *This month is for you [the first of months, you shall make it the first month of the year]* (Ex. 12:2):
    B. You count by it, but the nations of the world will not count by it. [They use the solar calendar, you the lunar one.]

2. A. R. Levi in the name of R. Yose b. R. Ilai: "It is merely natural that someone who presently is great should count by what is great, and someone who presently is small should count by what is small.
    B. "Accordingly, Esau [Rome] counts by the sun, because it is great, while Jacob [Israel] counts by the moon, for it is small."
    C. Said R. Nahman, "That really is a good omen. Esau counts by the sun, because it is great. But just as the sun rules by day but does not rule by night, so the wicked Esau rules in this world but not in the world to come.
    D. "Jacob counts by the moon, which is small, and just as the moon rules by night and also by day [making its appearance both by night and by day], so too will Jacob rule in this world and in the world to come."
    E. R. Nahman said, "So long as the light of the great luminary glows splendidly in the world, the light of the lesser luminary is not going to be noted. Once the light of the great light sets, then the light of the lesser one shines forth.
    F. "So too, as long as the light of the wicked Esau lasts, the light of Jacob will not be seen. Once the light of the wicked Esau sets, then the light of Jacob will shine forth.
    G. "That is in line with this verse: *Arise, shine [for behold, darkness shall cover the earth, and gross darkness the peoples, but upon you the Lord will arise, and his glory shall be seen upon you]* (Is. 60:1)."

Pesiqta Rabbati XV:XI.1=Pesiqta deRab Kahana V:XIV.3:

3. A. R. Simeon b. Yohai taught on Tannaite authority, "In three matters Moses had difficulty. The Holy One, blessed be He, showed him – as it were – with his finger: the candelabrum, the creeping things, and the moon.
    B. "As to the candelabrum: This *is the work of the candlestick* (Num. 8:4).
    C. "The creeping things: This *is what is unclean for you among the creeping things that creep on the earth* (Lev. 11:29).
    D. "The moon: This *month is for you [the first of months]* (Ex. 12:2)."

We remain focused upon the dative of possession, for you, and Nos. 1, 2 go over that point. Israel, but not the nations, calculate the calendar through the moon. No. 2 makes the recurrent point about the eschatological significance of that fact. No. 3 moves on to the next word, this, explaining why the demonstrative is used.

Pesiqta Rabbati XV:XXI.2=Pesiqta deRab Kahana V:XV.1:

1. A. R. Simlai, and it has been taught in the name of R. Samuel, "Every month on the beginning of which the [Braude and Kapstein, p. 116:] the conjunction of the new moon does not take place before noon, one cannot see [the moon] before evening."

   B. R. Samuel bar Yeba, R. Aha in the name of R. Samuel bar Nahman: "In the year in which the Israelites went forth, the beginning of the lunar month and the vernal equinox coincided [*sic!*]"

2. A [Explaining the procedure for receiving testimony of the appearance of the new moon, with reference to the demonstrative statement, *This month (=moon) is for you*] **R. Berekhiah**, R. Hiyya bar Ba in the name of R. Yohanan: "The Holy One, blessed be He, cloaked himself in a cloak bearing fringes and put Moses on one side and Aaron on the other, calling Michael and Gabriel [to demonstrate the procedure for receiving testimony on the appearance of the new moon]. He appointed them messengers to proclaim the new moon and said to them, 'On what side did you see the moon? Was it before the sun or after the sun? Was it to the north or to the south? How high was it? Where was it inclining? How thick was the cresent?'

   B. "He said to them, 'This is the procedure, as you see it here, is the way in which people should intercalate the year down below: through an elder, with witnesses, through the use of a cloak bearing show-fringes.'"

No. 1 seems to make the point that the new moon on the occasion on which the Israelites went out of Egypt coincided with the vernal equinox (March 21), which is not possible. On that basis Braude and Kapstein reject what we have and choose to translate: "began on the same day of the week." But the sages at hand seem to wish to say that it was a miracle. No. 2 reverts to the stress on this moon, indicating that in so stating matters, God was explaining to Moses the proper procedure for receiving testimony as to the appearance of the new moon.

Pesiqta Rabbati XV:XXII.1=Pesiqta deRab Kahana V:XVI.1:

1. A. *This month is for you [the first of months, you shall make it the first month of the year]* (Ex. 12:2):] R. Nahman and R. Eleazar b. R. Yose and R. Aha:

   B. One of them said, "[Reading the letters for month to sound like the word, *innovation:*] "Said the Holy One, blessed be He, to Israel, 'There will be an innovation as to redemption for you in the age to come.'"

   C. The other said, "It will be an innovation as to the age to come that you will have here.

   D. "Just as, in the age to come, *Then the eyes of the blind will be opened* (Is. 35:5), so now, *And all the people saw the sounds* (Ex. 20:18).

   E. "Just as in the age to come, *The ears of the deaf will be unstopped* (Is. 35:5), so here, *And they said, Everything which the Lord has spoken we shall do and we shall hear* (Ex. 24:7).

F. "Just as in the age to come, *Then the lamb will skip like a ram* (Is. 35:6), so now, *Moses brought forth the people out of the camp to meet God and they stood below the mountain* (Ex. 19:17).

G. "Just as in the age to come, *The tongue of the dumb shall sing* (Is. 35:6), so here: *All the people sang together* (Ex. 19:8).

The earlier tendency to compare the coming redemption to the redemption from Egypt is now made still more concrete. Each detail of Isaiah's vision is applied to the account of the Exodus from Egypt. The innovation that bears the point is from C forward.

Pesiqta Rabbati XV:XXIII.1=Pesiqta deRab Kahana V:XVII.1:

1. A. *Speak to the whole community of Israel and say to them, On the tenth day of this month [let each man take a lamb or a kid for his family, one for each household, but if a household is too small for one lamb or one kid then the man and his nearest neighbor may take one between them. They shall share the cost, taking into account both the number of persons and the amount each of them eats. Your lamb or kid must be without blemish, a yearling male. You may take equally a sheep or a goat. You must have it in safe keeping until the fourteenth day of this month, and then all the assembled community of Israel shall slaughter the victim between dusk and dark. They must take some of the blood and smear it on the two doorposts and on the lintel of every house in which they eat the lamb. On that night they shall eat the flesh roast on the fire; they shall eat it with unleavened cakes and bitter herbs. You are not to eat any of it raw or even boiled in water, but roasted, head, shins, and entrails. You shall not leave any of it till morning; if anything is left over until morning, it must be destroyed by fire]* (Ex. 12:1-10):

   B. Said R. Yohanan, "Is the lamb not suitable only when taken from the fold? Why say to designate it on the tenth day, [even though it will not be used until the fourteenth, four days later]?

   C. "This teaches that the lambs were tied up to the Israelites' beds from the tenth day, and the Egyptians would come in and see them and [realizing what was about to happen,] their souls would expire."

2. A. R. Hiyya son of R. Ada/**Aha** of Jaffa: *"[Moses summoned all the elders of Israel and said to them,] Draw out and get sheep for your families and slaughter the Passover* (Ex. 12:21):

   B. "'The requirement is that each one of you draw out the god of an Egyptian and slaughter it in his presence, [Braude and Kapstein, p. 118: even as the Egyptian...speaks up in protest].'"

3. A. R. Helbo in the name of R. Yohanan: "Here you say, *On the tenth day of this month* (Ex. 12:3), and later on: *The people went up from the Jordan on the tenth day* (Joshua 4:19)."

   B. R. Hiyya in the name of R. Yohanan: "The act of taking the lamb is what sustained the Israelites at the Jordan, and the act of eating it is what protected them in the days of Haman.

   C. *"And they shall eat the meat on that night* (Ex. 12:8). *On that night the sleep of the king was troubled* (Est. 6:1)."

Pesiqta Rabbati XV:XXIV.1=Pesiqta deRab Kahana V:XVII.4:

4. A. R. Berekhiah in the name of R. Abbahu: "Nahum the son of R. Simai in Tarsus gave this exposition: *"...let each man take [a lamb or a kid for his family, one for each household]* – the *man* here is the Holy One, blessed be He, as it is said, *The Lord is a man of war* (Ex. 15:3).

   B. "[Since the meaning is that they must "take" the Holy One, blessed be He, we ask:] with what does one acquire him? With the two daily continual offerings [one in the morning, the other at dusk,] *a lamb for the house of the fathers, a lamb for the house of the fathers* (Ex. 12:3)"

5. A. Said R. Yudan in the name of R. Simon, "No one ever spent the night in Jerusalem while still bearing sin. How so? The daily whole-offering of then morning would effect atonement for the sins that had been committed overnight, and the daily whole-offering of dusk would effect atonement for the transgressions that had been committed by day.

   B. "In consequence, no one ever spent the night in Jerusalem while still bearing sin.

   C. "What is the verse of Scripture that makes that point? *Righteousness will spend the night in it* (Is. 1:21)."

Nos. 1, 2 links the preparations of the slaughter of the lamb as a Passover offering to the punishment of the Egyptians for their idolatry. No. 1 sets the stage for No. 2. No. 3 then broadens the frame of reference still further. The merit acquired on the occasion of the first Passover sustained the Israelites at two further crises, as shown. No. 4 draws the parallel between the Passover and the daily whole-offering, morning and night, and at this point Braude and Kapstein insert Ex. 29:39: *The one lamb you offer in the morning, the other at dusk* , at which point they further read, *The one lamb in the ancestral House, the other lamb in that House, in the Temple*, which they give as Ex. 12:3. None of this is in Mandelbaum's text, but it does clarify the passage. No. 5 forms an appendix to No. 4. The daily whole-offering effects atonement for sins of the community.

Pesiqta Rabbati XV:XXV.1=Pesiqta deRab Kahana V:XVIII.1:

1. A. [Interpreting the combination of the word for *month*, as new, hence, renewal, and the word for *first*, in the verse, *This month is for you the first of months, you shall make it the first month of the year*], R. Berekhiah in the name of R. Isaac: "*New* (Ex. 12:3): Renew your deeds, for [otherwise] the head and *first* of all will come.

   B. "The *first* is Nebuchadnezzar, the wicked, of whom it is written: *You are the head of gold* (Dan. 2:38).

   C. "The *first* is the wicked Esau, of whom it is written, *The first came forth red* (Gen. 25:25).

   D. "Who will exact vengeance for you from the first? It is the first: *I the Lord am the first and the last, I am he* (Is. 41:4).

   E. "Who will exact vengeance for you from Media [Haman]? [It is the kingdom mentioned when the cited verse speaks of] *the tenth*, [at Ex. 12:3]."

2. A.   Said R. Abin, "The *ten* alludes to [the ten thousand talents of silver to be paid to Ahasuerus] by Haman and his ten sons.

   B.   "Who will exact vengeance for you from them?

   C.   "The two guardians, Mordecai and Esther, Mordecai on the outside, Esther on the inside.

   D.   "Who will exact vengeance for you from Greece? The sons of the Hasmoneans, who offered the two daily whole-offerings every day.

   E.   "Who will exact vengeance for you from Edom? Natronah [that is, the guard].

   F.   "*And he shall serve as a guard for you to the fourteenth day of the month* (Ex. 12:6)."

3. A.   [Reverting back to the verse cited above, *"The first came forth red"* (Gen. 25:25):] said the Holy One, blessed be He, "His father called him the greater: *And he called Esau, his son, the greater* (Gen. 27:1).

   B.   "And his mother called him the greater: *Rebecca took the clothing of Esau, her son, the greater* (Gen. 27:15).

   C.   "But I shall call him the lesser: *And lo, I have made you least among the nations* (Ob. 1:2).

   D.   "Since they call him the greater, in accord with the size of the ox is the measure of the slaughterer: *The Lord has a sacrifice in Bosrah, a great slaughter in the land of Edom* (Is. 34:6)."

   E.   Said R. Berekhiah, "[We read the verse:] 'There will be a great slaughterer in the land of Edom' [namely, God himself]."

The eschatological reading of the matter of Ex. 12:2ff. brings us to the two who are called first, Nebuchadnezzar and Esau, and that accounts for No. 1. No. 2 then raises the question of redemption: who will save Israel and punish the oppressor. That the passage is not particular to our setting is clear, since at No. 1 no one has referred to Haman, Mordecai, and Esther. But the goal, as always, is Edom, and that requires us to ring the changes on the four monarchies. The climax comes at No. 3: God himself will exact punishment of Edom/Rome.

Pesiqta Rabbati XV:XXV.4=Pesiqta deRab Kahana V:XIX.1:

1. A.   [Continuing the account of the punishment of Edom:] *You are not to eat any of it raw* – that is, not merely half-cooked, or merely *or even boiled in water, but roasted, head, shins, and entrails.*

   B.   [Edom, together with] its dukes, its hyparchs, and its generals.

   C.   *Your wealth, your staple wares, your imports, your sailors and your helmsmen, your caulkers, your merchants, and your warriors, all your ship's company, all who were with you were flung into the sea on the day of your disaster; at the cries of your helmsmen the troubled waters tossed* (Ez. 27:27-28):

   D.   Said R. *Samuel bar R.* Isaac, "*All your ship's company* encompasses even those who had been of my company and had gone and joined your company – even they *were flung into the sea on the day of your disaster.*"

2. A. *This is the way in which you must eat it: you shall have your belt fastened, your sandals on your feet and your staff in your hand, and you must eat in urgent haste. It is the Lord's Passover* (Ex. 12:11):

   B. Said R. Samuel bar Nahman, "Since in this world, *you must eat in urgent haste,* in the world to come what is written?

   C. *"But you shall not come out* in urgent haste *nor leave like fugitives; for the Lord will march at your head, your rearguard will be Israel's God* (Is. 52:12)."

The exposition of the verse brings us back to Pesiqta deRab Kahana V:IX, which treats the same specification in the same way, and with the same effect: the eschatologization of the theme. No. 2 then applies the fixed notion that the exodus serves as model and counterpart to to the final redemption.

Part Two

LITERARY STRUCTURES OF PESIQTA RABBATI
AND PESIQTA DeRAB KAHANA

Chapter Seven

Recurrent Literary Structures
of Pesiqta Rabbati

I. Introduction

A literary structure is a set of rules that dictate to an authorship recurrent conventions of expression, organization, or proportion that are *extrinsic* to the message of the author or authorship. The conventions at hand bear none of the particular burden of the author's personal and particular message, so they are not idiosyncratic. They convey in their context the larger world-view expressed within the writing in which they are used, so they prove systemic and public. That is because a literary structure conforms to rules that impose upon the individual writer a limited set of choices about how he will convey whatever message he has in mind. Or the formal convention will limit an editor or redactor to an equally circumscribed set of alternatives about how to arrange received materials. These conventions then form a substrate of the literary culture that preserves and expresses the world-view and way of life of the system at hand.

A structure in literature thus will dictate the way in which diverse topics or ideas come to verbal expression. It follows that we cannot know that we have a structure if the text under analysis does not repeatedly resort to the presentation of its message through that disciplined syntactic pattern (or other structure that organizes fixed components of discourse, e.g., materials taken from some other and prior document), external to its message on any given point. And, it follows, quite self-evidently, that we do know that we have a structure when the text in hand repeatedly follows recurrent conventions of expression, organization, or proportion *extrinsic* to the message of the author. The adjective "recurrent" therefore constitutes a redundancy when joined to the noun "structure." For a structure – in our context, a persistent syntactic pattern, rhetorical preference, logical composition – by definition recurs and characterizes a variety of passages. Like Pesiqta deRab Kahana, Pesiqta Rabbati comprises large-scale literary structures.

How do we know that fact? It is because, when we divide up the undifferentiated columns of words and sentences and point to the boundaries that separate one completed unit of thought or discourse from the next such completed composition, we produce rather sizable statements conforming to a single set of syntactic and other formal patterns. On the basis of what merely appears to us to be patterned or extrinsic to particular meaning and so entirely formal, we cannot allege that we have in hand a fixed, literary structure. Such a judgment would prove subjective. Nor shall we benefit from bringing to the text at hand recurrent syntactic or grammatical patterns shown in other texts, even of the same canon of literature, to define conventions for communicating ideas in those other texts. Quite to the contrary, we find guidance in a simple principle:

A text has to define its own structures for us.

Its authors do so by repeatedly resorting to a given set of linguistic patterns and literary conventions – and no others. On the basis of a survey of recurrent choices, we may account for the "why this, not that" of literary forms. On that same basis of inductive evidence alone we test the thesis that the authors at hand adhere to a fixed canon of literary forms. If demonstrably present, we may conclude that these forms will present an author or editor with a few choices on how ideas are to be organized and expressed in intelligible – again, therefore, public – compositions. When, as in the present exercise, we draw together and compare two distinct documents, each one to begin with has to supply us with evidence on its own literary structures. We conduct a survey in detail for our sample of Pesiqta Rabbati and then review the findings already in hand for Pesiqta deRab Kahana.

So we look for large-scale patterns and point to such unusually sizable compositions as characteristic. Why? Because they recur and define discourse, *pisqa* by *pisqa*. Indeed, as we shall now see, a given *pisqa* is made up of a large-scale literary structure, which in a moment I shall describe in detail. In all, what I mean when I claim that Pesiqta Rabbati, like Pesiqta deRab Kahana, is made up of large-scale literary structures is simple. When we divide a given *pisqa*, or chapter, of Pesiqta Rabbati into its subdivisions, we find these subdivisions stylistically cogent and well-composed, always conforming to the rules of one out of three possible formal patterns. To identify the structures of the document before us, we had best move first to the analysis of a single *pisqa*. We seek, within that *pisqa*, to identify what holds the whole together. The second step then is to see whether we have identified something exemplary, or what is not an example of a fixed and formal pattern, but a phenomenon that occurs in fact only once or at random. For the first exercise, we take up *Pisqa* One, and for the second, Two through Five, then Fifteen. I do not cite the texts already translated in the earlier part of this book. A bird's eye view of the whole of Pesiqta Rabbati shows it to be a formally uniform document, so that sample suffices for the purposes of working out the argument of this book.

II. Pesiqta Rabbati *Pisqa* 1

1. Pesiqta Rabbati *Pisqa* 1 I:I

"May our master teach us" – *yelammedenu rabbenu* – introduces a discourse on a matter of law, following a highly conventional and restrictive form: question with the formal introduction, followed by our masters have taught us, with a legal formulation, and then a secondary thematic development. No. 1 presents us with the colloquy, *May our master instruct us...our masters have taught us...*, followed at No. 2 by a secondary point not generated by the primary colloquy. We note that the theme of the *pisqa* as a whole, the New Moon, does not generate in the legal component of the *pisqa* a thesis that will dominate discourse later on. There is no correlation whatsoever between the legal problem and the thematic exposition that follows. No. 3 likewise pursues its own interests, without intersecting with any point that will follow.

2. Pesiqta Rabbati *Pisqa* 1 I:II

We should expect to have an intersecting-verse fully expounded and then brought into relationship with a base-verse. But that anticipated form is not realized. We do have a brief feint in that direction at No. 1, for No. 1 intends to draw into juxtaposition Ps. 42:1-4 and Lev. 16:1ff. We have an allusion to the matter, in that the two verses – intersecting, base – are cited. But then the authorship refers us to another discourse, without copying that other discourse. In a fully realized execution of the intersecting-verse/base-verse construction, we should have not only an exposition of the intersecting-verse, which we do have here, but also an explicit introduction, at the outset, of the base-verse, which should be Is. 66:22-24. That verse does occur at the end, but no preparation has announced that it is going to be the centerpiece of discussion. The result is an exceedingly defective exercise in which base-verse is ignored, even though a powerful message concerning its ultimate meaning is exposed by the intersecting-verse.

Nos. 3, 4, 5, 6, 7, 8 cite the intersecting-verse, With my whole being I thirst for God, and impute meanings to that verse. Hence the form is simple: citation of a verse, statement of the meaning or application of that verse. No. 9 is tacked on to No. 8 because of thematic reasons. No. 10 continues No. 9. No. 11 pursues the same program of exegesis of what we call the intersecting-verse. Then No. 11 brings us back to the lection for the Sabbath that coincides with the New Moon. But that lection has not been cited, so we cannot imagine that we have a sizable exposition of an intersecting-verse and then its juxtaposition with a base-verse, simply because the "base-verse" in this case is cited only at the end. The theme of a yearning of Israel to union with God is a rather general one. There is no sustained exposition of a proposition that opens the base-verse in a fresh way. True, there is a powerful proposition, which is that in the end of time the New Moon will enter the status of a pilgrim festival. But it is difficult for me to see how the formal characteristics of the composition match the cogency of the programmatic intent. The one formal possibility is that I:I is intended to introduce the base-verse, the presence of which is then taken for granted in the execution of I:II. But I find no evidence in the document before us that that is the intent. There is no continuity in either form or program between I:I and I:II.

Later on we shall contrast this execution of the intersecting-verse/base-verse form with the execution of that same form in Leviticus Rabbah and Pesiqta deRab Kahana. Overall, it suffices to note that in Leviticus Rabbah there will be a full and sustained inquiry into the many and diverse meanings of the intersecting-verse, and only then the base-verse comes into view and its meaning is revised by the intersection. In Pesiqta deRab Kahana, by contrast, the intersecting-verse always focuses upon a single point, the point that the authorship wishes to make with reference to the base-verse. So the articulation is intellectually economical and disciplined, by contrast to the intellectually promiscuous character of the use of the form in Leviticus Rabbah. In our document, the formal discipline is lost altogether; there is neither a systematic treatment of the intersecting-verse nor a highly purposeful intersection, making a single stunning point, such as we note in the two prior compilations, respectively.

3. Pesiqta Rabbati *Pisqa* 1 I:III

We have now an exposition of the base-verse, which is Is. 66:22-24. Formally, we find precisely the formal plan characteristic of the foregoing: citation of a verse, a few words that impute meaning to that verse. Once more we shall notice how our authorship contrasts with that of Pesiqta deRab Kahana. For the exegetical form employed in Pesiqta deRab Kahana, in its syntactic traits identical to the one before us, yields a single message, an implicit syllogism repeated many times over. In our document (as in Leviticus Rabbah), by contrast, the exegetical form permits an authorship to say pretty much whatever it wants on a given theme, and does not impose the requirement to state in yet another, new way an established syllogism. These distinctions become important in Chapter Eleven.

4. Pesiqta Rabbati *Pisqa* 1 I:IV

I:IV.1-2 seem to me to continue the preceding, that is, I:III.4.

5 Pesiqta Rabbati *Pisqa* 1 I:V

This subdivision continues the foregoing.

6. Pesiqta Rabbati *Pisqa* 1 I:VI

This subdivision continues the established theme, the importance of living in the Land of Israel.

7. Pesiqta Rabbati *Pisqa* 1 I:VII

What I said just now applies here.

III. The Forms of Pesiqta Rabbati *Pisqa* 1

We may now review the results of the form-analysis. We have defined the following formal preferences:

1. Legal colloquy:

May our master instruct us...our masters have taught us..., followed by a secondary lesson.

2. Exegesis of a verse

A verse is cited and then given a secondary or imputed meaning, e.g., Another matter + verse + a few words that state the meaning of that verse or its concrete application.

3. Intersecting-verse/base-verse (hypothetical)

We should expect to find a base-verse, e.g., Is. 66:22-24, cited, then an intersecting-verse, e.g., Ps. 42:1-4, used to impute to the former some more profound meaning than is obvious at the surface. This form, not realized here, is suggested and of course elsewhere validated as a routine option. That is why it must take its place within the formal repertoire, even though our sample does not present us with an instance in which it is used.

IV. The Thematic Program and Proposition of Pesiqta Rabbati *Pisqa* 1: Syllogism, Collage, or Scrapbook?

Before proceeding to test our form-analytical hypothesis, we have now to ask whether the *pisqa* at hand presents a cogent statement of its own, or whether it constitutes a collection of thematically joined but syllogistically distinct statements. Let us review the propositions of our pisqa:

I:I: If one forgot to include a reference to the New Moon in the Grace after Meals. Other rules about the Grace after Meals for the New Moon. The New Moon is equivalent to a festival.

I:II: Israel thirsts for God, who bestows blessings of a natural order and also will bring salvation. Leading to 8.B: When will you restore the glory of going up on the three pilgrim festivals to see the face of God. Ultimately the New Moon will be equivalent to a pilgrim festival.

I:III: Interpretation of Is. 66:22-24: can people really come to Jerusalem every New Moon and every Sabbath? Other problems in that same framework.

I:IV: On what account will Israel enjoy all this glory? Because of the merit of dwelling in the Land of Israel. The resurrection of those who are buried in the Land.

I:V: More on the resurrection of those who are buried in the Land.

I:VI: More on the resurrection of those who are buried in the Land.

I:VII: Secondary expansion of a detail in the foregoing. More on the resurrection of those who are buried in the Land. When will the Messiah come.

We may now ask whether our *pisqa* forms a highly cogent syllogism, with a proposition systematically proven by each of the components; whether it forms a collage, in which diverse materials seen all together form a cogent statement; or whether it constitutes a scrapbook in which thematically continuous materials make essentially individual statements of their own. Among these three choices, the second seems to me, in balance, to apply to *Pisqa* One. We certainly do not find a single cogent statement, an implicit syllogism repeated over and over in the several components of the *pisqa*. But we do have more than a mere scrapbook on a common theme. For the basic point, the equivalence of the New Moon to a pilgrim festival, is made both at the legal passage, I:I, and the exegetical one, I:II-III. I:IV-VII then form a mere appendix, tacked on without much good reason. So we may judge our *pisqa* to be an imperfectly executed collage, one that, in the aggregate, really does make its point.

V. The Order of the Forms of *Pisqa* 1

The legal colloquy appears first of all, at **I:I**. If **I:II** had worked out an intersecting-verse/base-verse composition, then that would have constituted the form to appear second in sequence. **I:III** presents an exegesis of the base-verse on its own terms. It follows that as a matter of hypothesis, we should expect the order of types of forms to be, first, a legal colloquy, which will introduce the theme and possibly also the thesis; second, the intersecting-verse/base-verse form, which will allow the theme, and possibly the thesis, to come to expression in exegetical, rather than legal terms; and, third, the exegetical form, which allows the base-verse to be spelled out on its own. Miscellanies then will come at the end. So there would appear to be a preferred order of types of units of discourse. But a large-scale test of a sizable sample is now needed.

VI. Testing the Form-Analytical Hypothesis: Five Experiments

1. Introduction

My hypothesis is in three parts. First, I propose to test the proposition that Pesiqta Rabbati in the main, though not wholly, comprises four recurrent literary structures, **I.** legal colloquy, **II.** base-verse/intersecting-verse, **III.** exegetical, and, as we shall see in a moment, **IV.** syllogistic argument for a proposition through the composition of a list of facts, all of them sustained by proofs of Scripture. Second, it would appear that the *pisqa* of Pesiqta Rabbati, while not a closely argued and cogent syllogistic statement, also is not a mere scrapbook, but does, in the aggregate if not in detail, point toward a distinctive conclusion. Third, the ideal order would place the legal colloquy first, the intersecting-verse/base-verse second, then the exegetical form third, followed by whatever supplementary materials seemed required for a complete statement.

That three-part hypothesis now requires testing. For that purpose we turn to the other four *pisqaot* that I have translated and undertake exactly the same procedure that produced our original hypothesis. If the proposed formal repertoire and program of cogent discourse encompasses the bulk of what is before us, then we find justification to postulate the same formal character for the entirety of the document. My comments on the selected *pisqaot* focus upon form-analytical issues: why do I think a given unit of thought falls into one of the three classifications adduced to date. The upshot of what is to follow had best be stated at the outset. We shall see that our original hypothesis does encompass most of the materials of the sample of five *pisqaot* under study.

2. Pesiqta Rabbati *Pisqa* 2

1. *Legal Colloquy*

   II:I: when is one obligated to kindle the lamp in celebration of Hanukkah? Where; use of light; why one does so; why recite the Hallel-psalms.

2. *Exegesis of a Verse*

   II:III-IV: Ps. 149:5 + in what glory will they exult + Is. 57:2, 21. My best sense is that we deal with an exegesis of Ps. 149:5. II:IV continues the foregoing. At the end Ps. 30:1 makes a minor point in connection with the foregoing. It is not central to the exegetical program concerning Ps. 149:5.

   II:V works on the conflict between 2 Sam. 7:5 and 1 Chr. 17:4 to make the point that David did not build the Temple, but Solomon did. The reason for that fact is then made clear. What is explained is how the Psalm can refer to the house of David, when Solomon built it.

   II:VI goes over the same ground. David is credited with the Temple, so Ps. 30:1.

3. *Intersecting-verse/Base-verse (hypothetical)*

   I see no instance of this form in Pisqa II.

4. *Proposition Proved by a List of Verses*

   This is a form not noted earlier. We have a proposition, proved by the facts amassed in a list of facts provided by verses. Thus: II:II: How many occasions for rededication through the kindling of lights are there: seven; so too II:VII, which goes over the same ground. The list ends with its own point of emphasis.

5. *The Thematic Program and Proposition of Pesiqta Rabbati Pisqa 2:
    The Pisqa as Syllogism, Collage, or Scrapbook*

    II:I presents no clear hypothesis. The principle of aggregation is
    merely thematic. I see no hypothesis. **II:II-II:IV** present an
    exegesis of Ps. 149:5. The return to Ps. 30:1 makes no basic
    point. The basic point is that when deceased, the righteous endure
    and praise God. That hypothesis, though not everywhere present,
    does take pride of place. **II:V** includes David in the credit for the
    building of the Temple. This is not wholly out of phase with
    II:IV. II:VI pursues precisely the same matter. **II:VII** lists
    seven acts of dedication, going over the ground of **II:II.** The
    dedication of the world to come will involve a kindling of lights.
    It is difficult to see the *pisqa* as a whole as a cogent statement,
    although the central theme of David's getting credit for the house
    that Solomon built should not be missed. But the correspondence
    of the legal inquiry, **II:I**, with the syllogism to follow, **II:IIff.**, is
    hardly so striking as in *Pisqa* 1. Yet the eschatological interest of
    II:I.3.H should not be missed, and that does recur at **II:II,
    II:VII.** In the balance, however, it is difficult to regard *Pisqa* 2 as
    a collage, which, through the aggregation of diverse materials,
    creates a single powerful effect. That does not seem to me to be
    the case. We have something more than a scrapbook but
    considerably less than a collage, and, in any event, nothing
    remotely approaching a cogent syllogistic statement.

6. *The Order of Types of Units of Discourse*

    Our final question is whether the types of units of discourse follow
    a fixed order.

II:I	=	legal syllogism/Type I
II:II	=	list proving a proposition/Type IV
II:III	=	exegesis of verse/Type III
II:IV	=	exegesis of verse/Type III
II:V	=	exegesis of verses/Type III
II:VI	=	exegesis of verse/Type III
II:VII	=	list proving a proposition/Type IV

    The answer is that – so far as I can see – they do not. We seem to
    have no instance of Type II, and the order of Types III and IV is not
    regular.

3. Pesiqta Rabbati *Pisqa* 3

1. *Legal Colloquy*

III:I: What do we do with left-over oil of a Hanukkah-lamp? The answer derives from a decree of elders. The outcome is that one should obey the decree of elders. Even God is bound by the decree of elders. This is illustrated by Num. 7:54, which has Ephraim first, then Manasseh. Thus the younger brought prior to the elder, just as the younger was blessed before the elder.

2. *Exegesis of a Verse*

While we have numerous exegeses of specific verses, e.g., Gen. 13:1ff., 20:1ff., in regard to Lot, at **III:III**, Gen. 48:1ff., in regard to Jacob and Joseph and the blessing of his sons, at **III:IV**, the thrust of the whole is to clarify the important point of the base-verse, the placing of the younger first, the elder second. And that, for its part, serves to illustrate the power of the decree of the sage, in this case, Jacob. So while the Pisqa contains its share of exegeses of verses, its principal building blocks make use of these exegeses in the larger enterprise of spelling out the meaning of the intersection of the intersecting-verse and the base-verse.

3. *Intersecting-verse/Base-verse*

III:II: Qoh. 12:11/Num. 7:54 goes over precisely the point important at **III:I**. The decree of the elders is primary: *The words of the wise are as goads.* The intersecting-verse and its language are spelled out with care. The climactic statement is that the words of Torah and the words of scribes enjoy the same authority. **III:III** continues the exposition of the intersecting-verse, then shifts into an exposition of the theme of Abraham and Lot, which has no clear point of contact with our verse. But the important point is that Lot and the woman of Zarephath made the same statement, which is that *the words of sages are like goads* – and that is the point that is important. This then yields, at **III:IV**, the important point, which is that Jacob decreed that the younger was to come first. That is the issue of our base-verse, which places the younger first, then the elder son of Joseph.

III:V: Here we have a systematic exposition of the base-verse, Num. 7:54ff., in its own terms.

4. *Proposition Proved by a List of Verses*

I see no example of this form in the present *pisqa*.

5. *The Thematic Program and Proposition of Pesiqta Rabbati Pisqa 2: The Pisqa as Syllogism, Collage, or Scrapbook*

III:I, II make the same point, and do so very cogently: the words of Torah and the words of scribes enjoy the same authority. **III:III, IV** go over precisely the same ground and prove the same point of other cases. III:IV brings us back to Jacob with Manasseh and Ephraim, which is where we began. So far as the parts are meant to point toward a single, whole proposition, which is that the younger precedes the elder, and that there are lessons to be learned from that fact, *Pisqa* 3 constitutes a highly cogent statement of an implicit syllogism.

6. *The Order of Types of Units of Discourse*

Our final question is whether the types of units of discourse follow a fixed order.

III:I	=	legal syllogism/Type I
III:II	=	intersecting-verse/base-verse/Type II
III:III	=	intersecting-verse/base-verse/Type II
III:IV	=	intersecting-verse/base-verse/Type II
III:V	=	exegesis of verses/Type III

The answer is that – so far as I can see – they do: type I, II, and III – in that order. Everything now works: disciplined forms, following the "right" order, and making a single point in a number of different ways. The contrast to the foregoing is striking.

4. Pesiqta Rabbati *Pisqa* 4

1. *Legal Colloquy*

IV:I: Does one make mention of Hanukkah in the Prayer-service covering Additional Offerings? Indeed so. Where does one do so? In the Prayer of Thanksgiving. All the wonders God has done were on account of the merit of the tribal progenitors, including the building of the house. This ends with the base-verse, which is 1 Kgs. 18:30-32: the twelve stones that Elijah took for his altar.

2. *Exegesis of a Verse*

I see no component of the composition that focuses upon the exegesis of a verse, though, of course, many of the large-scale statements draw upon exegeses of Scripture.

3. *Intersecting-verse/Base-verse*

IV:III: Is. 66:1-2 is drawn into juxtaposition with 1 Kgs. 18:30-32. The main point is that the tribal progenitors' merit stands behind the good things that are discussed here.

4. *Proposition Proved by a List of Verses*

IV:II: Hos. 12:14 refers to Moses, Elijah. They were alike in all regards. That includes the one important here, which is that both Moses and Elijah built altars of twelve stones, corresponding to the number of tribal progenitors. While this composition ends with our base-verse, in fact it is a sustained list of facts, of which our base-verse constitutes one. We cannot regard this sizable list as an instance of the intersecting-verse/base-verse construction, and it certainly does not constitute merely a sequence of exegesis of verses of Scripture.

5. *The Thematic Program and Proposition of Pesiqta Rabbati Pisqa 2: The Pisqa as Syllogism, Collage, or Scrapbook*

The main point is that the merit of the tribal progenitors accounts for all of the good things that have happened to Israel, and that will happen. While that point is stated at **IV:I:3**, the legal question does not relate to it. The correspondence or equivalency of Moses and Elijah, **IV:II**, while drawing upon the fact contributed by the base-verse as a pertinent fact, does not restate the proposition. That composition makes its own, distinctive point. IV:III works on the base-verse and its exposition, and it also alludes, at **IV:III.1.S** to the proposition, the focus is on the exposition of the history of the destruction of the Temple, not upon the centrality of the merit of the twelve tribal progenitors. So, in all, we have not even a collage but a scrapbook. And that is despite the repeated allusions to the proposition that the compositor of the whole has clearly wished to establish.

6. *The Order of Types of Units of Discourse*

Our final question is whether the types of units of discourse follow a fixed order.

IV:I	=	legal syllogism/Type I
IV:II	=	list proving a proposition/Type IV
IV:III	=	intersecting-verse/base-verse/Type II

The answer is that – so far as I can see – they do not. Still, where there is a list, it does intervene between the legal colloquy and the exegetical form that finds a place in the whole, just as is the case above. Seen as a whole *Pisqa* 4 shows us the opposite of *Pisqa* 3: where nothing works, nothing works.

5. Pesiqta Rabbati *Pisqa 5*

1. *Legal Colloquy*

V:I raises the question of the procedure of presenting the lection in both Hebrew and Aramaic translation. May the one who does the one do the other too? No, that may not be done. The final proof-text, Hos. 8:12, leads to **V:II**, which introduces our theme, the setting up of the tabernacle. What follows is that the legal colloquy does not contribute a dominant proposition or even a theme. The whole thing has been included only because of the connection to **V:II** at Hos. 8:12 (**V:I2.H** connecting to **V:III.1.A**, Another interpretation of the verse.... And that passage has been introduced because in its propositional list, it makes reference, among other matters, to the setting up of the tabernacle. Its point is that if one is prepared to give his life for something, then that thing will be credited to him.

2. *Exegesis of a Verse*

V:IV works on the exegesis of Song 4:16. I do not see how that verse serves as an intersecting-verse for Num. 7:1. The sole point of contact is thematic, as the exegesis unfolds, and the allusion to the altar at Num. 7:1 accounts for the inclusion in our *pisqa* of the entire construction. **V:V** goes its own way in interpreting Song 5:1. Only at **V:V.6** do we come back to our base-verse, and then the intersection is a solid and important one. While at No. 1 **V:VII** interprets some of the language of the base-verse, in fact we have a syllogism demonstrated by a long list of facts/proof-texts. **V:X** presents a fine interpretation of the juxtaposition of two verses, Num. 7:1 and Num. 6:24. The meaning of each is clarified in light of the other.

3. *Intersecting-verse/Base-verse*

V:III weaves Prov. 30:4 together with Num. 7:1. The point of contact is at the ascent of Moses to heaven. Intersecting-verse is applied to Moses, Elijah, and to God. The composition, however, does not seem to me to make any single point, and the way in which the base-verse is recast by its encounter with the intersecting-verse so as to yield an important new proposition is hardly self-evident to me. The main point is that Moses has established the tabernacle as God's residence, but that point is submerged among many others. **V:IV-V** ends with the intersection of Song 4:16 and Num. 7:1. Then the point is that the union of bride, Israel, and groom, God, took place when Moses finished the tabernacle, focussing upon the dual-sense of the word KLH as finish and also as bride. But this point is tacked on and hardly the centerpiece of interest. It is as though the redactor has made use of the sizable exegesis of Song 4:16ff. not because that exegesis has imposed its sense or meaning or even theme on the base-verse, but only because of the adventitious occurrence of the base-verse in the other composition. Still, that is a matter of judgment. **V:VI** makes better use of this form to contrast Qoh. 2:21 with Num. 7:1. It makes the point that while Bezallel made the tabernacle, Moses got credit for it. But no reason is given or lesson adduced. So the potential of the form is hardly realized. **V:IX** invokes Song 3:11 along with Num. 7:1, but does not spell out the lessons it wishes to impart; then proceeds to Ps. 85:9, now going over the ground of how the tabernacle reconciled God and Israel. That point is repeated in the unfolding of the pericope.

4. *Proposition Proved by a List of Verses*

   V:II rests on the point that God credited Moses with those things for which he was prepared to give his life, including the setting up of the tabernacle. **V:VII-VIII-IX** work out a sequence of examples for the proof of the proposition that a certain construction bears a specified meaning. This philological inquiry does not provide the exegesis of any one text, nor do the appearances of a variety of texts yield a fresh meaning for any one or even the lot of them. The centerpiece of discourse is an inquiry into the meaning of words, as diverse examples of a given type prove that meaning. The reason for the insertion of the whole, which comes at **V:IX.7**, the building of the tabernacle caused the nations to say, "Woe," should not be confused with the principle of cogency of the entire composition, which derives from the word-study.

5. *The Thematic Program and Proposition of Pesiqta Rabbati Pisqa 5: The Pisqa as Syllogism, Collage, or Scrapbook*

   V:I makes the point that what is particular to Israel is the Oral Torah meaning in particular the Mishnah. **V:II** stresses that Moses got credit for those matters for which he was ready to give his life. Moses established God's residence on earth when he set up the tabernacle, **V:III**. **V:IV** pursues its own theme, which is the diversity of offerings on the altar. **V:V** presents its exegesis of Song 5:1, never making a point pertinent to what has gone before. Only at the end does V:V allude to our base-verse, making the point that with the setting up of the altar Israel married God. **V:VI** points out that Bezalel did the work but Moses got the credit. It does not say why. **V:VII-IX** take up the meaning of the words, *and it came to pass*. The important point of intersection comes at the end: the building of the tabernacle brought woe to the nations. **V:X** explains why the blessings of Num. 6:24 are juxtaposed with the building of the tabernacle, Num. 7:1. The tabernacle is the source of various blessings for Israel. **V:XI** underlines this same point again and again. While a number of the compositions make the same point – e.g., the tabernacle as a source of blessings – the *pisqa* as a whole constitutes not a collage but a scrapbook, joined only by the theme of the tabernacle, but presenting no cogent proposition or even a coherent statement of any kind.

6. *The Order of Types of Units of Discourse*

Our final question is whether the types of units of discourse follow a fixed order.

V:I	=	legal syllogism/Type I
V:II	=	list proving a proposition/Type IV
V:III	=	Intersecting-verse/base-verse/Type II
V:IV	=	exegesis of verse/Type III
V:V	=	exegesis of verses/Type III [but, for reasons already given, one may wish to classify V:IV-V as a massive statement in the form of the intersecting-verse/base-verse/Type II]
V:VI	=	intersecting-verse/base-verse/Type II
V:VII	=	list proving a proposition/Type IV
V:VIII	=	list proving a proposition/Type IV
V:IX	=	list proving a proposition/Type IV
V:X	=	exegesis of verse/Type III
V:XI	=	intersecting-verse/base-verse/Type II

The answer is that – so far as I can see – they do not. Once more: where nothing works, nothing works.

6. Literary Structures of a *Pisqa* Shared by Pesiqta Rabbati with Pesiqta deRab Kahana: Pesiqta Rabbati *Pisqa* 15

Let us now conduct the same inquiry of our example of the shared *pisqa*. We wish to know whether a *pisqa* that appears in both Pesiqta Rabbati and Pesiqta deRab Kahana exhibits traits of formal preference – types of units of discourse, order of the types – and logical cogency (or lack of the same) characteristic, also, of the *pisqaot* that occur only in Pesiqta Rabbati. I follow the numbering system of Pesiqta deRab Kahana.

1. *Legal Colloquy*

None.

2. *Exegesis of a Verse*

V:XI is the point at which we begin the exegesis of the base-verse in its own terms. The redemption will be through an unusual means. V:XII works on Ex. 12:1 in its own way. V:XIII interprets Ex. 12:2 in a different way, specifically, Israel is in charge of the calendar and is the authority over the moon's seasons.

V:XIV interprets the base-verse in its own way. V:XV deals with the base-verse. V:XVI goes over the word for month, meaning, innovation. V:XVII turns to a later clause in the base-verse. V:XVIII deals with the base-verse once more, again with interest in the word for month/new. V:XIX goes on to a later part of the base-verse, but only to make the established point.

3. *Intersecting-verse/Base-verse*

V:I introduces Ps. 104:19 to underline the use of the lunar calendar on the part of Israel. V:II invokes Prov. 40:5 and makes the point that Israel is in charge of the lunar calendar. V:III appeals to Prov. 13:12-14 on hope deferred/desire fulfilled to make the point that *This month* , Ex. 12:1-2, marked the end of hope deferred and the beginning of desire fulfilled. V:VII presents an exegesis of Ex. 12:1 in line with Song 2:8-10, making the point that Israel will be redeemed in Nisan. V:VIII-X continue the same exercise.

4. *Proposition Proved by a List of Verses*

I am inclined to find in the redemption-in-*This month* sequence, V:IV-VI, a list pointing to a single proposition, which is that redemption will take place in Nisan. The exegesis of the diverse verses that are adduced otherwise has no bearing upon the base-verse, and we cannot see these entries as examples of the intersecting-verse/base-verse construction. For the intersecting-verse never reaches the base-verse and imposes no fresh meaning or perspective upon it. Rather, it makes its own point, which, at the end, serves the larger proposition at hand: redemption in Nisan. The formal trait of the entire sequence is the tacking on of *When did this take place? In this month* + *Ex. 12:2*. That is a redactional flourish, but it does justify including the item in the present sequence and makes of the whole simply a list of proofs for the proposition at hand.

5. *The Thematic Program and Proposition of Pesiqta Rabbati Pisqa 15: The Pisqa as Syllogism, Collage, or Scrapbook*

Pisqa 15 is not a composite on a common theme, e.g., a collage, but presents a tight syllogism, which is repeated in one way or another, on every component of the *pisqa*. Israel's special status is underlined by the use of the lunar calendar, over which Israel has control, V:I, II. The hope deferred, V:III, was for redemption, which began to be fulfilled in the month under discussion. *This month*, Nisan, will be the month in which redemption will take place, as it did in Egypt, V:IV-VI. V:VII maintains that Nisan is the month of redemption, but that Israel has to be patient. V:VIII works out a messianic theme on its own, without reverting to the base-verse. **V:IX-X** continue the foregoing. The redemption will be an innovation in some way, so **V:XI**. The waxing and the waning of the moon stand, **V:XII**, for Israel's fortunes. **V:XIII** stresses that it is Israel that is in charge of the lunar calendar. Israel appeals to the moon, the nations to the sun, **V:XIV**, and ultimately Israel will be in charge. **V:XV** goes over the same point. **V:XVI** goes over the familiar point that Israel's coming redemption will represent an innovation. **V:XVII** goes over the theme of redemption, though the proposition at hand goes its own way and emphasizes the atonement for sins that is involved in the daily whole-offering. **V:XVIII** reverts to the proposition that the renewal of the month of Nisan marks redemption. **V:XIX** compares the first redemption in Nisan with the coming redemption in Nisan. This time it will not be in haste. I cannot imagine within the genre at hand a more cogent and single-minded statement of one basic point.

6. *The Order of Types of Units of Discourse*

Our final question is whether the types of units of discourse follow a fixed order.

V/XV:I	=	intersecting-verse/base-verse/Type II
V/XV:II	=	intersecting-verse/base-verse/Type II
V/XV:III	=	intersecting-verse/base-verse/Type II
V/XV:IV	=	list proving a proposition/Type IV
V/XV:V	=	list proving a proposition/Type IV
V/XV:VI	=	list proving a proposition/Type IV
V/XV:VII	=	intersecting-verse/base-verse/Type II
V/XV:VIII	=	intersecting-verse/base-verse/Type II
V/XV:IX	=	intersecting-verse/base-verse/Type II
V/XV:X	=	intersecting-verse/base-verse/Type II
V/XV:XI	=	exegesis of verse/Type III
V/XV:XII	=	exegesis of verse/Type III
V/XV:XIII	=	exegesis of verse/Type III
V/XV:XIV	=	exegesis of verse/Type III
V/XV:XV	=	exegesis of verse/Type III
V/XV:XVI	=	exegesis of verse/Type III
V/XV:XVII	=	exegesis of verse/Type III
V/XV:XVIII	=	exegesis of verse/Type III
V/XV:XIX	=	exegesis of verse/Type III

The answer is that – so far as I can see – the order is absolutely fixed: first type II, then type III. As we shall see in the next chapter, that is the formal preference of the redactors of Pesiqta deRab Kahana. We cannot demonstrate that that same preference characteristically appealed to the framers of Pesiqta Rabbati. Now, where everything synchronizes, the whole works with facility: rhetorical form and logical cogency joining to register with great force a single implicit syllogism.

VII. Summary: Recurrent Literary Structures: Types of Units of Discourse, their Order, and their Cogency

We may classify all the large-scale compositions of Pesiqta Rabbati within four literary structures. These are the legal colloquy, which itself follows a fairly restrictive pattern in that the form opens with a narrowly legal question, which moves toward a broader, propositional conclusion; the intersecting-verse/base-verse construction, the exegetical form, and the propositional list. The intersecting-verse/base-verse construction itself is composed of a variety of clearly formalized units, e.g., exegesis of verses of Scripture and the like. The exegetical form, for its part, is remarkably simple, since it invariably consists of the citation of a verse of Scripture followed by a few words that impute to that verse a given meaning; this constant beginning may then be followed by a variety of secondary accretions which themselves exhibit no persistent formal traits. The propositional list is remarkably cogent in both its formal traits and its principle of cogency.

It goes without saying that the order of the types of forms is not fixed. In Pesiqta Rabbati we find one fixed order: the legal colloquy always comes first. But even that form serves diverse purposes, since, as we noted, in some *pisqaot* it announces a proposition which will be spelled out and restated in exegetical form as well, while in others the legal colloquy introduces a theme but no proposition in connection with that theme. From that point we may find anything and its opposite: propositional lists, then, intersecting-verse/base-verse-compositions, then exegetical statements, or any other arrangement. The significance of that fact emerges in the sharply disciplined order of the types of forms in Pesiqta deRab Kahana *Pisqa* 5/Pesiqta Rabbati *Pisqa* 15. I have already demonstrated that that fixed order characterized the first of the two Pesiqtas throughout.

The matter of cogency invokes a somewhat more subjective judgment. Yet I find it difficult to discover as a general or indicative trait of Pesiqta Rabbati a sustained effort at making a cogent and single statement. That – as we shall shortly see – indeed does mark Pesiqta de Rab Kahana beginning to end. That fact is suggested by our survey of the cogency of the *pisqaot* of Pesiqta Rabbati that we have reviewed. Among the three analogies which I proposed – syllogism, collage, or scrapbook – we could invoke all three. That means that the authorship of the document as a whole found itself contented with a variety of types of logical discourse. Some of the *pisqaot* appeared to treat a single topic, but only in a miscellaneous way. The propositions associated with that topic would scarcely cohere to form a single cogent statement. In that case I found we had a scrapbook. Other *pisqaot* seemed to wish to draw a variety of statements into juxtaposition so that, while not coherent, when viewed all together, those statements would form a single significant judgment upon a theme, hence, a collage. While I cannot demonstrate beyond a doubt the correctness of my assignment of a given *pisqa* to a given classification, I think that, overall, we are on firm ground in making these assignments: *Pisqa* 1, collage; *Pisqa* 2, scrapbook on a single theme; *Pisqa* 3, syllogism; *Pisqa* 4, scrapbook; *Pisqa* 5, scrapbook. So we find everything and its opposite. The contrast to Pesiqta Rabbati *Pisqa* 15=Pesiqta deRab Kahana *Pisqa* 5 is then stunning: there we see what a *pisqa* looks like when the authorship has made not merely a composite but a single and uniform composition. In a moment we shall see that the entirety of Pesiqta deRab Kahana follows suit.

The conclusion may be stated very briefly. The authorship of Pesiqta Rabbati has made use of a fixed and limited repertoire of large-scale literary structures – four in all. These it has ordered in diverse ways, so the authorship found no important message to be delivered through the sequence in which the types of forms would be utilized. The same authorship pursued a variety of modes of cogent discourse, sometimes appealing to the theme to hold together whatever materials they chose to display, sometimes delivering a rather general message in connection with that theme, and, on occasion, choosing to lay down a very specific syllogism in connection with a theme. These traits revealed by our survey take on significance when we compare Midrash to Midrash, that is to say, Pesiqta Rabbati to Pesiqta deRab Kahana. For it is now self-evident that, confronted with a *pisqa* lacking all identification, we could readily and easily distinguish a *pisqa* particular to Pesiqta Rabbati from one shared with Pesiqta deRab Kahana, and that on more than a single basis. And, it goes without saying, we should have no difficulty whatsoever in picking out a *pisqa* that may fit into either of the two Pesiqtas from a *pisqa* that would belong to Sifra, Sifré to Numbers, Genesis Rabbah, Leviticus Rabbah, The Fathers According to Rabbi Nathan, the Tosefta, the Mishnah, the Yerushalmi, or the Bavli. Each document exhibits its distinctive and definitive traits of rhetoric and logic.

Chapter Eight

Recurrent Literary Structures of Pesiqta deRab Kahana:

Types of Units of Discourse and their Order

I. Defining Pesiqta deRab Kahana

The brief comparisons, now executed in Chapters Six and Seven, call to our attention the close relationship between the two Pesiqtas. Our task is now to distinguish the one from the other, which, in the end, will serve to define each in its own distinctive terms and so permit us to compare the one with the other. We have no better way of definition for analytical purposes than the route of comparison. The reason is that the ordinary means of definition of a document – information on the time and place and intention of authorship, for example – prove unavailable. That is why we are left to work with internal evidence. For no document in the canon of Judaism produced in late antiquity do we have a named author. No writing in that canon contains within itself a statement of a clearcut date of composition, a defined place or circumstance in which a book is written, a sustained and on-going argument to which we readily gain access, or any of the other usual indicators by which we define the authorship, therefore the context and the circumstance, of a book.

There is a reason for that fact. The purpose of the sages who in the aggregate created the canonical writings of the Judaism of the dual Torah is served by not specifying differentiating traits such as time, place, and identity of the author or the authorship. The canon – "the one whole Torah of Moses, our rabbi" – presents single books as undifferentiated episodes in a timeless, ahistorical setting: Torah revealed to Moses by God at Mount Sinai, but written down long afterward. That theological conviction about the canon overall denies us information to introduce the book at hand, that is, to say what it is. Without the usual indicators, then, how then are we to read our document on its own terms, so as to answer the question: what is this book? When, where, why was it written? What does it mean?

When we do turn to the internal evidence of Pesiqta deRab Kahana, we ask its authorship for guidance on what they proposed to accomplish in their composition. My insistence upon an inductive reading of internal evidence requires me first to classify, then to specify the internal evidence of choice. The evidence of a document of late antiquity will fall into three classifications:

rhetoric, recurrent modes or patterns of expression; topic, the program of systematic exposition of a limited number of themes; and logic, the principle that joins one sentence to the next in an intelligible proposition or syllogism and that imparts cogency and integrity to the document in each of its parts and as a whole. We have already treated the rhetoric and the logic of discourse of our sample of Pesiqta Rabbati. Only when we have a clear picture of the implications of the counterpart-document's own traits of plan and program may we move beyond the limits of the writing and ask about the context in which the document at hand finds its location.

Among the three definitive or indicative traits of a piece of sustained writing, rhetoric, logic, and topic, the first is the easiest to characterize, since, as I said in Chapter Seven, it is, by definition, recurrent and repetitive.[1] The logic or principle of cogent discourse, which imparts (in the mind of the authorship) intelligibility comes to formal expression in rhetoric, so we commonly move from description of rhetoric to analysis of the logical foundations of rhetoric. And, under normal circumstances, the third and most difficult point of entry into a definition of the document is its topical program. For that is in the nature of things diffuse, since the authorship treats more than a single topic, and it is, furthermore, the indicative trait of the document least likely to form connections to other documents, authorships' preferring, after all, to say something fresh or at least something old in a new way. We take up that matter in a later chapter.

II. Sorting Out Internal Evidence: An Inductive Approach

Rhetoric provides internal evidence, to be inductively construed. The document rests upon clearcut choices of formal and rhetorical preference, so it is, from the viewpoint of form and mode of expression, cogent. Formal choices prove uniform and paramount. How to discover the forms of discourse? To begin with, as was our procedure with Pesiqta Rabbati, I analyze one *pisqa*, to show its recurrent rhetorical patterns and structures. These as a matter of hypothesis I describe and categorize. Then, I proceed to survey two more *pisqaot* to see whether or not a single cogent taxonomic structure provides a suitable system of classification for diverse units of discourse. We then proceed to survey the entirety of Pesiqta deRab Kahana, that is, *Pisqaot* 1-28, presented in my complete translation. If one taxonomy serves all and encompasses the bulk of the units of discourse at hand, I may fairly claim that Pesiqta deRab Kahana does constitute a cogent formal structure, based upon patterns of rhetoric uniform

---

[1] And, I repeat, persists from age to age. The pseudepigraphic character of large tracts of the canonical writings of the Judaism of the dual Torah must stand as a given in all research, and not solely because of the parlous state of the manuscript evidence. All historical judgments of description, analysis, and interpretation that claim to relate to a determinate time and place must rest therefore on those indicative traits that characterize the document as a whole. These mark the document *ab origine* because they define its character and integrity. They then dictate to the pseudepigraphs how they shall frame their contribution, later on, to the received writing.

and characteristic throughout. The importance of that fact will lie on the very surface. For on that basis we can describe – and we shall be able to – the incremental message, the cumulative effect, of the formal traits of speech and thought revealed in the uniform rhetoric and syntax of the document. The framers or redactors followed a set of rules which we are able to discern. These rules lead us deep into the interiority of our authorship: people say things the way they mean to say them, and how they express their ideas imparts meaning to what they say.

III. Literary Structures of Pesiqta deRab Kahana *Pisqa* 6

For Pesiqta deRab Kahana I use some analytical language slightly different from that used above, and that language requires definition at the outset. Specifically, I refer, first, to contrastive-verse and base-verse, and these prove to be the prime building blocks of rhetorical analysis. The base-verse is the recurrent verse of Scripture that defines the point of recurrent reference for all *pisqaot* but two or three. I call it base-verse simply because it forms the basis of all discourse and imparts unity to each *pisqa*. The contrastive-verse is the same as the intersecting-verse of Pesiqta Rabbati; in this document it functions quite conventionally, as a verse that will be introduced to clarify the meaning of the base-verse. The contrast between the one and the other then yields a syllogism, and the purpose of the whole, as I shall show, is that syllogistic discourse. Thus it is the contrastive-verse, by reason of its well-defined function. While in the body of the translation, I have used the language appropriate in earlier documents, hence intersecting-verse and base-verse, here a more exact usage is required, because, as I have noted, the function of the intersecting-verse in Leviticus Rabbah, which is to permit extended discussion of everything but the base-verse, here shifts to a functionally well defined purpose, just as in Pesiqta Rabbati the form shifts once more, now using the intersecting-verse for less well defined purposes. In Pesiqta deRab Kahana the function of the outside verse (here: contrastive-verse) is to establish the main point of the syllogism, and it is in the intersecting of the contrastive-verse and the base-verse that that syllogism is brought to clear statement. We shall see, overall, that Pesiqta deRab Kahana presents its syllogisms in a far more powerful and direct medium of rhetoric than does Leviticus Rabbah, earlier, or Pesiqta Rabbati, later on.

Second, I refer to an implicit syllogism. By syllogism I mean a proposition that forms the recurrent principle a *pisqa* wishes to express and to prove in the way its authorship deems plausible and compelling. It is implicit because it is never stated in so many words, yet it is readily recognized and repeatedly imputed to one set of verses after another. The implicit syllogism, as we shall see, reaches expression in one of two ways, one through what I call propositional form, the other through exegetical form. Let me state with appropriate emphasis the rhetorical program represented by the two forms we shall now discern. *Both are ways of stating in the idiom our authorship has chosen, in the media of expression they have preferred, and through the modes of demonstration and evidentiary proof they deem probative, a truth they never spell out but always take for granted we shall recognize and adopt.*

We now proceed to the first of our three complete *pisqaot* and conduct precisely the same exercise of translation and analysis that we have already accomplished for Pesiqta Rabbati.

VI:I

1. A. *If I were hungry, I would not tell you, for the world and all that is in it are mine. [Shall I eat the flesh of your bulls or drink the blood of he-goats? Offer to God the sacrifice of thanksgiving and pay your vows to the Most High. If you call upon me in time of trouble, I will come to your rescue and you shall honor me]* (Ps. 50:12-15):

   B. Said R. Simon, "There are thirteen traits of a merciful character that are stated in writing concerning the Holy One, blessed be He.

   C. "That is in line with this verse of Scripture: *The Lord passed by before him and proclaimed, The Lord, the Lord, God, merciful and gracious, long-suffering and abundant in goodness and truth; keeping mercy unto the thousandth generation, forgiving iniquity, transgression, and sin, who will be no means clear* (Ex. 34:6-7).

   D. "Now is there a merciful person who would hand over his food to a cruel person [who would have to slaughter a beast so as to feed him]?

   E. "One has to conclude: *If I were hungry, I would not tell you.*"

2. A. Said R. Judah bar Simon, "Said the Holy One, blessed be He, 'There are ten beasts that are clean that I have handed over to you [as valid for eating], three that are subject to your dominion, and seven that are not subject to your dominion.

   B. "'Which are the ones that are subject to your dominion? *The ox, sheep, and he-goat* (Deut. 14:4).

   C. "'Which are the ones not subject to your dominion? *The hart, gazelle, roebuck, wild goat, ibex, antelope, and mountain sheep* (Deut. 14:5).

   D. "'Now [in connection with the sacrificial cult] have I imposed on you the trouble of going hunting in hills and mountains to bring before me an offering of one of those that are not in your dominion?

   E. "'Have I not said to you only to bring what is in your dominion and what is nourished at your stall?'

   F. "Thus: *If I were hungry, I would not tell you.*"

3. A. Said R. Isaac, "It is written, *[The Lord spoke to Moses and said, Give this command to the Israelites:] See that you present my offerings, the food for the food-offering of soothing odor, to me at the appointed time. [Tell them: This is the food-offering which you shall present to the Lord: the regular daily whole-offering of two yearling rams without blemish. One you shall sacrifice in the morning and the second between dusk and dark]* (Num. 28:1-4).

   B. "Now is there any consideration of eating and drinking before Me?

   C. "'Should you wish to take the position that indeed there is a consideration of eating and drinking before me, derive evidence to the contrary from my angels, derive evidence to the contrary from my ministers: *...who makes the winds your messengers, and flames of fire your servants* (Ps. 104:4).

D.   "'Whence then do they draw sustenance? From the splendor of the Presence of God.

E.   "'For it is written, *In the light of the presence of the King they live* (Prov. 16:15).'"

F.   R. Haggai in the name of R. Isaac: *"You have made heaven, the heaven of heavens...the host...and you keep them alive* (Neh. 9:6, meaning, you provide them with livelihood [Leon Nemoy, cited by Braude and Kapstein, p. 125, n. 4]."

4.   A.   Said R. Simeon b. Laqish, "It is written, *This was the regular whole-offering made at Mount Sinai, a soothing odor, a food-offering to the Lord* (Num. 28:6).

B.   "[God says,] 'Now is there any consideration of eating and drinking before Me?

C.   "'Should you wish to take the position that indeed there is a consideration of eating and drinking before me, derive evidence to the contrary from Moses, concerning whom it is written, *And he was there with the Lord for forty days and forty nights. Bread he did not eat, and water he did not drink* (Ex. 34:28).

D.   "'Did he see me eating or drinking?

E.   "'Now that fact yields an argument *a fortiori*: now if Moses, who went forth as my agent, did not eat bread or drink water for forty days, is there going to be any consideration of eating and drinking before me?

F.   "Thus: *If I were hungry, I would not tell you."*

5.   A.   Said R. Hiyya bar Ba, "'Things that I have created do not need [to derive sustenance] from things that I have created, am I going to require sustenance from things that I have created?

B.   "'Have you ever in your life heard someone say, 'Give plenty of wine to this vine, for it produces a great deal of wine'?

C.   "'Have you ever in your life heard someone say, 'Give plenty of oil to this olive tree, for it produces a great deal of oil'?

D.   "'Things that I have created do not need [to derive sustenance] from things that I have created, am I going to require sustenance from things that I have created?'

E.   "Thus: *If I were hungry, I would not tell you."*

6.   A.   Said R. Yannai, "Under ordinary circumstances if someone passes though the flood of a river, is it possible for him to drink a mere two or three *logs* of water? [Surely not. He will have to drink much more to be satisfied.]

B.   "[God speaks:] 'But as for Me, I have written that a mere single *log* of your wine shall I drink, and from that I shall derive full pleasure and satisfaction.'"

C.   R. Hiyya taught on Tannaite authority, *"The wine for the proper drink-offering shall be a quarter of a hin for each ram; you are to pour out this strong drink in the holy place as an offering to the Lord* (Num. 28:7).

     D.   "This statement bears the sense of drinking to full pleasure, satisfaction, and even inebriation."

7.   A.   Yose bar Menassia in the name of R. Simeon b. Laqish, "When the libation was poured out, the stoppers [of the altar's drains] had to be stopped up [Braude and Kapstein, p. 126: so that the wine overflowing the altar would make it appear that God could not swallow the wine fast enough]."

     B.   Said R. Yose bar Bun, "The rule contained in the statement made by R. Simeon b. Laqish is essential to the proper conduct of the rite [and if the drains are not stopped up, the libation offering is invalid and must be repeated]."

8.   A.   [God speaks:] "I assigned to you the provision of a single beast, and you could not carry out the order. [How then are you going to find the resources actually to feed me? It is beyond your capacity to do so.]'

     B.   "And what is that? It is *the Behemoth on a thousand hills* (Ps. 50:10)."

     C.   R. Yohanan, R. Simeon b. Laqish, and rabbis:

     D.   R. Yohanan said, "It is a single beast, which crouches on a thousand hills, and the thousand hills produce fodder, which it eats. What verse of Scripture so indicates? *Now behold Behemoth which I made...Surely the mountains bring him forth food* (Job 40:15)."

     E.   R. Simeon b. Laqish said, "It is a single beast, which crouches on a thousand hills, and the thousand hills produce all sorts of food for the meals of the righteous in the coming age.

     F.   "What verse of Scripture so indicates? *Flocks shall range over Sharon and the Vale of Achor be a pasture for cattle; they shall belong to my people who seek me* (Is. 65:10)."

     G.   Rabbis said, ""It is a single beast, which crouches on a thousand hills, and the thousand hills produce cattle, which it eats.

     H.   "And what text of Scripture makes that point? *And all beasts of the field play there* (Job 40:20)."

     I.   But can cattle eat other cattle?

     J.   Said R. Tanhuma, *"Great are the works of our God* (Ps. 111:2), how curious are the works of the Holy One, blessed be He."

     K.   And whence does it drink?

     L.   It was taught on Tannaite authority: R. Joshua b. Levi said, "Whatever the Jordan river collects in six months it swallows up in a single gulp.

     M.   "What verse of Scripture indicates it? *If the river is in spate, he is not scared, he sprawls at his ease as the Jordan flows to his mouth* (Job 40:23)."

     N.   Rabbis say, "Whatever the Jordan river collects in twelve months it swallows up in a single gulp.

     O.   "What verse of Scripture indicates it? *he sprawls at his ease as the Jordan flows to his mouth* (Job 40:23).

     P.   "And that suffices merely to wet his whistle."

     Q.   R. Huna in the name of R. Yose: "It is not even enough to wet his whistle."

     R.   Then whence does it drink?

S.   R. Simeon b. Yohai taught on Tannaite authority, *"And a river flowed out of Eden* (Gen. 2:10), and its name is Yubal, and from there it drinks, as it is said, *That spreads out its roots by Yubal* (Jer. 17:8).

T.   It was taught on Tannaite authority in the name of R. Meir, *"But ask now the Behemoth* (Job 12:7) – this is *the Behemoth of the thousand hills* (Ps. 50:10), *and the fowl of the heaven will tell you* (Job 12:7), that is the *ziz*-bird (Ps. 50:10), *or speak to the earth that it tell you* (Job 12:8) – this refers to the Garden of Eden. Or *let the fish of the sea tell you* (Job 12:8) – this refers to Leviathan.

U.   *"Who does not know among all these that the hand of the Lord has done this* (Job 12:9)."

9.   A.   "I gave you a single king, and you could not provide for him. [How then are you going to find the resources actually to feed me? It is beyond your capacity to do so.] And who was that? It was Solomon, son of David."

     B.   *The bread required by Solomon in a single day was thirty kors of fine flower and sixty kors of meal* (1 Kgs. 5:2).

     C.   Said R. Samuel bar R. Isaac, "These were kinds of snacks. But as to his regular meal, no person could provide it: *Ten fat oxen* (1 Kgs 5:3), fattened with fodder, *and twenty oxen out of the pasture and a hundred sheep* (1 Kgs 5:3), also out of the pasture; *and harts, gazelles, roebucks, and fatted fowl* (1 Kgs. 5:3)."

     D.   What are these fatted fowl?

     E.   R. Berekhiah in the name of R. Judah said, "They were fowl raised in a vivarium."

     F.   And rabbis say, "It is a very large bird, of high quality, much praised, which would go up and be served on the table of Solomon every day."

     G.   Said R. Judah bar Zebida, "Solomon had a thousand wives, and every one of them made a meal of the same dimensions as this meal. Each thought that he might dine with her."

     H.   "Thus: *If I were hungry, I would not tell you.*"

10. A.   "One mere captive I handed over to you, and you could barely sustain him too. [How then are you going to find the resources actually to feed me? It is beyond your capacity to do so.]"

     B.   And who was that? It was Nehemiah, the governor:

     C.   *Now that which was prepared for one day was one ox and six choice sheep, also fowls were prepared for me, and once in ten days store of all sorts of wine; yet for all this I demanded not the usual fare provided for the governor, because the service was heavy upon this people* (Neh. 5:18).

     D.   What is *the usual fare provided for the governor?*

     E.   Huna bar Yekko said, "[Braude and Kapstein, p. 114:] It means gourmet food carefully cooked in vessels standing upon tripods."

     F.   "Thus: *If I were hungry, I would not tell you.*"

11. A.   It has been taught on Tannaite authority: **The incense is brought only after the meal** (M. Ber. 6:6).

B. Now is it not the case that the sole enjoyment that the guests derive from the incense is the scent?

C. Thus said the Holy One blessed be He, "My children, among all the offerings that you offer before me, I derive pleasure from you only because of the scent: *the food for the food-offering of soothing odor, to me at the appointed time.*

The passage commences with what is clearly the contrastive-verse, Ps. 50:12, which stands in stark contrast to the base-verse, Num. 28:1ff., because what the latter requires, the former denigrates. No. 1 is open-ended, in that it does not draw us back to the base-verse at all. It simply underlines one meaning to be imputed to the contrastive-verse. No. 2 pursues the theme of the base-verse – the selection of beasts for the altar – and reverts to the intersecting one. Nos. 3, 4 and 5 then draw us back to the base-verse, but in a rather odd way. They treat it as simply another verse awaiting consideration, not as the climax of the exercise of explication of the many senses of the contrastive-verse. The purpose of the composition before us is not to explore the meanings of the contrastive-verse, bringing one of them to illuminate, also, the base-verse. The purpose is to make a single point, to argue a single proposition, through a single-minded repertoire of relevant materials, each of which makes the same point as all the others. In Chapter Eleven we shall return to this matter and draw conclusions important in the comparison of Pesiqta deRab Kahana, Leviticus Rabbah and Pesiqta Rabbati.

I see No. 5 as the conclusion of the main event, that is to say, the contrastive-verse has laid down its judgment on the sense of the base-verse and established the syllogism. No. 6 then underlines that single point by saying that the natural world presents cases in which considerable volumes of food or drink are necessary to meet this-worldly requirements. How then can we hope to meet the supernatural requirements of God? That point, made at No. 6, 8, 9, and 10, is essentially secondary to what has gone before. So we have a composition of two elements, Nos. 1-5, the systematic exposition of the base-verse in terms of the single proposition of the intersecting-verse, then No. 6-10, the secondary point that reenforces the main one. No. 11 resolves the enormous tension created by the contrast between the base-verse and the contrastive-verse. I do not need the food, but I get pleasure from the smell. Further discussion of the importance of these results is once more postponed to Chapter Eleven.

The foregoing anaysis has presented us with our first hypothetical rhetorical pattern, one formed out of the comparison and contrast of two verses of Scripture, with the result that a well-formed syllogism emerges. Let me now offer a clear description of the rhetorical pattern I believe underlies **VI:I.**

1. **The Propositional Form: The implicit syllogism is stated through the intervention of an contrastive-verse into the basic proposition established by the base-verse.**

This form – which corresponds to the intersecting-verse/base-verse form of Pesiqta Rabbati – in Pesiqta deRab Kahana ordinarily cites the base-verse, then a contrastive-verse. Sometimes the base-verse is not cited at the outset, but it is always used to mark the conclusion of the *pisqa*. The sense of the latter is read into the former, and a syllogism is worked out, and reaches intelligible expression, through the contrast and comparison of the one and the other. There is no pretense at a systematic exegesis of the diverse meanings imputed to the contrastive-verse, only the comparison and contrast of two verses, the external or intersecting- and the base-verses, respectively. The base-verse, for its part, also is not subjected to systematic exegesis. This represents, therefore, a strikingly abstract and general syllogistic pattern, even though verses are cited to give the statement the formal character of an exegesis. But it is in no way an exegetical pattern. The purpose of this pattern is to impute to the base-verse the sense generated by the intersection of the base-verse and the contrastive-verse. Since the contrastive-verse dictates the sense to be imputed to the base-verse, therefore its fundamental proposition, we should further expect that the contrastive-verse/base-verse form will come first in the unfolding of a *pisqa*, as it does here. For any further exposition of a proposition will require a clear statement of what, in fact, is at stake in a given *pisqa*, and that, as I said, is the contribution of the contrastive-verse/base-verse form.

VI:II

1. A. *A righteous man eats his fill, [but the wicked go hungry]* (Prov. 13:25):
   B. This refers to Eliezer, our father Abraham's servant, as it is said, *Please let me have a little water to drink from your pitcher* (Gen. 24:17) – one sip.
   C. *...but the wicked go hungry:*
   D. This refers to the wicked Esau, who said to our father, Jacob, *Let me swallow some of that red pottage, for I am famished* (Gen. 28:30).

2. A. *[And Esau said to Jacob, Let me swallow some of that red pottage, for I am famished* (Gen. 25:30):]
   B. Said R. Isaac bar Zeira, "That wicked man opened up his mouth like a camel. He said to him, 'I'll open up my mouth, and you just toss in the food.'
   C. "That is in line with what we have learned in the Mishnah: **People may not stuff a camel or force food on it, but may toss food into its mouth [M. Shab. 24:3].**"

3. A. Another interpretation of the verse, *A righteous man eats his fill:*
   B. This refers to Ruth the Moabite, in regard to whom it is written, *She ate, was satisfied, and left food over* (Ruth 2:14).

    C.   Said R. Isaac, "You have two possibilities: either a blessing comes to rest through a righteous man, or a blessing comes to rest through the womb of a righteous woman.

    D.   "On the basis of the verse of Scripture, *She ate, was satisfied, and left food over*, one must conclude that a blessing comes to rest through the womb of a righteous woman."

    E.   *...but the wicked go hungry:*

    F.   This refers to the nations of the world.

4. A.   Said R. Meir, "Dosetai of Kokhba asked me, saying to me, "What is the meaning of the statement, '*...but the wicked go hungry?'*

    B.   "I said to him, 'There was a gentile in our town, who made a banquet for all the elders of the town, and invited me along with them. He set before us everything that the Holy One, blessed be He, had created on the six days of creation, and his table lacked only soft-shelled nuts alone.

    C.   "What did he do? He took the tray from before us, which was worth six talents of silver, and broke it.

    D.   "I said to him, 'On what account did you do this? [Why are you so angry?]'

    E.   "He said to me, 'My lord, you say that we own this world, and you own the world to come. If we don't do the eating now, when are we going to eat [of every good thing that has ever been created]?'

    F.   "I recited in his regard, *...but the wicked go hungry.*"

5. A.   Another interpretation of the verse, *A righteous man eats his fill, [but the wicked go hungry]* (Prov. 13:25):

    B.   This refers to Hezekiah, King of Judah.

    C.   They say concerning Hezekiah, King of Judah, that [a mere] two bunches of vegetables and a *litra* of meat did they set before him every day.

    D.   And the Israelites ridiculed him, saying, "Is this a king? *And they rejoiced over Rezin and Remaliah's son* (Is. 8:6). But Rezin, son of Remaliah, is really worthy of dominion."

    E.   That is in line with this verse of Scripture: *Because this people has refused the waters of Shiloah that run slowly and rejoice with Rezin and Remaliah's son* (Is. 8:6).

    F.   What is the sense of *slowly*?

    G.   Bar Qappara said, "We have made the circuit of the whole of Scripture and have not found a place that bears the name spelled by the letters translated *slowly*.

    H.   "But this refers to Hezekiah, King of Judah, who would purify the Israelites through a purification-bath containing the correct volume of water, forty *seahs*, the number signified by the letters that spell the word for slowly."

    I.   Said the Holy One, blessed be He, "You praise eating? *Behold the Lord brings up the waters of the River, mighty and many, even the king of Assyria and all his glory, and he shall come up over all his channels and go over all his bands and devour you as would a glutton* (Is. 8:7)."

6. A.   *...but the wicked go hungry:* this refers to Mesha.

B.   *Mesha, king of Moab, was a* noked (2 Kgs. 3:4).   What is the sense of *noked*? It is a shepherd.

C.   *"He handed over to the king of Israel a hundred thousand fatted lambs and a hundred thousand wool-bearing rams* (2 Kgs. 3:4)."

D.   What is the meaning of wool-bearing rams?

E.   R. Abba bar Kahana said, "Unshorn."

7.   A.   Another interpretation of the verse, *A righteous man eats his fill, [but the wicked go hungry]* (Prov. 13:25):

B.   This refers to the kings of Israel and the kings of the House of David.

C.   *...but the wicked go hungry* are the kings of the East:

D.   R. Yudan and R. Hunah:

E.   R. Yudan said, "A hundred sheep would be served to each one every day."

F.   R. Hunah said, "A thousand sheep were served to each one every day."

8.   A.   Another interpretation of the verse, *A righteous man eats his fill* (Prov. 13:25):

B.   this refers to the Holy One, blessed be He.

C.   Thus said the Holy One blessed be He, "My children, among all the offerings that you offer before me, I derive pleasure from you only because of the scent: *the food for the food-offering of soothing odor, to me at the appointed time."*

Our contrastive-verse now makes the point that the righteous one gets what he needs, the wicked go hungry, with a series of contrasts at Nos. 1, 2, 3, 5, 6, 7, leading to No. 8: the Holy One gets pleasure from the scent of the offerings. I do not see exactly how the contrastive-verse has enriched the meaning imputed to the base-verse.   What the compositors have done, rather, is to use the contrastive-verse to lead to their, now conventional, conclusion, so 8.C appears tacked on as a routine conclusion, but, as before, turns out to be the critical point of cogency for the whole. Then the main point is that God does not need the food of the offerings; at most he enjoys the scent. The same point is made as before at **VI:I.11**: what God gets out of the offering is not nourishment but merely the pleasure of the scent of the offerings. God does not eat; but he does smell. The exegesis of Prov. 13:25, however, proceeds along its own line, contrasting Eliezer and Esau, Ruth and the nations of the world, Hezekiah and Mesha, Israel's kings and the kings of the East, and then God – with no contrast at all.

VI:III

1.   A.   *You have commanded your precepts to be kept diligently* (Ps. 119:4):

B.   Where did he give this commandment? In the book of Numbers. [Braude and Kapstein, p. 132: *"In Numbers you did again ordain...* Where did God again ordain? In the Book of Numbers."]

C.   What did he command?

D.   *To be kept diligently* (Ps. 119:4): *The Lord spoke to Moses and said, Give this command to the Israelites: See that you present my offerings, the food for the food-offering of soothing odor, to me at the appointed time.*

E. That is the same passage that has already occurred [at Ex. 29:38-42] and now recurs, so why has it been stated a second time?

F. R. Yudan, R. Nehemiah, and rabbis:

G. R. Yudan said, "Since the Israelites thought, 'In the past there was the practice of making journeys, and there was the practice of offering daily whole-offerings. Now that the journeying is over, the daily whole-offerings also are over.'

H. "Said the Holy One, blessed be He, to Moses, 'Go, say to Israel that they should continue the practice of offering daily whole-offerings.'"

I. R. Nehemiah said, "Since the Israelites were treating the daily whole-offering lightly, said the Holy One, blessed be He, to Moses, 'Go, tell Israel not to treat the daily whole-offerings lightly.'"

J. Rabbis said, "[The reason for the repetition is that] one statement serves for instruction, the other for actual practice."

2 . A. R. Aha in the name of R. Hanina: "It was so that the Israelites should not say, 'In the past we offered sacrifices and so were engaged [in studying about] them, but now that we do not offer them any more, we also need not study about them any longer.'

B. "Said the Holy One, blessed be He, to them, 'Since you engage in studying about them, it is as if you have actually carried them out.'"

3 . A. R. Huna made two statements.

B. R. Huna said, "All of the exiles will be gathered together only on account of the study of Mishnah-teachings.

C. "What verse of Scripture makes that point? *Even when they recount [Mishnah-teachings] among the gentiles, then I shall gather them together* (Hos. 8:10)."

D. R. Huna made a second statement.

E. R. Huna said, *"From the rising of the sun even to the setting of the sun my name is great among the nations, and in every place offerings are presented to my name, even pure-offerings* (Malachi 1:11). Now is it the case that a pure-offering is made in Babylonia?

F. "Said the Holy One, blessed be He, 'Since you engage in the study of the matter, it is as if you offered it up.'"

4 . A. Samuel said, *"And if they are ashamed of all that they have done, show them the form of the house and the fashion of it, the goings out and the comings in that pertain to it, and all its forms, and write it in their sight, that they may keep the whole form of it* (Ez. 43:11).

B. "Now is there such a thing as the form of the house at this time?

C. "But said the Holy One, blessed be He, if you are engaged in the study of the matter, it is as if you were building it.'"

5 . A. Said R. Yose, "On what account do they begin instruction of children with the Torah of the Priests [the book of Leviticus]?

B. "Rather let them begin instruction them with the book of Genesis.

C.   "But the Holy One, blessed be He, said, 'Just as the offerings [described in the book of Leviticus] are pure, so children are pure. Let the pure come and engage in the study of matters that are pure.'"

6. A.   R. Abba bar Kahana and R. Hanin, both of them in the name of R. Azariah of Kefar Hitayya: "[The matter may be compared to the case of] a king who had two cooks. The first of the two made a meal for him, and he ate it and liked it. The second made a meal for him, and he ate it and liked it.

    B.   "Now we should not know which of the two he liked more, except that, since he ordered the second, telling him to make a meal like the one he had prepared, we know that it was the second meal that he liked more.

    C.   "So too Noah made an offering and it pleased God: *And the Lord smelled the sweet savor* (Gen. 8:21).

    D.   "And Israel made an offering to him, and it pleased the Holy One, blessed be He.

    E.   "But we do not know which of the two he preferred.

    F   "On the basis of his orders to Israel, saying to them, *See that you present my offerings, the food for the food-offering of soothing odor, to me at the appointed time,* we know that he preferred the offering of Israel [to that of Noah, hence the offering of Israel is preferable to the offering of the nations of the world]."

7. A.   R. Abin made two statements.

    B.   R. Abin said, "The matter may be compared to the case of a king who was reclining at his banquet, and they brought him the first dish, which he ate and found pleasing. They brought him the second, which he ate and found pleasing. He began to wipe the dish.

    C.   *"I will offer you burnt-offerings which are to be wiped off* (Ps. 66:15), like offerings that are to be wiped off I shall offer you, like someone who wipes the plate clean."

    D.   R. Abin made a second statement:

    E.   "The matter may be compared to a king who was making a journey and came to the first stockade and ate and drank there. Then he came to the second stockade and ate and drank there and spent the night there.

    F.   "So it is here. Why does the Scripture repeat concerning the burnt-offering: *This is the Torah of the burnt-offering* (Lev. 3:5), *It is the burnt-offering* Lev. 6:2)? It is to teach that the whole of the burnt-offering is burned up on the fires [yielding no parts to the priests]."

The rhetorical pattern now shifts. We have interest in the contrast between our base-verse and another one that goes over the same matter. That contrast, to be sure, is invited by Ps. 119:4. But that contrastive-verse does not function in such a way as to lead us to our base-verse, but rather, as is clear, to lead us to the complementary verse for our base-verse. That is, therefore, a different pattern from the one we have identified. The exegesis moves from text to context. We have two statements of the same matter, in Numbers and in Exodus, as indicated at No. 1. Why is the passage repeated? No. 1 presents a systematic composition on that question, No. 2 on another. No. 3 serves as an appendix to

No. 2, on the importance of studying the sacrifices. But No. 3 obviously ignores our setting, since it is interested in the Mishnah-study in general, not the study of the laws of the sacrifices in particular. No. 4 goes on with the same point. No. 5 then provides yet another appendix, this one on the study of the book of Leviticus, with its substantial corpus of laws on sacrifice. No. 6 opens a new inquiry, this time into the larger theme of the comparison of offerings. It has no place here, but is attached to No. 7. That item is particular to Leviticus 6:2, but it concerns the same question we have here, namely, the repetition of statements about sacrifices, this timed Lev. 3:5, 6:2. So Nos. 6, 7 are tacked on because of the congruence of the question, not the pertinence of the proposition. In that case we look to No. 1 for guidance, and there we find at issue is the convergence of two verses on the same matter, and that is what stands behind our composition.

The rhetorical pattern is hardly clear. I see a problem – the convergence of verses – but not a pattern that would precipitate expectation of recurrent examples.

VI:IV

1. A. *...the regular daily whole-offering of two yearling rams without blemish:*
   B. [Explaining the selection of the lambs,] the House of Shammai and the House of Hillel [offered opinions as follows:]
   C. The House of Shammai say, "Lambs are chosen because the letters that spell the word for lamb can also be read to mean that 'they cover up the sins of Israel,' as you read in Scripture: *He will turn again and have compassion upon us, he will put our iniquities out of sight* (Micah 7:19)."
   D. And the House of Hillel say, "Lambs are selected because the letters of the word lamb can yield the sound for the word, *clean*, for they clean up the sins of Israel.
   E. "That is in line with this verse of Scripture: *If your sins are like scarlet, they will be washed clean like wool* (Is. 1:18)."
   F. Ben Azzai says, "...*the regular daily whole-offering of two yearling rams without blemish* are specified because they wash away the sins of Israel and turn them into an infant a year old."

2. A. *[...the regular daily whole-offering of] two [yearling rams without blemish. One you shall sacrifice in the morning and the second between dusk and dark]:*
   B. *Two a day* on account of [the sins of] the day.
   C. *Two a day* to serve as intercessor for that day: *They shall be mine, says the Lord of hosts, on the day that I do this, even my own treasure, and I will spare them, as a man spares his son who serves him* (Malachi 3:17).
   D. *Two a day* meaning that they should be slaughtered in correspondence to that day in particular.
   E. *Two a day* meaning that one should know in advance which has been designated to be slaughtered in the morning and which at dusk.

3. A. ...*a daily whole-offering:*

   B. Said R. Yudan in the name of R. Simon, "No one ever spent the night in Jerusalem while still bearing sin. How so? The daily whole-offering of the morning would effect atonement for the sins that had been committed overnight, and the daily whole-offering of dusk would effect atonement for the transgressions that had been committed by day.

   C. "In consequence, no one ever spent the night in Jerusalem while still bearing sin.

   D. "And what verse of Scripture makes that point? *Righteousness will spend the night in it* (Is. 1:21)."

4. A. R. Judah bar Simon in the name of R. Yohanan: "There were three statements that Moses heard from the mouth of the Almighty, on account of which he was astounded and recoiled.

   B. "When he said to him, *And they shall make me a sanctuary [and I shall dwell among them]* (Ex. 25:8), said Moses before the Holy One, blessed be He, 'Lord of the age, lo, the heavens and the heavens above the heavens cannot hold you, and yet you yourself have said, *And they shall make me a sanctuary [and I shall dwell among them] .*'

   C. "Said to him the Holy One, blessed be He, 'Moses, it is not the way you are thinking. But there will be twenty boards' breadth at the north, twenty at the south, eight at the west, and I shall descend and shrink my Presence among you below.'

   D. "That is in line with this verse of Scripture: *And I shall meet you there* (Ex. 25:20).

   E. "When he said to him, *My food which is presented to me for offerings made by fire [you shall observe to offer to me]* (Num. 28:2), said Moses before the Holy One, blessed be He, 'Lord of the age, if I collect all of the wild beasts in the world, will they produce one offering [that would be adequate as a meal for you]?

   F. "'If I collect all the wood in the world, will it prove sufficient for one offering,' as it is said, *Lebanon is not enough for altar fire, nor the beasts thereof sufficient for burnt-offerings* (Is. 40:16).

   G. "Said to him the Holy One, blessed be He, "Moses, it is not the way you are thinking. But: *You shall say to them, This is the offering made by fire [he lambs of the first year without blemish, two day by day]* (Num. 28:3), and not two at a time but one in the morning and one at dusk, as it is said, *One lamb you will prepare in the morning, and the other you will prepare at dusk* (Num. 28:4).'

   H. "And when he said to him, *When you give the contribution to the Lord to make expiation for your lives* (Ex. 30:15), said Moses before the Holy One, blessed be He, 'Lord of the age, who can give redemption-money for his soul?

   I. "'*One brother cannot redeem another* (Ps. 49:8), *for too costly is the redemption of men's souls* (Ps. 49:9).'

   J. "Said the Holy One, blessed be He, to Moses, 'It is not the way you are thinking. But: *This they shall give* – something like this [namely, the half-shekel coin] they shall give."

The rhetorical pattern is clear: the base-verse is analyzed, clause by clause. The point that is made is that the offerings achieve expiation and serve as intercessors. That is the same proposition that the contrastive-verse wishes to establish. The exegesis of the components of the base-verse accounts for the miscellany with which our *pisqa* draws to a close. But the point is cogent. The daily whole-offering effects atonement for sins of the preceding day. No. 1 makes that point in one way, No. 2 in another. Deriving from elsewhere, No. 3, bearing in its wake No. 4, says the same thing yet a third time. So the miscellany is a composite but makes a single point in a strong way.

The form in its purest exemplification would give us the base-verse clause by clause, with each of the clauses subjected to amplification and exposition. The rhetorical pattern then may be described as follows:

2. The Exegetical Form: The implicit syllogism is stated through a systematic exegesis of the components of the base-verse on their own.

That proposition is taken to be the message established by the base-verse. So the base-verse now serves as the structural foundation for the pericope. This form cites the base-verse alone. A syllogism is worked out, and reaches intelligible expression, through the systematic reading of the individual components of the base-verse. The formal traits: [1] citation of a base-verse, [2] a generalization or syllogistic proposition worked out through details of the base-verse. We know this form full well in Pesiqta Rabbati.

We should moreover anticipate that the exegetical form will follow in sequence upon the propositional form, since the propositional form through the interplay of contrastive-verse and base-verse establishes the theorem to be worked out, and only then does the exegetical form undertake the secondary amplification of that same message, now in terms of the base-verse alone. If this scheme is a sound one, then we should always find the sequence [1] propositional and [2] exegetical form. But as we recall, the compelling power of that ordinarily fixed order, which seems to me logical, does not impress the authorship of Pesiqta Rabbati.

Whether or not the authorship of Pesiqta deRab Kahana required for the accomplishment of its purpose more than the two forms identified here will be seen in below, when we survey the entire document's rhetorical character. First we have to test the hypothesis framed here concerning the identification and definition of the recurrent rhetorical patterns of choice. At issue are two matters. First, we wish to know whether the formulations we have defined in fact dictate the mode of discourse at all, and this in regard to both the pattern of formulating ideas and also the sequence by which the two hypothetical forms or patterns occur, first one, then the other. Second, we want to find out whether these are not only necessary but also sufficient, or whether we shall have to define (not invent) yet other formal patterns to account for the recurrent modes by which intelligible propositions are framed.

IV. Literary Structures of Pesiqta deRab Kahana Pisqaot 14 and 22

So far as I can see, the large units of *Pisqa* 6 all fall within the two patterns for formal compositions that we have now identified. Do these suffice or are other formal patterns to be defined? To answer these questions we proceed to two further *pisqaot*, selected at random. In Chapter Eleven, moreover, I conduct a test by examining a *pisqa* that occurs also in another document, that is, Pisqa 27, which is shared with Leviticus Rabbah. This will allow us a negative test, since, if my claim is correct that Pesiqta deRab Kahana is the work of a distinctive authorship, which has made its singular choices as to rhetoric, then a *pisqa* not particular to that authorship should exhibit different traits altogether. In Chapter Eleven I show that that is indeed the case. But I did not wish to repeat the same *pisqa* here.

Since my principal purpose is to test our hypothetical scheme of the rhetorical patterns of the document, the principal point of exposition addresses the question of whether we deal with propositional form, exegetical form, or some other.

XIV:I

1. A. *Therefore hear me you men of understanding, far be it from God that he should do wickedness, and from the almighty that he should do wrong. [For according to the work of a man he will requite him, and according to his ways he will make it befall him]* (Job 34:10-11):

   B. R. Azariah, R. Jonathan bar Haggai in the name of R. Samuel bar R. Isaac, "[With reference to the verse, *Then Jacob became angry and upbraided Laban. Jacob said to Laban, 'What is my offense? What is my sin, that you have hotly pursued me? Although you have felt through all my goods, what have you found of all your household goods? Set it here before my kinsmen and your kinsmen that they may decide between us two'* (Gen. 31:36-37),] Better the captiousness of the fathers than the irenic obsequiousness of the sons.

   C. "[We learn the former from this verse:] *Then Jacob became angry and upbraided Laban. Jacob said to Laban, 'What is my offense? What is my sin, that you have hotly pursued me?'* [Gen. R. 74:10 adds: You might imagine that, in consequence, there would be a brawl. But in fact there was nothing but an effort at reconciliation. Jacob made every effort to reconcile his father-in-law: *Although you have felt through all my goods, what have you found of all your household goods? Set it here before my kinsmen and your kinsmen that they may decide between us two.*]

   D. "[We learn about] the irenic obsequiousness of the sons from the case of David:

   E. *"And David fled from Naioth in Ramah and came and said before Jonathan, What have I done? What is my iniquity? and what is my sin before your father, that he seeks my life?* (1 Sam. 20:1).

F.   "Even while he is trying to reconcile with the other, he mentions bloodshed.

G.   Said R. Simon, "Under ordinary circumstances, when a son-in-law is living with his father in law and then proceeds to leave the household of his father in law, is it possible that the father-in-law will not find in his possession even the most minor item?   But as to this [Jacob], even a shoelace, even a knife, was not found in his possession.

H.   "That is in line with this verse of Scripture: *Although you have felt through all my goods, what have you found of all your household goods? Set it here before my kinsmen and your kinsmen that they may decide between us two.*

I.   "Said the Holy One, blessed be He, 'By your life!   In the very language by which you have rebuked your father-in-law, I shall rebuke your children: *What wrong did your fathers find in me that they went far from me and went after worthlessness and became worthless?*"

The issue before us is whether the contrastive-verse opens up any aspect of the base-verse.   Clearly, the first point of interest is the use of the word "hear," shared by Job 34:10 and Jer. 2:4.   But what is to be heard?   It is that there is good reason for what God does (Job 34:10), and it must follow that God's complaint – there must be good reason for what man does – is justified.   That seems to me a solid basis for classifying the composition as **the Propositional Form.**   The implicit syllogism – there is a common bond of rationality that accounts for God's and man's deeds – is stated through the intervention of an contrastive-verse into the basic proposition established by the base-verse.

XIV:II

1.   A.   *[For the simple are killed by their turning away, and the complacence of fools destroys them;] but he who listens to me will dwell secure, and will be at ease, [without dread of evil]* (Prov. 1:33):

B.   There are four categories of hearing.

C.   There is one who listens and loses, there is one who listens and gains, one who does not listen and loses, one who does not listen and gains.

D.   There is one who listens and loses: this is the first Man: *And to Man he said, Because you listened to the voice of your wife* (Gen. 3:17).

E.   What did he lose? *For you are dust and to dust you will return* (Gen. 3:19).

F.   ...who listens and gains: this is our father, Abraham: *Whatever Sarah says to you, Listen to her voice* (Gen. 21:12).

G.   How did he gain? *For through Isaac will you have descendents* (Gen. 21:12)

H.   ...who does not listen and gains: this refers to Joseph: *And he did not listen to her, to lie with her* (Gen. 39:11).

I.   How did he gain? *And Joseph will place his hand over your eyes* (Gen. 46:4).

J.   ...who does not listen and loses: this refers to Israel: *They did not listen to me and did not pay attention* (Jer. 7:26).

K. What did they lose? *Him to death, to death, and him to the sword, to the sword* (Jer. 15:2).

2. A. Said R. Levi, "The ear is to the body as the kiln to pottery. Just as in the case of a kiln, when it is full of pottery, if you kindle a flame under it, all of the pots feel it,

B. "so: *Incline your ear and go to me and listen and let your souls live* (Is. 55:3)."

The choice of the contrastive-verse is accounted for by the reference at Prov. 1:33 to "he who listens will dwell secure." The proposition is that listening to God will produce a gain to a faithful people, in the model of Abraham. The category, once more, is **the Propositional Form.**

XIV:III

1. A. *If you are willing and listen, you shall eat the good of the land; but if you refuse and rebel, [you shall be devoured by the sword; for the mouth of the Lord has spoken]* (Is. 1:19-20):

B. *[...you shall eat the good of the land:]* You shall eat carobs.

C. Said R. Aha, "When an Israelite has to eat carobs, he will carry out repentance.

D. Said R. Aqiba, "As becoming is poverty for a daughter of Jacob as a red ribbon on the breast of a white horse."

2. A. Said R. Samuel bar Nahman, "Even while a palace is falling, it is still called a palace, and even when a dung heap rises, it is still called a dung heap.

B. "Even while a palace is falling, it is still called a palace: *Hear the word of the Lord, O House of Jacob, and all the families of the House of Israel* (Jer. 2:4-6). When while they are declining, he still calls them *the House of Israel*.

C. "...and even when a dung heap rises, it is still called a dung heap: *Behold the land of the Chaldeans – this is the nation that was nothing* (Is. 23:13) – would that they were still nothing!"

3. A. Said R. Levi, The matter may be compared to the case of a noble woman who had two family members at hand, one a villager, the other a city-dweller. The one who was a villager, [when he had occasion to correct her,] would speak in words of consolation: 'Are you not the daughter of good folk, are you not the daughter of a distinguished family?'

B. "But the one who was a city-dweller, [when he had occasion to correct her,] would speak in words of reprimand: 'Are you not the daughter of the lowest of the poor, are you not the daughter of impoverished folk?'

C. "So too in the case of Jeremiah, since he was a villager, from Anathoth, he would go to Jerusalem and speak to Israel in words of consolation [and pleading,] *Hear the word of the Lord, O House of Jacob, [and all the families of the House of Israel. Thus says the Lord: "What wrong did your fathers find in me that they went far from me and went after worthlessness and became worthless? They did not say, "Where is the*

> *Lord who brought us up from the Land of Egypt, who led us in the wilderness, in a land of deserts and pits, in a land of drought and deep darkness, in a land that none passes through, where no man dwells?"]* (Jer. 2:4-6).

D. "'These are the improper deeds which your fathers did.'

E. "But Isaiah, because he was a city dweller, from Jerusalem, would speak to Israel in terms of reprimand: *Hear the word of the Lord, you rulers of Sodom, attend, you people of gomorrah, to the instruction of our God* (Is. 1:10).

F. "'Do you not come from the mold of the people of Sodom?'"

4. A. Said R. Levi, "Amoz and Amaziah were brothers, and because Isaiah was the son of the king's brother, he could speak to Israel in such terms of reprimand,

B. "in line with this verse: *A rich man answers impudently* (Prov. 18:23)."

The contrastive-verse once more focuses attention on listening, and that is the link to the base-verse. The implicit proposition is announced in that same verse: If you listen, you prosper, and if not, you lose out, so XIV:III.1. No. 2 leads us directly into our base-verse, commenting on the language that is used. No. 3, 4 then amplify that point by comparing Jeremiah and Isaiah. These form a secondary amplification of the theme; the proposition derives from No. 1. The category once more is **the Propositional Form.**

XIV:IV

1. A. Said R. Levi, "The matter may be compared to the case of a noble lady who [as her dowry] brought into the king two myrtles and lost one of them and was distressed on that account.

B. "The king said to her, 'Take good care of this other one as if you were taking care of the two of them.'

C. "So too, when the Israelites stood at Mount Sinai, they said, *Everything that the Lord has spoken we shall do and we shall hear* (Ex. 24:7). They lost the *we shall do* by making the golden calf.

D. "Said the Holy One, blessed be He, be sure to take care of the *we shall listen* as if you were taking care of both of them.'

E. "When they did not listen, the Holy One, blessed be He, said to them, *Hear the word of the Lord, O House of Jacob, [and all the families of the House of Israel. Thus says the Lord: 'What wrong did your fathers find in me that they went far from me and went after worthlessness and became worthless? They did not say, "Where is the Lord who brought us up from the Land of Egypt, who led us in the wilderness, in a land of deserts and pits, in a land of drought and deep darkness, in a land that none passes through, where no man dwells?"]* (Jer. 2:4-6)."

2. A. [A further comment on the verse, *Hear the word of the Lord* (Jer. 2:4-6):] before you have to listen to the words of Jeremiah.

B. Listen to the words of the Torah, before you have to listen to the words of the prophet.

C. Listen to the words of prophecy before you have to listen to words of rebuke.

D. Listen to words of rebuke before you have to listen to words of reprimand.

E. Listen to words of reprimand before you have to listen to *the sound of the horn and the pipe* (Dan. 3:15).

F. Listen in the land before you have to listen abroad.

G. Listen while alive, before you have to listen when dead.

H. Let your ears listen before your bodies have to listen.

I. Let your bodies listen before your bones have to listen: *Dry bones, hear the word of the Lord* (Ez. 37:4).

3. A. R. Aha in the name of R. Joshua b. Levi, "Nearly eight times in Egypt the Israelites [Braude and Kapstein, p. 270:] stood shoulder to shoulder].

B. "What is the scriptural verse that indicates it? *Come, let us take counsel against* him (Ex. 1:10).

C. "On that account [God] took the initiative for them and redeemed them: *And I came down to save* him *from the hand of the Egyptians* (Ex. 3:8)."

4. A. R. Abin, R. Hiyya in the name of R. Yohanan: "It is written, *My mother's sons were displeased with me, they sent me to watch over the vineyards; so I did not watch over my own vineyard* (Song 1:6).

B. "What brought it about that I watched over the vineyards? It is because *I did not watch over my own vineyard.*

C. "What brought it about that in Syria I separate dough-offering from two loaves? It is because in the Land of Israel I did not properly separate dough-offering from one loaf.

D. "I thought that I should receive a reward on account of both of them, but I receive a reward only on account of one of them.

E. "What brought it about that in Syria I observe two days for the festivals? It is because in the Land of Israel I did not properly observe one day for the festivals.

F. "I thought that I should receive a reward on account of both of them, but I receive a reward only on account of one of them."

G. R. Yohanan would recitre the following verse of Scripture in this connection: *And I also gave them ordinances that were not good* (Ez. 20:25).

This is a classic example of **the Exegetical Form.** The implicit syllogism is stated through a systematic exegesis of the components of the base-verse on their own. Formally, we know we are in fresh territory because No. 1 does not begin with the citation of any verse at all, and it clearly does not carry forward any prior discussion. So it stands at the head of a unit composed on a different formal paradigm from the foregoing ones. No. 1 presents a powerful comment on our base-verse. The proposition is that when Israel listens, they prosper, and when they do not listen, they lose out, just as before. But God is bound by reason and so expects man to be, hence, "What wrong...?" No. 2 moves in its own direction, but its contrast between listening to A so that you

will not have to listen to B makes its point with great power as well. The
relevance of Nos. 3, 4 is hardly self-evident. Speculation that these items
illustrate entries on the catalogue of No. 2 is certainly not groundless. And No.
4 is explicit that obeying ("listening") yields rewards, and not obeying,
penalties.

XIV:V

1. A. It is written, *Thus said the Lord, What wrong did your fathers find in me
   that they went far from me and went after worthlessness and became
   worthless?* (Jer. 2:5)

   B. Said R. Isaac, "This refers to one who leaves the scroll of the Torah and
   departs. Concerning him, Scripture says, *What wrong did your fathers
   find in me that they went far from me.*

   C. "Said the Holy One, blessed be He, to the Israelites, 'My children, your
   fathers found no wrong with me, but you have found wrong with me.

   D. "'The first Man found no wrong with me, but you have found wrong with
   me.'

   E. "To what may the first Man be compared?

   F. "To a sick man, to whom the physician came. The physician said to
   him, 'Eat this, don't eat that.'

   G. "When the man violated the instructions of the physician, he brought
   about his own death.

   H. "[As he lay dying,] his relatives came to him and said to him, 'Is it
   possible that the physician is imposing on you the divine attribute of
   justice?'

   I. "He said to them, 'God forbid. I am the one who brought about my own
   death. This is what he instructed me, saying to me, 'Eat this, don't eat
   that,' but when I violated his instructions, I brought about my own death.

   J. "So too all the generations came to the first Man, saying to him, 'Is it
   possible that the Holy One, blessed be He, is imposing the attribute of
   justice on you?'

   L. "He said to them, 'God forbid. I am the one who has brought about my
   own death. Thus did he command me, saying to me, *Of all the trees of
   the garden you mate eat, but of the tree of the knowledge of good and
   evil you may not eat* (Gen. 2:17). When I violated his instructions, I
   brought about my own death, for it is written, *On the day on which you
   eat it, you will surely die* (Gen. 2:17).'

   M. "[God's speech now continues:] 'Pharaoh found no wrong with me, but
   you have found wrong with me.'

   N. "To what may Pharaoh be likened?

   O. "To the case of a king who went overseas and went and deposited all his
   possessions with a member of his household. After some time the king
   returned from overseas and said to the man, 'Return what I deposited with
   you.'

   P. "He said to him, 'I did not such thing with you, and you left me nothing.'

   Q. "What did he do to him? He took him and put him in prison.

   R. "He said to him, 'I am your slave. Whatever you left with me I shall
   make up to you.'

   S. "So, at the outset, said the Holy One, blessed be He, to Moses, *Now go
   and I shall send you to Pharaoh* (Ex. 3:10).

T.   "That wicked man said to him, *Who is the Lord that I should listen to his voice? I do not know the Lord* (Ex. 2:5).

U.   "But when he brought the ten plagues on him, *The Lord is righteous and I and my people are wicked* (Ex. 9:27).

V.   "[God's speech now continues:] 'Moses found no wrong with me, but you have found wrong with me.'

W.   "To what may Moses be compared?

X.   "To a king who handed his son over to a teacher, saying to him, 'Do not call my son a moron."

Y.   What is the meaning of the word moron?

Z.   Said R. Reuben, "In the Greek language they call an idiot a moron."

AA. [Resuming the discourse:] "One time the teacher belittled the boy and called him a moron. Said the king to him, 'With all my authority I instructed you, saying to you, Do not call my son a fool,' and yet you have called my son a fool. It is not the calling of a smart fellow to go along with fools. [You're fired!]'

BB. "Thus it is written, *And the Lord spoke to Moses and to Aaron and commanded them concerning the children of Israel* (Ex. 6:13).

CC. "What did he command them? He said to them,'Do not call my sons morons.' But when they rebelled them at the waters of rebellion, Moses said to them, *Listen, I ask, you morons* (Num. 20:10).

DD. "Said the Holy One, blessed be He, to them, 'With all my authority I instructed you, saying to you, Do not call my sons fools,' and yet you have called my sons fools. It is not the calling of a smart fellow to go along with fools. [You're fired!]'

EE. "What is written is not *You* [singular] *therefore shall not bring,* but *you* [plural] *therefore shall not bring* (Num. 20:12). [For God said,] 'Neither you nor your brother nor your sister will enter the Land of Israel.'

FF. "[God's speech now continues:] Said the Holy One, blessed be He, to Israel, 'Your fathers in the wilderness found no wrong with me, but you have found wrong with me.'

GG. "'I said to them, *One who makes an offering to other gods will be utterly destroyed* (Ex. 22:19), but they did not do so, but rather, *They prostrated themselves to it and worshipped it* (Ex. 32:8).

HH. "After all the wicked things that they did, what is written, *And the Lord regretted the evil that he had considered doing to his people* (Ex. 32:14)."

2.   A.   Said R. Judah bar Simon, "Said the Holy One, blessed be He, to Israel, 'Your fathers in the wilderness found no wrong with me, but you have found wrong with me.

     B.   "'I said to them, *For six days you will gather [the manna] and on the seventh day it is a Sabbath, on which there will be no collecting of manna* (Ex. 16:26).

     C.   "'But they did not listen, but rather: *And it happened that on the seventh day some of the people went out to gather manna and did not find it* (Ex. 16:27).

     D.   "'Had they found it, they would have gathered it [and violated His wishes, so He did not give manna on the seventh day, therefore avoiding the occasion of making them sin].'"

We have yet another perfect example of **the Exegetical Form.** The sustained and powerful story amplifies the statement, *What wrong did your fathers find in me.* The point is that the fathers found no fault with God, which makes the actions of Jeremiah's generation all the more inexplicable. The movement from the first Man to Pharaoh, then Moses and Aaron, leads then to Israel, and the complaint is remarkably apt: it has to do with the forty years in the wilderness, to which Jeremiah makes reference! So the story-teller has dealt with both parts of the complaint. First, the fathers found no fault with their punishment, that is, the forty years they were left to die in the wilderness, and, second, the forty years were a mark of grace. So complaining against God is without rhyme or reason. I cannot imagine a better example of a sustained amplification, through exegesis of intersecting-verses, parables, and syllogisms, of the basic proposition. While implicit, that proposition could not come to more explicit demonstration than it does in this exquisite composition.

XIV:VI

1. A. *...they went far from me and went after worthlessness and became worthless?* (Jer. 2:5)
   B. Said R. Phineas in the name of R. Hoshaiah, "For they would drive out those who did return to God.
   C. "That is in line with this verse of Scripture: *Therefore I chased him away from me* (Neh. 13:28), [Braude and Kapstein, p. 272 add: they chased away and made go far from me those who would have returned to me]."

The **exegetical form** characterizes this exposition of a further clause in the base-verse. The exegesis of a clause of the base-verse imparts to the message a still deeper dimension. The basic proposition seems to me the same as before.

XIV:VI

1. A. *...and went after worthlessness and became worthless?* (Jer. 2:5):
   B. Said R. Isaac, "The matter may be compared to the case of a banker, against whom a debit was issued, and he was afraid, saying, 'Is it possible that the debit is for a hundred gold coins or two hundred gold coins.'
   C. "Said the creditor to him, 'Do not fear, it covers only a kor of bran and barley, and in any event it's already been paid off.'
   D. "So said the Holy One, blessed be He, to Israel, My children, as to the idolatry after which you lust, *it is nothing of substance, but they are nought, a work of delusion* (Jer. 10:15).
   E. "But not like these is *the portion of Jacob, for he is the creator of all things, Israel are the tribes of his inheritance; the Lord of hosts is his name* (Jer. 10:16)."

The conclusion turns the final clause on its head. Since the Israelites went after what was worthless, it is easy for God to forgive them, and God does forgive them. This is fresh, but it does not change the formal pattern: the base-verse is systematically worked out.

Clearly, the entire *pisqa* works out its implicit proposition through first the intervention of a contrastive-verse, which imparts to the base-verse the fundamental proposition to be expounded, and then the systematic exposition of the base-verse, which reads the implicit proposition into – but also in terms of – that verse. We proceed to the second of the three test-*pisqaot*.

XXII:I

1. A. It is written, *Will you not revive us again [that your people may rejoice in you? Show us your steadfast love, O Lord, and grant us your salvation]* (Ps. 85:6-7):
   B. Said R. Aha, "May your people and your city rejoice in you."

2. A. *And Sarah said, God has made joy for me; everyone who hears will rejoice with me* (Gen. 21:6):
   B. R. Yudan, R. Simon, R. Hanin, R. Samuel bar R. Isaac: "If Reuben is happy, what difference does it make to Simeon? So too, if Sarah was remembered, what difference did it make to anyone else? For lo, our mother Sarah says, *everyone who hears will rejoice with me* (Gen. 21:6).
   C. "But this teaches that when our mother, Sarah, was remembered, with her many barren women were remembered, with her all the deaf had their ears opened, with her all the blind had their eyes opened, with her all those who had lost their senses regained their senses. So everyone was saying, 'Would that our mother, Sarah, might be visited a second time, so that we may be visited with her!'
   D. [Explaining the source of common joy,] R. Berekhiah in the name of R. Levi said, "She added to the lights of the heavens. The word *making* ['God has made joy'] is used here and also in the following verse: *And God made the two lights* (Gen. 1:16). Just as the word 'making' used elsewhere has the sense of giving light to the world, so the word 'making' used here has the sense of giving light to the world."
   E. "The word 'making' ['God has made joy'] is used here and also in the following verse: *And he made a release to the provinces* (Est. 2:18).
   F. "Just as the word 'making'; used there indicates that a gift had been given to the entire world, so the word 'making'; used there indicates that a gift had been given to the entire world."

3. A. R. Berekhiah in the name of R. Levi: "You find that when our mother, Sarah, gave birth to Isaac, all the nations of the world said, 'God forbid! It is not Sarah that has given birth to Isaac, but Hagar, handmaiden of Sarah, is the one who gave birth to him.'
   B. "What did the Holy One, blessed be He, do? He dried up the breasts of the nations of the world, and their noble matrons came and kissed the dirt at the feet of Sarah saying to her, 'Do a religious duty and give suck to our children.'
   C. "Our father, Abraham, said to her, 'This is not a time for modesty, but [now, go forth, and] sanctify the name of the Holy One, blessed be He, by sitting [in public] in the market place and there giving suck to children.'
   D. "That is in line with the verse: *Will Sarah give such to children* (Gen. 21:7).

E.   "What is written is not, *to a child*, but, *to children*.
F.   "And is it not an argument *a fortiori*: if in the case of a mortal, to whom rejoicing comes, the person rejoices and gives joy to everyone, when the Holy One, blessed be He, comes to give joy to Jerusalem, all the more so!
G.   *"I will greatly rejoice in the Lord [my soul shall exult in my God; for he has clothed me with the garments of salvation, he has covered me with the robe of righteousness, as a bridegroom decks himself with a garland, and as a bride adorns herself with her jewels. For as the earth brings forth its shoots, and as a garden causes what is sown in it to spring up, so the Lord God will cause righteousness and praise to spring forth before all the nations]* (Isaiah 61:10-11)."

The implicit syllogism maintains that when Jerusalem rejoices, everyone will have reason to join in. That point links the clause, "praise to spring forth before all the nations" to the statement, I will greatly rejoice in the Lord. It is at No. 2 that the proposition emerges, even though the contrastive-verse, Ps. 85:6-7, comes first. I do not regard the pericope as a good example of the contrastive-verse/base-verse form, even though the implicit proposition is very powerfully expounded.

XXII:II

1.   A.   *This is the day which the Lord has made; let us rejoice and be glad in it* (Ps. 118:24):
     B.   Said R. Abin, "But do we not know in what to rejoice, whether in the day or in the Holy One, blessed be He? But Solomon came along and explained, We shall rejoice in you: in you, in your Torah, in you, in your salvation."

2.   A.   Said R. Isaac, "In you (BK) [the Hebrew letters of which bear the numerical value of twenty-two, hence:] – in the twenty-two letters which you have used in writing the Torah for us.
     B.   "The B has the value of two, and the K of twenty."

3.   A.   For we have learned in the Mishnah:
     B.   **If one has married a woman and lived with her for ten years and not produced a child, he is not allowed to remain sterile [but must marry someone else]. If he has divorced her, he is permitted to marry another. The second is permitted to remain wed with her for ten years. If she had a miscarried, one counts from the time of the miscarriage. The man bears the religious duty of engaging in procreation but the woman does not. R. Yohanan b. Beroqah says, "The religious duty pertains to them both, for it is said, *And God blessed them* (Gen. 1:28)" [M. Yeb. 15:6].**

4.   A.   There was a case in Sidon of one who married a woman and remained with her for ten years while she did not give birth.

B. They came to R. Simeon b. Yohai to arrange for the divorce. He said to her, "Any thing which I have in my house take and now go, return to your father's household."

C. Said to them R. Simeon b. Yohai, "Just as when you got married, it was in eating and drinking, so you may not separate from one another without eating and drinking."

D. What did the woman do? She made a splendid meal and gave the husband too much to drink and then gave a sign to her slave-girl and said to her, "Bring him to my father's house."

E. At midnight the man woke up. He said to them, "Where am I?"

F. She said to him, "Did you not say to me, 'Any thing which I have in my house, take and now go, return to your father's household.' And that is how it is: I have nothing more precious than you."

G. When R. Simeon b. Yohai heard this, he said a prayer for them, and they were visited [with a pregnancy].

H. The Holy One, blessed be He, visits barren women, and the righteous have the same power.

I. "And is it not an argument *a fortiori:* if in the case of a mortal, to whom rejoicing comes, the person rejoices and gives joy to everyone, when the Holy One, blessed be He, comes to give joy to Jerusalem, all the more so! And when Israel looks forward to the salvation of the Holy One, blessed be He, all the more so!

J. *"I will greatly rejoice in the Lord [my soul shall exult in my God; for he has clothed me with the garments of salvation, he has covered me with the robe of righteousness, as a bridegroom decks himself with a garland, and as a bride adorns herself with her jewels. For as the earth brings forth its shoots, and as a garden causes what is sown in it to spring up, so the Lord God will cause righteousness and praise to spring forth before all the nations]* (Isaiah 61:10-11)."

The contrastive-verse at No. 1 expresses a rather general interest in the theme of rejoicing. No. 2 carries forward the opening element. The implicit syllogism is that when one rejoices, so does the other, however, and that is the main point of Nos. 1, 2, and is made explicit. No. 3 leads us into No. 4, which is the goal of the framer of the whole, since 4.I states precisely what the syllogism wishes to maintain.

XXII:III

1. A. The matter may be compared to the case of a noble lady, whose husband, sons, and sons-in-law went overseas. They told her, "Your sons are coming."

B. She said to them, "My daughters-in-law will rejoice."

C. "Here come your sons-in-law!"

D. "My daughters will rejoice."

E. When they said to her, "Here comes your husband," she said to them, "Now there is occasion for complete rejoicing."

F. So to, the former prophets say to Jerusalem, *"Your sons come from afar* (Is. 60:4)."

G. And she says to them, *"Let Mount Zion be glad* (Ps. 48:12)."

H. *"Your daughters are carried to you on uplifted arms* (Is. 60:4)."
I. *"Let the daughters of Judah rejoice* (Ps. 48:12)."
J. But when they say to her, *"Behold your king comes to you* (Zech. 9:9)," then she will say to him, "Now there is occasion for complete rejoicing."
K. *I will greatly rejoice in the Lord [my soul shall exult in my God; for he has clothed me with the garments of salvation, he has covered me with the robe of righteousness, as a bridegroom decks himself with a garland, and as a bride adorns herself with her jewels. For as the earth brings forth its shoots, and as a garden causes what is sown in it to spring up, so the Lord God will cause righteousness and praise to spring forth before all the nations]* (Isaiah 61:10-11).

The rhetorical pattern shifts. There is no pretense at commencing with a contrastive-verse. The parable forces our attention on the base-verse, with its statement, *I in particular shall rejoice* . So we deal with an exegetical form, in which the parabolic medium is used for the delivery of the exegetical message. The next component of the *pisqa* follows suit.

XXII:IV

1. A. The matter may be compared to the case of an orphan-girl who was raised in a palace. When the time came for her to be married, they said to her, "Do you have [for a dowry] anything at all?"
    B. She said to them, "I do indeed: I have an inheritance from father and I have an inheritance from my grandfather."
    C. So Israel has the merit left to them by Abraham, and they have the inheritance of our father Jacob:
    D. *He has clothed me with garments of salvation* (Is. 61:10) on account of the merit left by our father, Jacob: *And the hides of the offspring of goats she wrapped on his hands* (Gen. 27:16).
    E. *He has covered me with the robe of righteousness* (Is. 61:10) refers to the merit left by our father, Abraham: *I have known him to the end that he may command his children...to do righteousness* (Gen. 16:19).
    F. *...as a bridegroom decks himself with a garland, and as a bride adorns herself with her jewels* (Isaiah 61:10-11):
    G. You find that when the Israelites stood at Mount Sinai, they bedecked themselves like a bride, opening one and closing another eye [as a sign of modesty (Mandelbaum), and that merit the Israelites bequeathed to their children as well].

The next stage in the unfolding of discourse, that is the exposition of the clauses of our base-verse leads to yet another parable. The parable now underlines the Israelites' merit in expecting God's renewed relationship with them, this time deriving from Abraham, Jacob, and the whole of Israel at Sinai. The formal character of the parable is familiar in our document: first the general statement of matters, then the specific restatement in terms of Israel in particular.

The final component of the *pisqa* – third in line in formal types – presents us with a different rhetorical pattern entirely. In what follows, the base-verse of our *pisqa* plays no important role at all. Rather, the pericope is built upon a syllogism proved through a set of examples, that is, an exercise in list-making science. The syllogism is explicit, not implicit, and it has no important relationship to the *pisqa* at hand. The pericope is tacked on at the end only because our base-verse occurs in it. And yet, it must be added, the syllogism of the list is in general entirely congruent with the implicit syllogism before us.

XXII:V

1. A. In ten passages the Israelites are referred to as a bride, six by Solomon, three by Isaiah, and one by Jeremiah:

   B. Six by Solomon: *Come with me from Lebanon, my bride* (Song 4:8), *you have ravished my heart, my sister, my bride* (Song 4:9), *how beautiful is your love, my sister, my bride* (Song 4:10), *your lips drip honey, my bride* (Song 4:11), *a locked garden is my sister, my bride* (Song 4:12), and *I am come into my garden, my sister my bride* (Song 5:1).

   C. Three by Isaiah: *You shall surely clothe you with them as with an ornament and gird yourself with them as a bride* (Is. 49:18), the present verse, *as a bridegroom decks himself with a garland, and as a bride adorns herself with her jewels* (Isaiah 61:10-11), and *As the bridegroom rejoices over the bride* (Is. 62:5).

   D. One by Jeremiah: *The voice of joy and the voice of gladness, the voice of the bridegroom and the voice of the bride* (Jer. 33:11).

   E. Corresponding to the ten passages in which Israel is spoken of as a bride, there are ten places in Scripture in which the Holy One, blessed be He, clothed himself in a garment appropriate to each occasion:

   F. On the day on which he created the world, the first garment which the Holy One, blessed be He, put on was one of glory and majesty: *You are clothed with glory and majesty* (Ps. 104:1).

   G. The second garment, one of power, which the Holy One, blessed be He, put on was to exact punishment for the generation of the flood: *the Lord reigns, he is clothed with power* (Ps. 93:1).

   H. The third garment, one of strength, which the Holy One, blessed be He, put on was to give the Torah to Israel: *the Lord is clothed, he has girded himself with strength* (Ps. 93:1).

   I. The fourth garment, a white one, which the Holy One, blessed be He, put on was to exact punishment from the kingdom of Babylonia: *his raiment was as white snow* (Dan. 7:9).

   J. The fifth garment, one of vengeance, which the Holy One, blessed be He, put on was to exact vengeance from the kingdom of Media: *He put on garments of vengeance for clothing and was clad with zeal as a cloak* (Is. 59:17). Lo, here we have two [vengeance, zeal].

   K. The seventh garment, one of righteousness and vindication, which the Holy One, blessed be He, put on was to exact vengeance from the kingdom of Greece: *He put on righteousness as a coat of mail and a helmet of deliverance upon his head* (Is. 59:17). Here we have two more [coat of mail, helmet].

> L. The ninth garment, one of red, which the Holy One, blessed be He, put on was to exact vengeance from the kingdom of Edom [playing on the letters that spell both Edom and red]: *Why is your apparel red* (Is. 63:2).
>
> M. The tenth garment, one of glory, which the Holy One, blessed be He, put on was to exact bengeance from Gog and Mag: *This one that is the most glorious of his apparel* (Is. 63:1).
>
> N. Said the community of Israel before the Holy One, blessed be He, "Of all the garments you have none more beautiful than this, as it is said, *the most glorious of his apparel* (Is. 63:1)."

The composition has been worked out in its own terms and is inserted here only because of the appearance of our base-verse as a proof-text.

Now that we have worked out way through two *pisqaot* that are distinctive to Pesiqta deRab Kahana, we turn to one that is shared with Leviticus Rabbah. If my hypothesis concerning the rhetorical singularity of Pesiqta deRab Kahana is sound, then we should find the formal patterns that serve our document out of phase with those that serve the other document.

What is particular to the rhetorical plan of Pesiqta deRab Kahana, specifically, is the the Propositional Form, in which the implicit syllogism is both defined and then stated through the intervention of a contrastive-verse into the basic proposition established by the base-verse. My analysis of the rhetorical plan of Leviticus Rabbah repeatedly produced this observation:

> *The intersecting-verse in that document was subjected to systematic and protracted exegesis in its own terms and not in terms of the proposition to be imputed, also, to the base-verse at the end.*

By contrast, in Pesiqta deRab Kahana the contrastive-verse, which forms the counterpart to what I called the intersecting-verse in Leviticus Rabbah, is not subjected to sustained and systematic exegesis in its own terms. Quite to the contrary, as we have now seen many times, the contrastive-verse serves for the sole purpose of imposing upon the base-verse a very particular proposition, which then is repeated through a sequence of diverse contrastive-verses, on the one side, and also through a sustained reading of the successive components of the base-verse, on the other. We come then to a shared *pisqa* and pay close attention to how the contrastive-/intersecting-verse is treated.

V. The Rhetorical Plan of Pesiqta deRab Kahana

The upshot may be stated very simply. A *pisqa* in Pesiqta deRab Kahana systematically presents a single syllogism, which is expressed through, first the contrast of an external verse with the base-verse – hence, the Propositional Form, in which the implicit syllogism is stated through the intervention of an contrastive-verse into the basic proposition established by the base-verse, and then through the a systematic exegesis of the components of the base-verse on their own, hence through the Exegetical Form. In Leviticus Rabbah's *parashah* which is also Pesiqta deRab Kahana's *pisqa*, we find neither of these forms. Since these forms otherwise characterize our document, it follows that *Pisqa* 27 does not fit well with the rhetorical program of Pesiqta deRab Kahana, so far as the materials distinctive to our document, viewed whole, define that program. What is striking is that both components that prove relevant, *the intersecting-verse/base-verse construction* of Leviticus Rabbah=*the Propositional Form* made up of the contrastive-verse/base-verse construction of Pesiqta deRab Kahana, and also the Exegetical Form shared between both documents, with its clause by clause exegesis of the base-verse, prove remarkably disparate.

Since we have travelled a considerable distance from our point of departure, let me now briefly state the results of this exercise.

A. Pesiqta deRab Kahana's authorship resorted to three rhetorical patterns:

1. **The Propositional Form**: The implicit syllogism is stated through the intervention of an contrastive-verse into the basic proposition established by the base-verse.

2. **The Exegetical Form**: The implicit syllogism is stated through a systematic exegesis of the components of the base-verse on their own.

3. **The Syllogistic List**: The syllogism is explicit, not implicit, and is proven by a list of probative examples.

B. The nature of these rhetorical preferences also suggests that the order in which these types of forms occur will be as just now given, first the syllogism generated by the intersection of the contrastive- and base-verses, then the syllogism repeated through a systematic reading of the base-verse on its own, finally, whatever miscellanies the framers have in hand (or later copyists insert).

C. When we compare our document with another by examining a *pisqa* of Pesiqta deRab Kahana that is not unique to that composition but is shared with Leviticus Rabbah, we see that the definitive rhetorical traits of our document also prove distinctive. The hypothesis is simple:

Rhetorical analysis has yielded the proposition that Pesiqta deRab Kahana consists of twenty-eight syllogisms, each presented in a cogent and systematic way by the twenty-eight pisqaot, respectively. Each pisqa contains an implicit proposition, and that proposition may be stated in a simple way. It emerges from the intersection of an external verse with the base-verse that recurs through the pisqa, and then is restated by the systematic dissection of the components of the base-verse, each of which is shown to say the same thing as all the others.

To test this encompassing hypothesis of the rhetorical plan of Pesiqta deRab Kahana, both as to the types of forms of rhetoric and also the order of the types of forms, we now survey the entire document. Then we shall retest that hypothesis by reviewing the entire document's syllogistic program.

Let us now review the results of our original analysis of the several sample *pisqaot*. The plan here analyzed governs the large-scale formulation of complete units of discourse, which is to say, sustained and cogent discussions that are fully intelligible on their own. Each *pisqa* is made up of from four to twenty such subdivisions, and each subdivision is made up of from one to fifteen of the same. At issue in the formation of a complete document is the principle of cogency of the *pisqa*, viewed whole, and that is what I propose now to analyze through catalogues of the forms and order of the forms characteristic of whole *pisqaot*. Since no one maintains that the authorship of our document has made up each complete unit of thought of which it makes use, there is no need to analyze and classify the completed components of the subdivisions of the *pisqaot*. It was prior to their selection and arrangement in the subdivisions of the *pisqaot* that these ordinarily reached the form in which we have them. Not being part of the work of our authorship at formalization and arrangement, they do not require attention at this time. We address the *pisqa* and its subdivisions, their forms and the order of their forms, viewed from a perspective of the middle distance. Analysis of the formal patterns of the smallest whole and cogent components of discourse would carry us far from the task of *describing the document whole,* as to both its plan and its program, which I take to be the first and most important exercise of classification and definition.[2]

We have identified two rhetorical patterns and have further shown that they always occur in precisely the order indicated here: first No. 1, then No. 2, finally, No. 3.

1. **The Propositional Form: The implicit syllogism is stated through the intervention of a contrastive-verse into the basic proposition established by the base-verse.** This form cites the base-verse, then a contrastive-verse. Sometimes the base-verse is not cited at the outset, but it is always used to mark the conclusion of the *pisqa*. The sense of the latter is read into the former, and a syllogism is worked out, and reaches intelligible expression, through the contrast and comparison of the one and the other. There is no pretense at a systematic exegesis of the diverse meanings imputed to the contrastive-verse, only the comparison and contrast of two verses, the external or intersecting-

---

[2] I of course look forward to more systematic attention to the forms of the smallest whole units of discourse of which the subdivisions of the *pisqaot* are composed, and in my translation and presentation I paid some mind to that matter. But I see the task as quite distinct and the results as answering questions other than those before me here.

and the base-verses, respectively. The base-verse, for its part, also is not subjected to systematic exegesis. This represents, therefore, a strikingly abstract and general syllogistic pattern, even though verses are cited to give the statement the formal character of an exegesis. But it is in no way an exegetical pattern. The purpose of this pattern is to impute to the base-verse the sense generated by the intersection of the base-verse and the contrastive-verse.

2. **The Exegetical Form: The implicit syllogism is stated through a systematic exegesis of the components of the base-verse on their own.** That proposition is taken to be the message established by the base-verse. So the base-verse now serves as the structural foundation for the pericope. This form cites the base-verse alone. A syllogism is worked out, and reaches intelligible expression, through the systematic reading of the individual components of the base-verse. The formal traits: [1] citation of a base-verse, [2] a generalization or syllogistic proposition worked out through analysis and amplification of the details of the base-verse.

3. **The Syllogistic List:** Here the pericope is built upon a syllogism proved through a set of examples, accompanied by, or consisting of, verses of Scripture – that is, an exercise in list-making science. The syllogism is explicit, not implicit, and it has no important relationship to the *pisqa at* hand. The pericope is tacked on at the end only because the base-verse occurs in it. This form characterizes only a very few completed subdivisions of our document and ordinarily defines the principle of cogency for a smaller component of such a subdivision (one of my Arabic-numeral items, as against a Roman-numeral one).

As I have said, the first two forms occur in the same sequence, because the former of the two serves to declare the implicit syllogism, and the latter, to locate that implicit syllogism in the base-verse itself. The third will then be tacked on at the end. Otherwise it would disrupt the exposition of the implicit syllogism. That, at any rate, is how, in theories, the types of forms should lay themselves out.

Since we have analyzed four *pisqaot* and shown the probable formal and redactional plan of the document – first the proposition, generated by the intersection of an intersecting-verse and a base-verse, then the exegetical form, reviewing the implicit syllogism as it comes to the surface in each of the components of the base-verse – our task is now to review the consequent hypothesis as to the definitive forms and their fixed order and to see whether that hypothesis pertains to the entirety of our document. This review of the paramount formal traits of the principal divisions of Pesiqta deRab Kahana will therefore show both the characteristics of the formal patterns of all twenty-eight *pisqaot* and also to show the order in which the formal patterns persistently occur. We differentiate the five *pisqaot* shared with Leviticus Rabbah: Pesiqta deRab Kahana *pisqaot* 8 [Lev. R. 27], 9 [Lev. R. 28], 23 [Lev. R. 29], 26 [Lev. R. 20], and 27 [Lev. R. 30]. The following catalogues are so divided as to accomplish that purpose.

But I treat as identical, for the present purpose, the intersecting-verse/base-verse form of Leviticus Rabbah and the contrastive-verse/base-verse form of Pesiqta deRab Kahana. I further ignore the, to me striking, points of difference between the exegetical form and its inner cogency, revealed in our document, and the more discursive and discrete character of the equivalent form in Leviticus Rabbah. While the differences prove important in answering the question of the original location of the shared compositions, they do not contribute to a deeper understanding of the formal program of our document, since they require us to make distinctions on an other than totally-formal criterion and may lead us into subjective judgments, which are needless. The important issue is whether or not the formal program, grossly defined, of Pesiqta deRab Kahana holds for all twenty-eight *pisqaot* ultimately selected by its authorship.

1. The Types of Forms of Pesiqta deRab Kahana

A. *The Twenty-Three Pisqaot Unique to Pesiqta deRab Kahana* [all but 8, 9, 23, 26, 27]

1. **The Propositional Form** [syllogism generated through the impact of the contrastive-verse upon the reading of the base-verse and its theme]

   I:I-IV; II:I-VI; III:I-V; IV:I-V; V:I-X; VI:I-III; VII:I-IV (VII:X); X:I-VIII; XI:I-VI; XII:I-X; XII:I-VI; XIV:I-III;XV:I-V; XVI:I-VIII;XVII:I-V; XVIII:I; XIX:I-III [+IV?]; XX:I-IV; XXI:I-IV; XXII:I-III; XXIV:I-X; XXV:I; XXVIII:I-III.

   119

2. **The Exegetical Form** [exegesis of the elements of the base-verse in line with the implicit syllogism]

   I:V-VIII; II:VII-VIII; III:VII-XVI; IV:VII-X; V:XI-XVI, XVIII-XIX; VI:IV; VII:V-IX (+X), XI-XII; X:IX-X; XI:XII-XIII, XXV; XII:XI-XIII, XV-XXI [+XXII-XXV, new base-verse, but same form!]; XIII:XII-XV; XIV:IV; XV:VI-IX [+X]; XVI:IX-XI; XVII:VI-VIII; XVIII:II-VI; XIX:V-VI; XX:II-V, VIII; XXI:VI; XXII: none; XXIV:XI-XIII, XVI-XIX; XXV:II-IV; XXVIII:IV-X.

   102

3. **The Syllogistic List [the base-verse contributes a fact to prove a proposition independent of all verses on the list] [listed only where it is dominant in a subdivision of a *pisqa*]:**

   II:VIII; IV:VI.1; XII:XIV; XXII:V

   4

4. **Miscellanies [the form and presence of which I cannot explain]:**

   II:IX, VI:XVII; XI:XIV-XXIV [!]; XX:VI; XXI:V; XXIV:XIV-XV

   17

   242

   The percentage breakdown is as follows:
   Propositional form: 119 = 49%
   Exegetical form: 102 = 42%
   Syllogistic list: 4 = 1.6%
   Miscellanies [unclassifiable]: 17 = 7%

B. *The Five Pisqaot Shared with Leviticus Rabbah* [8, 9, 23, 26, 27]

1. **The Propositional Form [=intersecting-verse fully expounded in diverse terms, then brought to bear upon the base-verse to yield a syllogism]:**

   VIII:I-II; IX:I-VII; XXIII:I-VIII; XXVI:I-VI; XXVII:I-V

   28

2. **The Exegetical Form [=the elements of the base-verse are interpreted in diverse ways and yield disparate syllogisms]:**

   VIII:III-IV; IX:VIII-XII; XXIII:IX-XII; XXVI:VII-XII; XXVII:VI-X

   22

3. **The Syllogistic List [dominant in a subdivision of a *pisqa*]: None.**

4. **Miscellanies [the form and presence of which I cannot explain]: None.**

   The percentage breakdown is as follows:
   Propositional form: 28/50 = 56%
   Exegetical form: 22/50 = 44%
   Syllogistic list: –

Miscellanies [unclassifiable]" –

We may state the result very briefly.

1. As to types of forms in all but all but 8, 9, 23, 26., 27: the vast majority of all sizable subdivisions of the *pisqaot* are rhetorically either propositional or exegetical in form. There are some syllogistic lists of consequence, and a small number of miscallenies. The number of these is exaggerated by one huge composition, the one on Eleazar and Simeon b. Yohai, which is parachuted down, for reasons I cannot imagine.

2. As to types of forms in 8, 9, 23, 26., 27: the entire formal repertoire is comprised of the intersecting-verse/base-verse form, or the base-verse form as defined by Leviticus Rabbah, respectively. The smaller components of the principal subdivisions of the *pisqaot* of course exhibit diverse formal preferences.

2. The Order of the Types of Forms of Pesiqta deRab Kahana

The result for all *pisqaot,* both those unique to our document and those shared with Leviticus Rabbah, may be stated very simply. The propositional form *always* occurs first, and in the *pisqaot* shared with Leviticus Rabbah, the intersecting-verse/base-verse form always occurs first. There is a tendency for the intersecting-verse/base-verse items of Leviticus Rabbah in Pesiqta deRab Kahana to prove somewhat more prolix than those corresponding items in propositional form in our document, for reasons I have already explained. The exegetical form (Leviticus Rabbah: base-verse form) always follows the propositional form. No *pisqa* begins with the exegetical form and moves to the propositional form.

This review of the paramount formal traits of the principal divisions – *pisqaot* – of Pesiqta deRab Kahana has shown both the characteristics of the formal patterns of all twenty-eight *pisqaot* and also the order in which the formal patterns persistently occur: Pesiqta deRab Kahana is made up of propositional and exegetical compositions, presented in that order, in which an implicit syllogism is created out of the interplay of an intersecting-verse and a base-verse and then shown to inhere, also, in each of the components of the base-verse. Having characterized the two Pesiqtas, I may now compare them and place them into the still larger comparative context defined by the canon in which they occur. In Chapter Nine we compare the two Pesiqtas, and in Chapters Ten and Eleven we juxtapose to them Sifré to Numbers and Leviticus Rabbah, respectively. In that way we shall see how the several authorships of the four documents at hand have defined their work as to topic (Chapter Ten) and rhetoric and logic (Chapter Eleven).

Part Three

COMPARATIVE MIDRASH:
RHETORIC, LOGIC, TOPIC AND TEXTUALITY

Chapter Nine

Comparative Midrash [1]:
The Rhetorical and Logical Aspect

The Plan and Program of Pesiqta deRab Kahana and Pesiqta Rabbati

I. The Rhetorical Plans of the Two Pesiqtas

We may rapidly summarize the results in hand. Our interest in the plan of the two documents has been to effect a taxonomy of the units of discourse, then to ask whether in the case of each the types of units of discourse follow an order based on a redactor's preference for placing one type of form of a unit of discourse at the start of his larger composite, another type of form at the end. What we have seen is that Pesiqta Rabbati's authorship refers to four forms, the legal colloquy, the intersecting-verse/base-verse construction, the propositional list, and the exegetical form. These follow no fixed and conventional order. Pesiqta deRab Kahana's authorship makes extensive use of the second and the third types of form, much less common use of the fourth and none at all of the legal colloquy, which, in our context, is particular to the later of the two Pesiqtas. Except for the fixed practice of placing the legal colloquy at the outset of discourse, Pesiqta Rabbati's authorship as represented in our sample places no premium upon ordering its materials in one way rather than in some other. Pesiqta deRab Kahana's authorship, by contrast, follows the fixed preference of setting the intersecting-verse/base-verse form first, followed by the exegetical form. That authorship makes use of the intersecting-verse/base-verse form – which I therefore called the propositional form – to expose its syllogism, then the exegetical form to repeat or prove it.

II. Cogent Discourse in the Two Pesiqtas

Here too the available findings permit a rapid reprise. The pisqa in Pesiqta deRab Kahana commonly makes a single point, fully spelled out and carefully instantiated, which will be generated to begin with by that intersection. The *pisqa* in the later Pesiqta by contrast works through a fixed theme, but more often than not delivers miscellaneous messages concerning that theme, and, in any event, through its several components does not ordinarily argue in favor of (or against) a single important proposition. It follows that the *pisqa* of Pesiqta deRab Kahana proves remarkably cogent in its mode of discourse, repeatedly saying one thing through diverse media. The *pisqa* in the later Pesiqta tends to be propositionally diffuse, from the legal colloquy forward simply saying different things about one topic. The *pisqa* of Pesiqta Rabbati may fall into the category of a collage, with its cogent message made up of discrete yet mutually illuminating parts, or it may appear to be little more than a scrapbook on a single topic. But it rarely, if ever, exhibits that syllogistic integrity that won my admiration for the authorship of Pesiqta deRab Kahana. The *pisqa* of the earlier Pesiqta, by contrast, ordinarily presents a proposition worked out in a well-composed syllogism. In the final chapter we shall see the full weight and meaning of these facts.

III. The Topical Programs of the Two Pesiqtas

What of the matter of topic? Pesiqta deRab Kahana's blatant trait – which characterizes Pesiqta Rabbati as well – requires us to carry forward our comparative inquiry by paying close attention to the formation of the two documents' topical programs. For the single definitive trait of Pesiqta deRab Kahana as well as of Pesiqta Rabbati derives from the fundamental principle of organization and topical selection common to the two compilations. Each *pisqa* treats a single theme or topic, whether or not it brings to that topic a generative problematic to guide research into it. That principle guiding the programatic definition of the two Pesiqtas emerges from a simple account of the things the documents' framers have chosen as the programs. We begin with Pesiqta deRab Kahana, providing an account of that authorship's twenty-eight *pisqaot*, or propositions. Once we have reviewed them, we shall turn to an analysis of those internal data rapidly to define the document's programs. And, at the end, we revert to Pesiqta Rabbati with the same inquiry.

Were we to rely on the repertoire of the base-verses of either of the two Pesiqtas, we should not gain access to the program of the document. For the base-verse proves secondary and rests upon a prior fact, and it is that fact that accounts for the documents' programs, respectively. The reason is simple. While, in Leviticus Rabbah, by reference to the meeting of the contents of a given chapter of Leviticus with the proposition important to the framer of a *parashah* of Leviticus Rabbah, we can always explain the reason for the selection of the base-verse, in the two Pesiqtas internal evidence never suffices to account for that same matter. The identification of the *occasion* associated with that base-verse is the one fact not presented by the document itself. We have to appeal to the prior and external fact that a given passage serves as the synagogue lection on a given occasion to explain why a verse of said passage has been selected. Ample justification for introducing that fact at the very outset will rapidly present itself. Two items of the language that follows requires explanation. By Torah-lection I mean that a passage is read in the synagogue on a specified Sabbath. By prophetic lection I mean the same thing. The Sabbath that is so distinguished is then indicated as to its occasion.

Let me now survey the entire lectionary and therefore topical repertoire of Pesiqta deRab Kahana:

Pisqa   Base-verse
Topic or Occasion

1. *On the day Moses completed* (Num. 7:1)
   Torah-lection for the Sabbath of Hanukkah

2. *When you take the census* (Ex. 30:12)
   Torah-lection for the Sabbath of Sheqalim – first of the four Sabbaths prior to the advent of Nisan, in which Passover falls

3. *Remember Amalek* (Deut. 25:17-19)
   Torah-lection for the Sabbath of Zakhor – second of the four Sabbaths prior to the advent of Nisan, in which Passover falls

4. *Red heifer* (Num. 19:1ff.)
   Torah-lection for the Sabbath of Parah – third of of the four Sabbaths prior to the advent of Nisan, in which Passover falls

5. *This month* (Ex. 12:1-2)
   Torah-lection for the Sabbath of Hahodesh – fourth of the four Sabbaths prior to the advent of Nisan, in which Passover falls

6. *My offerings* (Num. 28:1-4)
   Torah-lection for the New Moon which falls on a weekday[1]

7. *It came to pass at midnight* (Ex. 12:29-32)
   Torah-lection for the first day of Passover

8. *The first sheaf* (Lev. 23:11)
   Torah-lection for the second day of Passover on which the first sheaves of barley were harvested and waved as an offering[2]

9. *When a bull or sheep or goat is born* (Lev. 22:26)
   Lection for Passover

---

[1] Abraham Goldberg, Pesiqta deRab Kahana, *Qiryat Sefer* 1967: 43:69, cited by Braude and Kapstein, p. 124, n. 1.

[2] Braude and Kapstein, p. 154, n. 1.

10. *You shall set aside a tithe* (Deut. 14:22)
     Torah-lection for Sabbath during Passover in the Land of Israel or for
     the eighth day of Passover outside of the Land of Israel[3]

11. *When Pharaoh let the people go* (Ex. 13:17-18)
     Torah-lection for the Seventh Day of Passover

12. *In the third month* (Ex. 19:1ff.)
     Torah-lection for Pentecost

13. *The words of Jeremiah* (Jer. 1:1-3)
     Prophetic lection for the first of three Sabbaths prior to the Ninth of
     Ab

14. *Hear* (Jer. 2:4-6)
     Prophetic lection for the second of three Sabbaths prior to the Ninth
     of Ab

15. *How lonely sits the city* (Lam. 1:1-2)
     Prophetic lection for the third of three Sabbaths prior to the Ninth of
     Ab

16. *Comfort* (Is. 40:1-2)
     Prophetic lection for the first of three Sabbaths following the Ninth
     of Ab

17. *But Zion said* (Is. 49:14-16)
     Prophetic lection for the second of three Sabbaths following the
     Ninth of Ab

18. *O afflicted one, storm tossed* (Is. 54:11-14)
     Prophetic lection for the third of three Sabbaths following the Ninth
     of Ab

19. *I even I am he who comforts you* (Is. 51:12-15)
     Prophetic lection for the fourth of three Sabbaths following the Ninth
     of Ab

20. *Sing aloud, O barren woman* (Is. 54:1ff.)
     Prophetic lection for the fifth of three Sabbaths following the Ninth
     of Ab

21. *Arise, shine* (Is. 60:1-3)
     Prophetic lection for the sixth of three Sabbaths following the Ninth
     of Ab

---

[3] *Ibid.*, p. 186, n. 1.

22. *I will greatly rejoice in the Lord* (Is. 61:10-11)
    Prophetic lection for the seventh of three Sabbaths following the Ninth of Ab

23. *The New Year*
    No base-verse indicated. The theme is God's justice and judgment.

24. *Return O Israel to the Lord your God* (Hos. 14:1-3)
    Prophetic lection for the Sabbath of Repentance between New Year and Day of Atonement

25. *Selihot*
    No base-verse indicated. The theme is God's forgiveness.[4]

26. *After the death of the two sons of Aaron* (Lev. 16:1ff.)
    Torah-lection for the Day of Atonement

27. *And you shall take on the first day* (Lev. 23:39-43)
    Torah-lection for the first day of the Festival of Tabernacles

28. *On the eighth day* (Num. 29:35-39)
    Torah-lection for the Eighth Day of Solemn Assembly

Before proceeding to interpret these data, we note three items that do not fit the pattern. This catalogue draws our attention to three eccentric *pisqaot*, distinguished by their failure to build discourse upon what I have called (for the sake of the initial analysis) the base-verse. These are No. 4, which may fairly claim that its topic, the red cow, occurs in exact verbal formulation in the verses at hand; No. 23, the New Year, and No. 25, *Selihot*. The last-named may or may not take an integral place in the structure of the whole. But the middle item, the New Year, on the very surface is essential to a structure that clearly wishes to follow the line of holy days onward through the the Sabbath of Repentance, the Day of Atonement, the Festival of Tabernacles, and the Eighth Day of Solemn Assembly. So while we may claim that No. 4 is no exception to the formal pattern and No. 25 may sustain more than a single explanation for its inclusion, therefore may come late in the formation of the document,[5] No. 23 forms an essential component of the pattern, therefore the statement, of the generative authorship and cannot be dismissed as a possible accretion later on. The rhetorically idiosyncratic traits of the *pisqa* therefore draw our attention and will provide a fundamental fact in the inductive examination of intrinsic evidence, which we now undertake.

---

[4] Goldberg, *op. cit.*, cited by Braude and Kapstein, links the *pisqa* at hand to the Fast of Gedaliah, on the third of Tishre, or to one of the days between New Year's Day and the Day of Atonement when the Torah is read.

[5] Here is where manuscript evidence extending over many centuries would prove helpful.

Let us now address to the internal evidence at hand a simple set of inductive questions, answered solely out of the facts before us. Is Pesiqta deRab Kahana (and, as we shall see, Pesiqta Rabbati, which follows the model of the earlier Pesiqta) organized around a text? The criterion is whether or not the authorship persistently refers to data outside of its own framework, appeals to an authority beyond itself. The answer on the surface is affirmative, in that the authorship quotes Scripture as its authority. We know that fact (as if we had to say so) because of the persistent pattern of invoking the language of citation, *as it is said, as it is written,* and the like, a powerful form of internal evidence. It is affirmative in a more profound sense, a sense deriving from the structure of language, syntax and sentence-formation. The authorship builds its cogent discourses (*pisqaot*) not on the foundation of syllogisms stated in the language and terms of the authorship alone, but rather, on the basis of syllogisms that refer to or borrow from another, prior writing. That writing we may call *the text* selected by the authorship of Pesiqta deRab Kahana for the foundation for a commentary. But I make that statement only with the proviso that the word *text* may refer to a variety of structures, not solely to Scripture. Each *pisqa* repeatedly refers to data clearly outside the frame of discourse of the authorship and treated as authoritative within that same frame. Pesiqta Rabbati, we know full well, follows suit.

The evidence read inductively indicates that we deal with a category of composition that persistently refers to some other, as my survey of the base-verses shows, hence Pesiqta deRab Kahana and Pesiqta Rabbati in a strictly formal sense constitutes a commentary to a text. But what is that *text*? And is it a text made up of a prior document, or words?

[1] It is not the Pentateuch, because a sizable sample of the *pisqaot* repeatedly refers to a prophetic passage.

[2] It is not the Prophetic writings for the same reason: many *pisqaot* appeal to the Pentateuch.

But [3] a further fact intervenes. Three of the twenty-eight *pisqaot* do not appeal to a recurrent verse of Scripture at all, and at least one of these forms an essential component of the unfolding structure.

So the fundamental structure, the "text" of our texts, also is not *Scripture.*

The internal evidence leads us to the limits of our text: the knowledge that we deal with a commentary but to a text other than Scripture.[6] Will the evidence of the documents tell us what that text is, if it is not Scripture? There is an implicit message intrinsic to the intrinsic evidence, inductively construed. We find it in the two *pisqaot* not built around a base-verse. These invoke the matter of the New Year and Selihot, and the former beyond all doubt points us toward the holy day. That piece of internal evidence – of a negative order – raises the probability that our document's text is constituted by the liturgical calendar. This is in two ways. First, the framers of the *pisqa* on the New Year have found in that topic the cogent proposition they wish to argue. Second, if we survey the cognate literature, we uncover the simple fact that other base-verses used as foundations for selections in our document are associated with other liturgical events, specifically assigned as synagogue lections for those special events.

That evidence is internal in that the contents of Pesiqta deRab Kahana have directed our attention to the set of base-verses under study rather than some other. And – we realize without the slightest doubt, the same fact pertains to Pesiqta Rabbati. But, it is clear, to make sense of those choices, rather than others, we have to refer to information provided by documents other than our own. The fact that the liturgical calendar dictates both lections and themes is not intrinsic to our documents. It is information we bring to the documents. But we go in search of that information because of the intrinsic traits of Pesiqta deRab Kahana and Pesiqta Rabbati, constructed inductively. What we find in the search directed by those intrinsic traits is simple. The liturgical calendar dictates lections and themes that also govern the organization of our document in particula.

Let me then underline the inductive character of this inquiry into internal data and their implications. If we had only Pesiqta deRab Kahana or Pesiqta Rabbati in hand, we should know the principles that do not apply and therefore we should readily explain why this, not that: exposition of neither pentateuchal nor prophetic passages, verse by verse; presentation of syllogisms arranged in accord with neither pentateucahl nor prophetic passages. The *pisqaot* that link up with holy days, moreover, tell us to why the document does the things it does do: *why this*, not only *why not that*. And – I have already made clear – the answers to these questions pertain without variation to the later Pesiqta as well.

---

[6] The amazing independence of our authorship is shown in this simple fact, since, in the extant canonical writings of the dual Torah, this is the first document to make use as its generative text neither of the written Torah, Scripture, nor of the first document of the oral Torah, the Mishnah. That is another example of the extraordinarily original minds of the framers of all of the documents of the initial phase of the dual Torah, that is, down to the end of late antiquity, for there is not a single document that imitates the structure of any other, and the most original of them all are the authorships that pretend to provide commentaries to received texts. But among these, the authorship that moved from a written text to one made up of the times and seasons of time must still stand out. I return to this matter in the comparative remarks of part viii.

Comparison with other documents furthermore highlights the importance of the internal traits on which I have laid emphasis. For other authorships prior to the one at hand,[7] moreover, did precisely what ours did *not* do, and none built a cogent unit of sustained and protracted discourse on the basis chosen by our authorship, that is, the character and theme of a holy day. The framers of Sifra and Sifré to Numbers and Sifré to Deuteronomy follow the verses of Scripture and attach to them whatever messages they wish to deliver. The authorship of Genesis Rabbah follows suit, though less narrowly guided by verses and more clearly interested in their broader themes. The framers of Leviticus Rabbah attached rather broad, discursive and syllogistic statements to verses of the book of Leviticus, but these verses do not follow in close sequence, one, then the next, as in Sifra and its friends. That program of exposition of verses of Scripture read in or out of sequence, of organization of discourse in line with biblical books, parallel to the Tosefta's and Talmuds' authorships exposition of passages of the Mishnah, read in close sequence or otherwise, we see, defines what our authorship has not done. It hardly requires explicit statement that Pesiqta Rabbati's authorship has followed the model of that of Pesiqta deRab Kahana – followed it but also, while imitating it, made its own revisions. But the revisions occur not in the program of the document, but, as we have already seen, in the plan.

Since the authorship at hand has rejected the principle of topical exposition joined to, and commonly precipitated by, verses of Scripture or sentences of the Mishnah, we find ourselves required to look, for the principle of topical and programmatic selection, elsewhere. We know what they did not do. But why this: what explains what they did do? We can answer that question too, solely by reference to our *pisqa* on the New Year. As I said, the presence of a *pisqa* devoted to the theme of a holy day directs our attention to holy days, particular Sabbaths and festivals, and since, in the other *pisqaot*, we do deal with selected verses of Scripture – pentateuchal or prophetic – we have reason to turn, at last, for a piece of evidence extrinsic to our document but entirely justified by the intrinsic evidence we have sifted. And when we ask about indicative traits of the selected base-verses that we do find, it is, as a matter of fact, that all of the selected base-verses, pentateuchal or prophetic, are in other documents of the same time and place identified with synagogual lections for specified holy days, special Sabbaths or festivals. The framers of Pesiqta Rabbati, as we shall see in a moment, did precisely the same thing, imitating the work of the framers of the first Pesiqta.

Drawing on statements occurring in the ancient writings, we identify the choices at hand with synagogue lections. We do not know how many synagogues, in what countries, followed the program before us. We know only

---

[7] In the final part of this chapter I outline the sequence of documents and identify the appropriate place of ours.

that there is a clear correlation between literary references[8] to what is read in the synagogue on holy days such as special Sabbaths and the topical program of our document. We therefore discover[9] entirely on the basis of an inductive examination of internal evidence what constitutes the generative text, the organizing principle, and the definitive structure of Pesiqta deRab Kahana. That text comprises a liturgical occasion of the synagogue, which is identical to a holy day, has told our authorship what topic it wishes to take up – and therefore also what verses of Scripture (if any) prove suitable to that topic and its exposition. What the authorship of Pesiqta Rabbati has done is to follow suit, with selections associated with the same liturgical occasions as those covered by the former of the two Pesiqtas, as well as with other ones.

Let me now briefly spell out the facts of the matter as these apply to Pesiqta deRab Kahana and to Pesiqta Rabbati. The documents' topical program breaks down in a clear pattern. We discern that pattern in a negative way, by noting that the base-verse is not consistently drawn from either of the two divisions of Scripture that provide lections for the synagogue, the Torah and the Prophetic writings; moreover at least two *pisqaot* do not appeal for a structural-redactional foundation to a base-verse at all. It follows that the overall foundation of the document does not follow the outlines of Scripture. The authorship of Pesiqta deRab Kahana and of Pesiqta Rabbati has selected a different and unprecedented definition of the generative structure. Internal evidence now fails, for nothing in the document itself tells us why this, not that: why these passages. My right hand column presents extrinsic evidence which, in the aggregate, requires only the conclusion unanimously reached by those who have studied our document (speaking now only of Pesiqta deRab Kahana, although Pesiqta Rabbati follows suit). The principle of selection and redaction derives not from passages of the Pentateuchal books, or from passages of Prophetic books but from passages selected because – it is unanimously held – synagogue liturgy identified them with particular Sabbath and festival occasions, as follows:

Adar-Nisan-Sivan

    Passover-Pentecost: *Pisqaot* 2-12 [possible exception: *Pisqa* 6]

Tammuz-Ab-Elul

    The Ninth of Ab: *Pisqaot* 13-22

Tishri

    Tishre 1-22: *Pisqaot* 23-28

---

[8] Not to mention contemporary practice, which can play no role in our analysis.

[9] The fact at hand is a given in all scholarship. What is important to me is how we reach it. As is clear, my interest is to find out the extent to which on the foundation of intrinsic evidence inductively construed we are able to define the document. That accounts for the protracted argument I have composed to reach a conclusion that, in its facticity, will surprise no one who has studied our document.

Only *Pisqa* 1 (possibly also *Pisqa* 6) falls out of synchronic relationship with a long sequence of special occasions in the synagogual lections.

To conclude, Pesiqta deRab Kahana follows the synagogual lections from early spring through fall, in the Western calendar, from late February or early March through late September or early October, approximately half of the solar year, 27 weeks, and somewhat more than half of the lunar year. On the very surface, the basic building block is the theme of a given lectionary Sabbath – that is, a Sabbath distinguished by a particular lection – and not the theme dictated by a given passage of Scripture, let alone the exposition of the language or proposition of such a scriptural verse. The topical program of the document may be defined very simply: expositions of themes dictated by special Sabbaths or festivals and their lections. What of the program of Pesiqta Rabbati?

Pesiqta Rabbati goes over precisely the same liturgical calendar in pretty much the same way. That is why I classify Pesiqta Rabbati as a secondary and imitative compilation, one which goes over the ground of the earlier Pesiqta at each point in its topical program, item by item. The imitative character of the later Pesiqta is proven by a simple fact. The authorship of Pesiqta Rabbati has simply recapitulated the liturgical program of the authorship of the earlier Pesiqta, providing (mainly) new compositions for the same occasions, whole or in part, that are covered by Pesiqta deRab Kahana. We should therefore not find surprising that in matters of rhetorical or formal composition (but not logical cogency) the authorship of Pesiqta Rabbati has learned so much as they have from their predecessors. Braude has provided us with a definitive statement of the topical program of Pesiqta Rabbati, which I now epitomize.[10]

Pisqa 1 treats the lesson for a New Moon which coincides with the Sabbath. Nos. 2-9 deal with the lessons read during the eight days of the Hanukkah festival. Nos. 10-16 deal with the five special Sabbaths, the first four coming prior to Passover (Sheqalim, Zakhor, Parah, HaHodesh), and finally, for the first Sabbath in Nisan. Nos. 17-19 [48, 49] take up the lessons for Passover. Nos. 20-25 cover lessons for Pentecost. Nos. 26-29/30 deal with three Sabbaths of mourning prior to the Ninth of Ab. Nos. 29/30A-37 deal with the lessons for the seven Sabbaths of Consolation after the Ninth of Ab. Nos. 38-47 take up the New Year, the Sabbath of Repentance, and the Day of Atonement. Nos. 51, 52 deal with Tabernacles and the Eighth Day of Solemn Assembly. No. 53 is not associated, in Braude's account, with a particular holy day or special occasion of the synagogue lections. In no way do the order or selections of passages of Pesiqta Rabbati differ from those of Pesiqta deRab Kahana. What we have is more of the same. I cannot point to many topics in Pesiqta Rabbati that will have surprised the authorship of Pesiqta deRab Kahana. To that fact I add a simple but prevailing impression. I also cannot point to many fresh themes and

---

[10] Wm. G. Braude, *Pesikta Rabbati* (New Haven and London, 1968: Yale University Pess), pp. 12-16.

concrete propositions concerning those themes specific by the authorship of Pesiqta Rabbati. The imitation is not solely rhetorical and topical, but, all the more so, propositional and even syllogistic.

The upshot of form-analysis and topical inquiry into the processes of laying out formalized material may be stated very simply. The formal repertoire of the two documents is pretty much the same. A single taxonomic system of formal classification serves them both, though requiring augmentation to be sure. The policy of arranging formalized materials in a consistent order is cogent, if not completely consistent, between the two. So, viewed as the outcome of a literary and formal policy dictating rules of how things would be formulated and ordered, the plan of Pesiqta deRab Kahana and that of Pesiqta Rabbati are if not one, then at least closely related. Formally and redactionally they fall into the same literary genus. In terms of topic they are pretty much identical. Where they differ, it is at the level of the logical cogency of the *pisqaot* of which each is made up.

IV. Comparative Midrash: The Two Pesiqtas Side by Side

Now that we know how the two Pesiqtas compare with one another, we ask we wonder whether we should have been able to pick out a *pisqa* primary to Pesiqta Rabbati and differentiate it from a *pisqa* shared by Pesiqta Rabbati with Pesiqta deRab Kahana. In terms of rhetoric (in the sense of large scale forms of syntactic conglomeration and aggregation) and logical cogency, we find no difficulty in identifying a *pisqa* shared by Pesiqta deRab Kahana and Pesiqta Rabbati apart from one particular to Pesiqta Rabbati. We may furthermore demonstrate that such a shared *pisqa* is primary to the earlier of the two Pesiqtas, in that it exhibits traits characteristic of other *pisqaot* in the earlier Pesiqta and absent in those dintinctive to the later Pesiqta. In terms of topic, we should not know why a given *pisqa* makes its appearance in one document rather than the other. The authorship of the later Pesiqta has made a number of choices. It has imitated the earlier Pesiqta by compiling materials that illuminate the liturgical lections. It has adopted the earlier Pesiqta's formal repertoire, while augmenting it with a form found elsewhere, the legal colloquy. Most strikingly – and I think the mark of the imitator and not the original intellect – the authorship of the later Pesiqta has not replicated the remarkably cogent mode of logical discourse of the earlier one. While the earlier authorship managed in many and diverse ways to say one thing concerning a given topic, the later compositors collected a great many diverse and essentially unrelated thoughts about one topic. The difference is between an authorship that has a very specific message which it wishes to register with great force and urgency, and one that plans only to collect and arrange important materials: the creative thinker as against the heir and successor, the formative mind as against the traditional one. The one substantial rhetorical innovation yielded by the comparison of the two Pesiqtas is the legal colloquy (which, of course, was in circulation prior to the composition of

Pesiqta Rabbati in any event). And the use of that rhetorical advance over the earlier Pesiqta proves random and not pointed, in that, in our sample, the point made in the legal colloquy ordinarily did not intersect with the points made in the exegetical passages. The *may our master teach us*-pericopae simply introduced a topic but imposed upon the treatment of that topic no paramount agenda. Once more, formal innovation makes a profoundly conservative and traditional frame of mind. Seen in context, Pesiqta deRab Kahana stands forth as an act of supreme imagination and fresh insight. For its authorship selected a new text – one drawn from liturgical circumstances and occasions, rather than words alone – and through that new text managed to speak as cogently and as coherently as did the authorship of Leviticus Rabbah, the closest associates of Pesiqta deRab Kahana's authorities. By contrast, compared to the authorship of the earlier Pesiqta, the later one has botched the opportunity of a fresh rhetorical conceit by treating it not as the occasion for linking law to theology, let alone by showing how, in deed, people act out the convictions of the Torah, but by merely making one miscellaneous point on a theme in a new way, another in an old: imitation in the mark of creative and imaginative rhetorical innovation. I find it difficult to suppress my admiration for the authorship of Pesiqta deRab Kahana, and, guided by its preferences in aesthetics, to express disappointment with the work of the later authorship.

Yet that is not the main issue before us, for there is a more important one, and, alas, it is one that the comparative study of midrash cannot settle. The real question is how we may distinguish not only the rhetorical and logical program of one Pesiqta from the other, but the topical one. By topic, in this case, I mean not merely subject-matter but proposition, on the one side, and premise, on the other. The reason, as is now, alas, all too clear, is that, in their different ways, the two authorships do not seem to me to say different things. The topical program of each document is distinguishable from that of the other, even while the formal and logical plans of the two documents permit us with facility to differentiate the one from the other. But the broad outlines of the message – the implicit propositions conveyed by the two documents – seem to me to encompass both documents quite comfortably. Not only so, but if we were to present to the framers of other compositions of ancient and even medieval Judaism as a set of propositions the specific points that the two authorships lay out, they would not find much surprising or incomprehensible. Quite to the contrary, the rhetorical forms and the logical underpinning of discourse may diverge from one document to the next, but the propositional program at this stage in its analysis looks to be uniform, if not from beginning to end in the unfolding of the canon, then at least from a certain point forward within that canon.

We may therefore wonder whether, from the remarkable statement adumbrated in the Talmud of the Land of Israel and fully exposed by the Talmud of Babylonia, many people within the canonical literature and its conventions found reason to differ from their predecessors. There seems to have been a broad and firm consensus, in which, as a matter of fact, our two Pesiqtas appear to find a perfectly comfortable place. I say "appears," because the analysis of that consensus, its principal components and their logical relationships, has yet to commence. In the context of the system of Judaism presented by the canon of late antiquity, summarized so handsomely by the Talmuds of the Land of Israel and of Babylonia, for example, none of the messages of the two Pesiqtas presents surprises. Indeed, all of them will strike the contemporary historian of Judaism as commonplaces, as indeed in later times they became. I can easily list propositions to which a variety of authorships – and even named authors in medieval and modern times – will readily accept. I cannot now account, within the framework of the actual literary documents, for the remarkable cogency of all of the documents, their consensus upon those shared propositions. What makes of the discrete documents a single canon is that iron consensus – for which I cannot account, and which, at this point, I cannot even describe. The way forward will require the description, analysis, and interpretation no longer of the discrete documents but of the canon as a whole. Where to begin and what to do I cannot now say.

From the Talmud of the Land of Israel, Genesis Rabbah, and Leviticus Rabbah, through Pesiqta deRab Kahana, onward to The Fathers According to Rabbi Nathan and the Talmud of Babylonia, a rather cogent set of statements may be discovered to define the premises of one writing after another. Specifically, the powerful interest in history and salvation, the recurring emphasis on the correspondence between Israel's holy way of life and the salvation of Israel in history, the reading of Scripture as an account of the present and future – these will have struck the compositors of diverse documents as not fresh but ineluctable and necessary. Compositors of writings of the two centuries from the Mishnah to the first of the two Talmuds, by contrast, will have found these premises surprising. For the authors of the Mishnah, with its close companion in the Tosefta, the compilers of tractate Abot, the author-compilers of Sifra to Leviticus – none of these circles of authorship took so keen an interest in the issue of salvation or in the correspondence between the biblical narrative and contemporary history. I have already offered an account of where, when, how, and why so complete a shift from one consensus to another took place. But I have yet to describe the fresh consensus not document by document, but as a cogent statement characteristic, as premise, of them all. The comparative study of midrash in the canon of the dual Torah has brought us to the question that clearly transcends the comparative method.

Chapter Ten

Comparative Midrash [2]: The Topical Aspect

Pesiqta Rabbati Compared to Pesiqta deRab Kahana and Sifre to Numbers on Num. 7:1

It Came to Pass When Moses Finished Setting up the Tabernacle

I. Comparing Midrash-Compilations

Now that we have undertaken a comparison of two closely related Midrash-compilations, we move to an altogether different sort of comparison. We take up not entire compilations, with attention to the comparison and contrast of their rhetorical, logical, and topical traits, but the exact opposite: diverse treatments of a single verse of Scripture, as these occur in a range of documents, whether or not related to one another. The systematic comparison of whole documents began, so far as I know, in the first volume of this study. That is not to suggest received scholarship has not affected the differentiation of documents. The opposite is true. Everyone knows that the so-called *yelammmedenu*-midrash is different from – say – a Tannaitic midrash-compilation. The so-called *Petihta*-form is subject to a sizable literature as well. But recognition of these distinctions among documents has made no perceptible difference to those who, at their whim, compare midrash-exegesis to midrash-exegesis, maintaining that the distinctions among documents make no difference and are essentially formal. The recognition that documents do follow one plan or program rather than some other has, to my knowledge, made slight impact upon inquiries before mine, as proved by the wide-spread position that the generative arena of discourse is the verse and its inherent traits, rather than the document and its authorship's intention and program. I call attention for one current and choice example to the position of James Kugel, who states,

> ...midrash is an exegesis of biblical verses, not of books. The basic unit of the Bible for the midrashist is the verse: this is what he seeks to expound, and it might be said that there simply is no boundary encountered beyond that of the verse until one comes to the borders of the canon itself.

As framed, Kugel's claim that there is no boundary between midrash-exegesis of a single verse and the entirety of the canon of Judaism seems uninformed. The documents we have reviewed demonstrate that the opposite is the fact. In yet another approach to the question, which draws us close to our theological agenda, Kugel maintains the twin positions that Midrash is the way every Jew reads Scripture and that what is at stake in Midrash is merely an academic exercise of clever erudition:

> Forever after, one cannot think of the verse or hear it recited without also recalling the solution to its problematic irritant–indeed, remembering it in the study-house or synagogue, one would certainly pass it along to others present, and together appreciate its cleverness and erudition. And so midrashic explications of individual verses no doubt circulated on their own, independent of any larger exegetical context. Perhaps in this sense it would not be inappropriate to compare their manner of circulating to that of jokes in modern society; indeed, *they were a kind of joking, a learned and sophisticated play about the biblical text,* and like jokes they were passed on, modified, and improved as they went, until a great many of them eventually entered into the common inheritance of every Jew, passed on in learning with the text of the Bible itself [italics supplied].

Kugel's claim that Midrash is a kind of erudite joke seems to me offensive to the very nature of Judaism. Kugel does not demonstrate that we deal with "a kind of joking," and nothing in the account I have provided of the character of Midrash, rabbinic or otherwise, supports Kugel's bizarre judgment. What I find stunning in the Midrash-compilations as well as in their contents, the midrash-exegeses is the urgency and immediacy of matters, that and not the cleverness and erudition demonstrated therein. Israel, the people of God, turned to with deep and everyday anxieties about salvation to Genesis, Leviticus, and the sacred calendar. I find nothing amusing, merely clever, or particularly erudite in what the sages found there. In my description, analysis, and interpretation of the midrash-compilations, I find messages of self-evident truth in response to questions of life and death. In this judgment of Kugel's I find no merit, since it treats as trivial and merely personal what is in fact a monumental theological statement of the founders of Judaism. Sages of the dual Torah were not mere scholars, clever erudites. They were holy men and they gave God's judgment, through the Torah, oral and written, to suffering Israel – then and now. As a believing and practicing Jew, that is my deepest conviction, on account of which I cannot find redeeming arguments in behalf of Kugel's amazing judgment. It calls into question the appreciation of Midrash among contemporary literary critics who claim to constitute continuators of Midrash for the reading of literature at large.

The comparison of discrete treatments of individual verses of themes of Scripture, by contrast, is routine. I also find that that other sort of comparison produces results that we cannot reasonably interpret. For it treats in a comparative way out of all documentary context, therefore in a manner defying all logic, matters that may not sustain comparison at all. That is the proposition of this second of my three exercises in comparative midrash. Let me explain.

When we compare what one authorship thinks important about a verse of Scripture with what another authorship, of the same religious world and of approximately the same period, chooses to emphasize in that same verse of Scripture, we must conclude that in hand are the results of the exegesis of different people talking about the same verse, but with an interest in utterly different things, to different people.[1] When we compare what one document and its authorship have to say about a given verse with what another composition and its writers find interesting and probative in that same verse, we must ask ourselves whether we have compared comparable entities. For prior to comparison comes the process of establishing *grounds* for comparison, and that demands that we show likeness. Once groups are demonstrated to be alike, then the points of difference become significant. If entities are utterly unlike, then what difference to us does the differences between them make?

In taxonomic terms, what is required is that we show that two specimens belong in a single genus, and then, only then, do we undertake the work of speciation. These simple rules of logic govern, also, in the field of comparing exegeses of verses of a common Scripture, as I shall now show in a striking case. When we examine what three authorships within the canon of Judaism say about one verse, we call into question the meaning of comparison of midrash as exegesis. For, as we shall now note, nothing in the reading of the verse produced by one group intersects with anything in the reading of the same verse yielded by the other: different people addressing a single thing but talking about different things to different people.

Comparative midrash[2] – that is, comparing exegeses of the same theme or verse of Scripture among the same circles of exegetes – can rest on solid foundations in logic.[3] The basis of comparison and contrast is established by points in common. Once we know that two things are like one another, then – and only then – do the points of difference become consequential. Two documents in the same canon surely bear broad affinities, having been selected by the consensus of the sages or the faithful as authoritative. They rely upon the opinion or judgment of sages of the same circle. They have been preserved and handed on by the same institutions of the faith. They presumably present

---

[1] Compare my "The Jewish Christian Argument in the First Century. Different People Talking about Different Things to Different People," *Crosscurrents*, 1985, 35:148-158.

[2] See my *Comparative Midrash: The Plan and Program of Genesis Rabbah and Leviticus Rabbah* (Atlanta, 1986: Scholars Press for Brown Judaic Studies).

[3] Compare Jonathan Z. Smith, "What a difference a difference makes," in *Take Judaism for Example* (Chicago, 1983: University of Chicago Press), ed. Jacob Neusner, and his equivalent paper in *"To See Ourselves as Others See Us:" Jews, Christians, "Others" in Late Antiquity* (Atlanta, 1985: Scholars Press: Studies in the Humanities), ed. by Jacob Neusner and Ernest S. Frerichs.

basically cogent convictions upon the meaning of Scripture. Accordingly, a variety of indicators justifies the judgment that the documents form a solid fit, bearing much in common. Then, it must follow, the work of comparison yields to the exercise of contrast. Being alike, the documents, in their treatment of precisely the same verse of Scripture, produce differences, and these differences make a difference. They tell us how one authorship wishes to read Scripture in one way, another in a different way. In the case at hand, however, the differences prove so profound and far-reaching that they call into question the very act of comparison.

In the present modest exercise, we compare the treatment of precisely the same verse by three groups of exegetes within the same religious world, that of the sages of the Judaism of the dual Torah. In their shared reading of Numbers 7:1, *"On the day when Moses had finished setting up the tabernacle...,"* we see strikingly different topical approaches to what is important in the verse at hand. The first group of exegetes we shall consider is that of Pesiqta Rabbati. The second is that behind Sifré to Numbers, the third, the exegetes represented in the compilation of Pesiqta deRab Kahana. One group of exegetes, that behind Sifré to Numbers, a close reading of selected passages of the book of Numbers concluded at an indeterminate point but possibly about ca. 400, asks one set of questions, the other, the authorship of Pesiqta deRab Kahana, possibly within the fifth century, finds a quite different point of interest in the same verse. The program of the former proves remarkably thin and routine, that of the latter, rich and imaginative and – unsurprisingly – highly argumentative and cogent. Indeed, as we shall see, despite several points shared between Sifré to Numbers and Pesiqta deRab Kahana, it is difficult to relate the message of the one to that of the other. The relationship of the exegetes in Pesiqta Rabbati to those in the other two documents proves equally random, though we shall not find surprising the affinity between the two Pesiqtas.

And that is a surprising result, since we have every reason to expect people who read Scripture within pretty much the same framework to seek in the same passage similar points of stress. But that is not what we shall now see. Indeed, were the theory to take shape that, within the circles of the sages of the dual Torah were profound differences on what required stress and what did not, the following comparison of exegeses – comparative midrash – would provide solid evidence. Quite how to sort out the amazing differences in approach, emphasis, and inquiry, that separate the authorship of Sifré to Numbers from that of Pesiqta Rabbati and of Pesiqta deRav Kahana remains a puzzle. I mean at this point only to raise the question of how both documents belong within the same canon and to ask what we can mean by canon when the authoritative writings relate so slightly as do these. The translations in both cases are my own.

Since my main interest is in the topical or propositional repertoire, I introduce each pericope with the topic I believe treated there, and a statement of the proposition at hand (where there is one). These I then compile for comparative purposes at the end.

II. Pesiqta Rabbati on Num. 7:1: A Reprise

Since the pertinent text – Pesiqta Rabbati *Pisqa 5* – has already been presented, it suffices simply to outline the way in which the editorship of Pesiqta Rabbati has chosen to treat the verse at hand. The following outline covers the main points.

1. The Torah's oral part is unique to Israel.

V:I.

1. A. May our master instruct us [concerning the correct procedure when one person reads aloud from the Hebrew of Scripture and another translates the passage into Aramaic for the community]?

   F. For the Torah has been given only in writing, as it is said, *I shall write on the tablets...* (Ex. 34:1).

   G. Said R. Judah the Levite, son of R. Shalom, "Said the Holy One, blessed be He, to Moses, 'How can you want the Mishnah to be written down? How are we to tell the difference between Israel and the nations of the world?

   H. "'It is written, *If I should write for him the larger part of my Torah, then he would have been seen as a stranger* (Hos. 8:12) – if so, they would have been held to be strangers [being unable to point to their knowledge of the Mishnah as evidence of their unique calling].'"

2. The tabernacle was credited to Moses, because he was prepared to give his life for it.

V:II.

1. A. Another interpretation of the verse, *If I should write for him the larger part of my Torah, then he would have been seen as a stranger* (Hos. 8:12):

   B. This is one of the three matters for which Moses was prepared to give his life, on account of which the Holy One, blessed be He, gave them in his name [in line with the sense of the verse, I should write *for him*, meaning, *in his name*].

   C. The three are the rule of justice, the Torah, and the building of the tabernacle in the wilderness.

3. Moses is comparable to God.

V:III.

1. A. Thus did R. Tanhuma b. R. Abba commence discourse: *Who has ascended heaven and come down?* [(Prov. 30:4):

   B. "This verse of Scripture is to be expounded with reference to God and Moses."

4. The children of Noah offered peace-offerings [and not whole-offerings].

V:IV.

2. A. R. Eliezer b. Pedat said, "The children of Noah offered peace-offerings [and not whole-offerings]."

   F. And R. Yose bar Hanina said, "They prepared them in the status of whole-offerings [burning up the entire animal and not keeping any portions for the sacrificer (who does the rite) and *sacrifier* (who benefits from the rite)]."

5. The tabernacle is comparable to the marriage canopy, in which God and Israel were united.

V:V.

1. A. *I have come into my garden, my sister, my bride* (Song 5:1):

   D. So too, when the tabernacle had been erected, the Israelites said, *"Let my beloved come into his garden* (Song 4:16)."

   E. The Holy One, blessed be He, sent to them and said, "Why are you concerned? *I have come into my garden, my sister, my bride* (Song 5:1)."

6. Bezalel made the tabernacle, but Moses got credit for it.

V:VI.

1. A. Another interpretation of the verse *And it came to pass on the day that Moses completed setting up the Tabernacle* (Num. 7:1-2):

   B. This is relevant to the following verse: *For there is a man whose labor is with wisdom and with knowledge and with skill* (Qoh. 2:21).

7. The tabernacle marked the reunion of God with the world, from which, in the sin of Adam, God had departed.

V:VII.

2. A. Said R. Joshua b. Levi, "The Holy One, blessed be He, stipulated with Israel while they were yet in Egypt that he would bring them out of Egypt only on condition that they make a tabernacle, in which he would bring his Presence to rest among them, as it is said, *And they shall know that I am the Lord their God, who has brought them forth out of the land of Egypt, that I may dwell among them* (Ex. 29:46).

5. A. "Therefore it is written here, *And it came to pass* (Num. 7:1), indicating that just as the Presence of God at the beginning of the creation of the world had been below, but had arisen upward by stages and then returned now to dwell below,

   B. "so now it would remain: *And it came to pass on the day that Moses completed setting up the Tabernacle.*"

8. Diverse meanings of the words, *And it came to pass.*

V: VIII-IX.

1. C. "Any passage in which the words, *And it came to pass* appear is a passage that relates unparalleled misfortune."

   D. Along these same lines said R. Simeon b. R. Abba in the name of R. Yohanan: "It may serve this meaning but also the opposite. Specifically, in any passage in which it says, *It came to pass in the days of*, speaks of distress without parallel.

9. The juxtaposition of the account of the tabernacle with the account of the priestly blessing is to show that the tabernacle brought a blessing.

V:X-XI.

1. B. What passage occurs just prior to this one? It is the blessing of the priests: *May the Lord bless you and keep you* (Num. 6:24).

   H. "But the evil eye had effect, so the tablets were broken, as it is said, *Moses broke them beneath the mountain* (Ex. 32:19).

   I. "When they came some time later and made the tabernacle, the Holy One, blessed be He, first handed over to them the priestly blessings, so that the evil eye should not have effect on them.

   J. "Therefore Scripture first wrote, *May the Lord bless you and keep you,* and then, *And it came to pass on the day that Moses completed setting up the Tabernacle.*"

III. Sifre to Numbers on Num. 7:1: Text and Program

The text we follow is *Sifré debe Rab. Sifré al sefer Bammidbar veSifré Zuta,* ed. by Haim Shaul Horovitz (Leipzig, 1917) [series title: *Schriften, herausgegeben von der Gesellschaft zur Foerderung der Wissenschaft des Judentums. Corpus Tannaiticum. Sectio Tertia: Continens Veterum Doctorum ad Pentateuchum Interpretationes Halachicas. Pars Tertia. Siphre d'Be Rab. Fasciculus primus: Siphre ad Numeros adjecto Siphre Zutta. Cum variis lectionibus et adnotationibus. Edidit* H. S. Horovitz]. There is no complete English translation of the document prior to mine.[4] We do not know when the document came to closure. All the named authorities belong to the age of the Mishnah, but we have no way of identifying the authentic from the pseudepigraphic attributions. In the model of the Tosefta,[5] a demonstrably Amoraic document, a large portion of which cites verbatim and comments on the

---

[4] Jacob Neusner and William Scott Green, *Sifré to Numbers. An American Translation* (Atlanta, 1986: Scholars Press for Brown Judaic Studies). I-III. I and II are now in print, covering *Pisqaot* 1-116, and III is expected in 1987.

[5] I have demonstrated that fact in my systematic comparison of the Tosefta to the Mishnah in my *History of the Mishnaic Law* (Leiden, 1974-1986: E. J. Brill) I-XLIII, and in my *Tosefta. Translated from the Hebrew* (N.Y., 1977-1986: Ktav) I-VI.

Mishnah and so is post-mishnaic, we may hardly assign the present composition to a period before the end of the fourth century.[6]

Sifré to Numbers makes use of two basic approaches, first, the syllogistic composition, which rests on the premise that Scripture supplies hard facts, which, properly classified, generate syllogisms. By collecting and classifying facts of Scripture, therefore, we may produce firm laws of history, society, and Israel's everyday life. The second maintains the fallibility of reason unguided by scriptural exegesis. Scripture alone supplies reliable basis for speculation. Laws cannot be generated by reason or logic unguided by Scripture. That is the recurrent polemic of the document – a point of interest completely outside of the imagination of the framers of Pesiqta deRav Kahana, as we shall see. They are arguing about different things, presumably with different people. For nothing in the program of questions addressed to the book of Numbers draws one group into alignment with the other: they simply do not raise the same questions or produce congruent answers. Whether or not the exegetical-eisegetical results can be harmonized is a separate question.[7]

1. Moses set up the tabernacle every day and took it down every night, until he finally left it standing.

XLIV:I.

1. A. *"On the day when Moses had finished setting up the tabernacle [and had anointed and consecrated it with all its furnishings and had anointed and consecrated the altar with all its utensils, the leaders of Israel, heads of their fathers' houses, the leaders of the tribes, who were over those who were numbered, offered and brought their offerings before the Lord, six covered wagons and twelve oxen, a wagon for every two of the leaders, and for each one an ox, they offered them before the tabernacle. Then the Lord said to Moses, 'Accept these from them, that they may be used in doing the service of the tent of meeting, and give them to the Levites, to each man according to his service.' So Moses took the wagons and the oxen and gave them to the Levites]"* (Num. 7:1-6):
   B. Scripture indicates that for each of the seven days of consecrating the tabernacle, Moses would set up the tabernacle, and every morning he would anoint it and dismantle it. But on that day he set it up and anointed it, but he did not dismantle it.

---

[6] Moses David Heer, *Midrash, Encyclopaedia Judaica* (Jerusalem, 1971: Keter Publishing Co), s.v. I have found no more authoritative statement on the present view of the dates of all midrash-compilations than Heer's. It is a question that will have in time to be reopened.

[7] That question demands attention in a far wider context than the present one. For it is the issue that when addressed will require us to ask what we mean by the canon, and, more important, what meanings inhere within the canon as a whole but not in some one of its parts: what holds the whole together that is not stated in any one component? I have no doubt whatever that that Judaism behind the systems of the several components of the canon of the dual Torah awaits systematic and rigorous definition; but at this writing I am uncertain about how to proceed.

C. R. Yose b. R. Judah: "Also on the eighth day he set it up and dismantled it, for it is said, *'And in the first month in the second year on the first day of the month the tabernacle was erected'* (Ex. 30:17). On the basis of that verse we learn that on the twenty-third day of Adar, Aaron and his sons, the tabernacle and the utensils were anointed."

This is the focus of interest: the meaning of the word KLH, that is, completed, and the same point will be made in Pesiqta deRab Kahana. But here it is the main point, since the exegete proposes to say what he thinks the simplest sense of the verse is. The second compilation of exegeses, by contrast, treats the matter in a much richer and more imaginative way.

2. Events on the first day of the month.

XLV:I.

2 . A. On the first day of the month the tabernacle was set up, on the second the red cow was burned [for the purification rite required at Num. 19], on the third day water was sprinkled from it in lieu of the second act of sprinkling, the Levites were shaved.

B. On that same day the Presence of God rested in the tabernacle, as it is said, *'Then the cloud covered the tent of meeting, and the glory of the Lord filled the tabernacle, and Moses was not able to enter the tent of meeting, because the cloud abode upon it'* (Ex. 40:34).

C. On that same day the heads offered their offerings, as it is said, *"He who offered his offering the first day..."* (Num. 7:12). Scripture uses the word "first" only in a setting when "first" introduces all of the days of the year.

D. On that day fire came down from heaven and consumed the offerings, as it is said, *"And fire came forth from before the Lord and consumed the burnt-offering and the fat upon the altar"* (Lev. 9:24).

E. On that day the sons of Aaron offered strange fire, as it is said, *"Now Nadab and Abihu, the sons of Aaron, each took his censer and put fire in it...and offered unholy fire before the Lord, such as he had not commanded them"* (Lev. 10:1).

F. *"And they died before the Lord..."* (Lev. 10:2): they died before the Lord, but they fell outside [of the tabernacle, not imparting corpse uncleanness to it].

G. How so? They were on their way out.

H. R. Yose says, "An angel sustained them, as they died, until they got out, and they fell in the courtyard, as it is said, *'And Moses called Mishael and Elzaphan, the sons of Uzziel the uncle of Aaron, and said to them, 'Draw near, carry your brethren from before the sanctuary out of the camp'"* (Lev. 10:4). What is stated is not, 'From before the Lord,' but, 'from before the sanctuary.'"

I. R. Ishmael says, "The context indicates the true state of affairs, as it is said, *'And they died before the Lord,'* meaning, they died inside and fell inside. How did they get out? People dragged them with iron ropes."

The exegete draws together a broad range of events which, in his view, all took place on one day. I do not detect an implicit syllogism that the exegete wishes to advance. To me we have nothing more than a scrapbook – a list of things with something in common, but a list that *proves* nothing more than that something in common. If we have an exercise in *Listenwissenschaft,* I cannot show it. But what is interesting – as the contrast will show in a moment – is what he does not say. He does not introduce the issue of Israel and Israel's redemption. Rather, he focuses upon the here and the now of what happened long ago. There is a perceived difference between the one-time historical event of the setting up of the tabernacle and the eternal and paradigmatic character of the event: its continuing meaning, not its one-time character at all. The tabernacle is not the paradigm of the natural world, and Israel's salvation simply plays no role in the passage. Now to the matter at hand.

The expansion and amplification of the base-verse runs through No. 1. From that point, No. 2, we deal with the other events of that same day, surveying the several distinct narratives which deal with the same thing, Ex. 40, Lev. 9-10, and so on. This produces the effect of unifying the diverse scriptural accounts into one tale, an important and powerful exegetical result. One of the persistent contributions of our exegetes is to collect and harmonize a diversity of verses taken to refer to the same day, event, or rule.

3. As the utensils were anointed, they were not sanctified. That was a separate operation. The manner of anointing. The effect.

XLIV:II.

1. A. *"...and had anointed and consecrated it with all its furnishings and had anointed and consecrated the altar with all its utensils":*
   B. Might I infer that as each utensil was anointed, it was sanctified?
   C. Scripture says, *"...and had anointed and consecrated it with all its furnishings and had anointed and consecrated the altar with all its utensils,"* meaning that not one of them was sanctified until all of them had been anointed. [The process proceeded by stages.]

Once more we shall see that the second exegesis – that of Pesiqta deRab Kahana – makes precisely this point. But it is swallowed up in a much different range of interest. The later document covers nearly everything in the earlier one, but makes nothing of what is constitutive of the received writing.

XLIV:II.

2. A. *"...and had anointed and consecrated it with all its furnishings and had anointed and consecrated the altar with all its utensils":*
   B. The anointing was done both inside and outside [of the utensil].

C. R. Josiah says, "Utensils meant to hold liquids were anointed inside and outside, but utensils meant to hold dry stuffs were anointed on the inside but not anointed on the outside."

D. R. Jonathan says, "Utensils meant to hold liquids were anointed inside and not outside, but utensils meant to hold dry stuffs not anointed.

E. "You may know that they were not consecrated, for it is said, *You shall bring from your dwellings two loaves of bread to be waved, made of two tenths of an ephah* (Lev. 23:17). Then when do they belong to the Lord? Only after they are baked." [The bread was baked in utensils at home, so the utensils have not been consecrated.]

The exegetes at Pesiqta deRab Kahana have no interest whatever in the details at hand. Theirs is not a search for concrete details.

XLIV:II.

3. A. Rabbi says, "Why is it said, *...and had anointed and consecrated it* ? And is it not already stated, '...and had anointed and consecrated it'?

    B. "This indicates that with the anointing of these utensils all future utensils were sanctified [so that the sanctification of the tabernacle enjoyed permanence and a future tabernacle or temple did not require a rite of sanctification once again]."

No. 1 clarifies the rite of sanctification, aiming at the notion that the act of consecration covered everything at once, leading to the future conclusion, at the end, that that act also covered utensils later on to be used in the cult. No. 3 goes over that same ground. No. 2 deals with its own issue, pursuing the exegesis of the verse at hand. Its interest in the consecration of the utensils is entirely congruent with No. 3, because it wants to know the status of utensils outside of the cult, and, while they serve the purpose of the cult as specified, still, they are not deemed to have been consecrated. That, sum and substance, is the message of the passage: this and that about not very much, apart from the sequence of events that took place on one and the same day, an effort to harmonize and unify diverse tales into a single set of cogent events.

IV. Pesiqta deRab Kahana on Num. 7:1: Text and Program

My translation of the critical text of Pisqta deRab Kahana published by Bernard Mandelbaum, *Pesikta de Rab Kahana. According to An Oxford Manuscript. With Variants from All Known Manuscripts and Genizoth Fragments and Parallel Passages. With Commentary and Introduction* (N.Y., 1962: The Jewish Theological Seminary of America) I-II. I have further followed Mandelbaum's notes and commentary, and he was kind enough to correct the first draft of my translation. I also consulted William G. (Gershon Zev) Braude and Israel J. Kapstein, *Pesikta de-Rab Kahana. R. Kahana's Compilation of Discourses for Sabbaths and Festal Days* (Philadelphia, 1975:

Jewish Publication Society of America).[8] The formal traits of the second compilation differ radically. Pesiqta deRab Kahana falls into precisely the same structural-formal classification as Genesis Rabbah and Leviticus Rabbah. It approaches the exegesis of the verse of primary interest, which I call the base-verse, by means of a secondary and superficially unrelated verse, which I call the intersecting-verse. The latter will be extensively treated, entirely on its own. Then the exegete will move from the intersecting-verse to the base-verse, showing how the verse chosen from some other passage in fact opens up the deeper meaning of the verse of primary concern. In what follows the intersecting-verse, Song 5:1, is chosen because it refers to "bride," and the word for " had finished" is formed of the letters KLH, which can be read as bride. So in the mind of the exegete, an appropriate intersecting-verse will speak of the same matter – KLH=finish or bride – and the rest follows. But, as we shall see, that intersecting-verse imparts its deepest meaning on the base-verse, and, in the present instance, the tabernacle on that account is taken as the place in which Israel entered the bridal canopy of God. The clear purpose of the authorship emerges in their treatment of the base-verse, Num. 7:1: teleological-eschatological, beginning, middle and end. The one thing important about the base-verse is the opposite of the main thing that struck the authorship of Sifré to Numbers: its interest in a one-time event on a particular day. To the authorship of Pesiqta deRav Kahana, Scripture presents eternal paradigms and not one-time history.[9]

1. In building the tabernacle, Moses has brought God down to earth.

I:I

1. A. *I have come back to my garden, my sister, my bride* (Song 5:1):

---

[8] Theirs is not a translation but an eisegetical rendition, more of a literary paraphrase than an academic translation. Moreover, the Hebrew text on which Braude's and Kapstein's translation is based appears to be eclectic, one that they appear to have chosen for the occasion, therefore is not readily available to scholars in general, rather than systematic and commonly accessible. Finally, because they have not analyzed the text into its constitutive components, they have translated (eisegetically) as though one clause derived from the last and led to the next, when, in fact, each component was worked out within its own framework and is not necessarily cogent with the others fore and aft. Consequently, their translation harmonizes constantly what seem to me discrete components of discourse. Their penchant for translating not the text but what they (not necessarily without reason) conceive to be its meaning makes the translation attractive and engaging, but in no way reliable as an account of what is there in the Hebrew. It has to be checked at every point, though I would not dismiss it as without value, even as a translation of the Hebrew. Its lack of accuracy on minor points makes little material difference as to its usefulness.

[9] Whether the authorship of Sifré to Numbers has a different definition of event and a different conception of history from that of Pesiqta deRab Kahana is a question we cannot follow in the present context.

B. R. Azariah in the name of R. Simon said, "[The matter may be compared to the case of] a king who became angry at a noble woman and drove her out and expelled her from his palace. After some time he wanted to bring her back. She said, 'Let him renew in my behalf the earlier state of affairs, and then he may bring me back.'

C. "So in former times the Holy One, blessed be He, would receive offerings from on high, as it is said, *And the Lord smelled the sweet odor* (Gen. 8:21). But now he will accept them down below."

2. A. *I have come back to my garden, my sister, my bride* (Song 5:1):
   B. Said R. Hanina, "The Torah teaches you proper conduct,
   C. "specifically, that a groom should not go into the marriage canopy until the bride gives him permission to do so: *Let my beloved come into his garden* (Song 4:16), after which, *I have come back to my garden, my sister, my bride* (Song 5:1)."

As we shall see, the intersecting-verse is fully exposed entirely in its own terms, before we are able to recover the base-verse and find out what we learn about that verse from the intersecting one.

3. A. R. Tanhum, son-in-law of R. Eleazar b. Abina, in the name of R. Simeon b. Yosni: "What is written is not, 'I have come into the garden,' but rather, *I have come back to my garden.* That is, 'to my [Mandelbaum:] canopy.'

   B. "That is to say, to the place in which the the principal [presence of God] had been located to begin with.

   C. "The principal locale of God's presence had been among the lower creatures, in line with this verse: *And they heard the sound of the Lord God walking about* (Gen. 3:8)."

4. A. *[And they heard the sound of the Lord God walking about* (Gen. 3:8):] Said R. Abba bar Kahana, "What is written is not merely 'going,' but 'walking about,' that is, 'walking away from.'"

   B. *And man and his wife hid* (Gen. 3:8):

   C. Said R. Aibu, "At that moment the first man's stature was cut down and diminished to one hundred cubits."

5. A. Said R. Isaac, "It is written, *The righteous will inherit the earth* (Ps. 47:29). Where will the wicked be? Will they fly in the air?

   B. "Rather, the sense of the clause, *they shall dwell thereon in eternity* is, they shall bring the presence of God to dwell on the earth."

6. A. [Reverting to 3.C,] the principal locale of God's presence had been among the lower creatures, but when the first man sinned, it went up to the first firmament.

   B. The generation of Enosh came along and sinned, and it went up from the first to the second.

   C. The generation of the flood [came along and sinned], and it went up from the second to the third.

D. The generation of the dispersion...and sinned, and it went up from the third to the fourth.

E. The Egyptians in the time of Abraham our father [came along] and sinned, and it went up from the fourth to the fifth.

F. The Sodomites..., and sinned, ...from the fifth to the sixth.

G. The Egyptians in the time of Moses...from the sixth to the seventh.

H. And, corresponding to them, seven righteous men came along and brought it back down to earth:

I. Abraham our father came along and acquired merit, and brought it down from the seventh to the sixth.

J. Isaac came along and acquired merit and brought it down from the sixth to the fifth.

K. Jacob came along and acquired merit and brought it down from the fifth to the fourth.

L. Levi came along and acquired merit and brought it down from the fourth to the third.

M. Kahath came along and acquired merit and brought it down from the third to the second.

N. Amram came along and acquired merit and brought it down from the second to the first.

O. Moses came along and acquired merit and brought it down to earth.

P. Therefore it is said, *On the day that Moses completed the setting up of the tabernacle, he anointed and consecrated it* (Num. 7:1).

The selection of the intersecting-verse, Song 5:1, rests, as I said, on the appearance of the letters KLT, meaning, completed, but yielding also the word KLH, meaning, bride. The exegete wishes to make the point that in building the tabernacle, Moses has brought God down to earth, 6.P. This he accomplishes by bringing the theme of "garden, bride" together with the theme of the union of God and Israel. The parable at 1.B then is entire apt, since it wishes to introduce the notion of God's having become angry with humanity but then reconciled through Israel in the sacrificial cult. 1.B then refers to the fall from grace, with Israel as the noble spouse who insists that the earlier state of affairs be restored. C then makes explicit precisely what is in mind, a very effective introduction to the whole. No. 2 pursues the exegesis of the intersecting-verse, as does No. 3, the latter entirely apropos. Because of 3.C, Nos. 4 is tacked on; it continues the exegesis of the proof-text but has no bearing on the intersecting-verse. But No. 5 does – at least in its proposition, if not in its selection of proof-texts. No. 6 then brings us back to 3.C, citing the language of the prior component and then making the point of the whole quite explicit. Even with the obvious accretions at No. 4, 5, the whole hangs together and makes its point – the intersecting-verse, Song 5:1, the base-verse Num. 7:1 – in a cogent way.

2. The tabernacle was the place of God's presence on earth.

I:II.

1. A. *King Solomon made a pavilion for himself* (Song 3:9) [The New English Bible: *The palanquin which King Solomon had made for himself was of wood from Lebanon. Its poles he made of silver, its head-rest of gold; its seat was of purple stuff, and its lining was of leather]:*

   B. *Pavilion* refers to the tent of meeting.

   C. *King Solomon made a ...for himself* he is the king to whom peace *(shalom/shelomoh)* belongs.

2. A. Said R. Judah bar Ilai, "[The matter may be compared to the case of] a king who had a little girl. Before she grew up and reached puberty, he would see her in the market place and chat with her, or in alleyways and chat with her. But when she grew up and reached puberty, he said, 'It is not fitting for the dignity of my daughter that I should talk with her in public. Make a pavilion for her, so that I may chat with her in the pavilion.'

   B. "So, to begin with: *When Israel was a child in Egypt, then in my love of him, I used to cry out* ((Hos 11:1). In Egypt they saw me: *And I passed through the land of Israel* (Ex. 12:12). At the sea they saw me: *And Israel saw the great hand* (Ex. 14:31). At Sinai they saw me: *Face to face the Lord spoke with you* (Deut. 5:4).

   C. "But when they received the Torah, they became a fully-grown nation for me. So he said, 'It is not appropriate to the dignity of my children that I should speak with them in public. But make me a tabernacle, and I shall speak from the midst of the tabernacle.'

   D. "That is in line with this verse: *And when Moses entered the tent of the presence to speak with God, he heard the voice speaking from above the cover over the ark of the tokens from between the two cherubim: the voice spoke to him* (Num. 7:89)."

3. A. *[The palanquin which King Solomon had made for himself was of wood from Lebanon. Its poles he made of silver, its head-rest of gold; its seat was of purple stuff, and its lining was of leather]...was of wood from Lebanon. Make for the tabernacle planks of acacia-wood as uprights* (Ex. 26:25).

   B. *Its poles he made of silver: The hooks and bands on the posts shall be of silver (Ex. 27:10).*

   C. *...its head-rest of gold: Overlay the planks with gold, make rings of gold on them to no hold the bars* (Ex. 26:29).

   D. *...its seat was of purple stuff: Make a veil of finely woven linen and violet, purple, and scarlet yarn* (Ex. 26:31).

   E. *...and its lining was of leather:*

   F. R. Yudan says, "This refers to the merit accruing on account of the Torah and the righteous."

   G. R. Azariah in the name of R. Judah bar Simon says, "This refers to the Presence of God."

4 . A. Said R. Aha bar Kahana, "It is written, *And there I shall meet with you* (Ex. 25:22),

B. "to teach that even what is on the outside of the ark-cover is not empty of God's presence."

5 . A. A gentile asked Rabban Gamaliel, saying to him, "On what account did the Holy One, blessed be He, reveal himself to Moses in a bush?"

B. He said to him, "If he had revealed himself to him in a carob tree or a fig tree, what might you have said? It is so as to indicate that there is no place in the earth that is empty of God's presence."

6 . A. R. Joshua of Sikhnin in the name of R. Levi: "To what may the tent of meeting be compared?

B. "To an oceanside cave. The sea tide flows and engulfs the cave, which is filled by the sea, but the sea is not diminished.

C. "So the tent of meeting is filled with the splendor of the presence of God."

D. Therefore it is said, *On the day that Moses completed the setting up of the Tabernacle, he anointed and consecrated it* (Num. 7:1).

Seen by itself, No. 1 has no bearing upon the larger context, but it does provide a good exegesis of Song 3:9 in terms of the theme at hand, the tabernacle. The point of No. 2 is that the purpose of the tabernacle was to make possible appropriate communication between a mature Israel and God. Then the two items are simply distinct workings of the theme of the tabernacle, one appeqaling to Song 3:9, the other, Num. 7:89.

The introduction at **I:II** of Song 3:9, with the explanation that palanquin refers to the tent of meeting, accounts for the exposition of No. 3, which reads each phrase of that intersecting-verse in line with the proof-texts concerning the tent of meeting. Had **I:II.1** been continued by No.3, we should have a smoother statement of the main point. No. 4 seems to me to flow from No. 3's interest in the tent of meeting; the point of contact is with the viewpoint that God's presence was in the tent. Then No. 5 is tacked on for obvious reasons, a story that makes the same point as the exegesis. No. 6 goes over the matter yet again. The force of 6.D is derived only from its redactional function, which is to direct our attention back to our base-verse. But while the theme – the tent of meeting or tabernacle – has been worked out, the base-verse in its own terms has not been discussed. Tacking it on is only for purpose of marking the finish of the discourse at hand.

3. Exegesis of Song 3:9-11.

I:III

1 . A. [Continuing the exegesis of the successive verses of Songf 3:9ff.] *Come out, daughters of Jerusalem, you daughters of Zion, come out and welcome King Solomon, wearing the crown with which his mother has*

crowned him, on his wedding day, on his day of joy (Song 3:11) [Braude and Kapstein: *Go forth, O younglings whose name Zion indicates that you bear a sign*]:

B. Sons who are marked [a play on the letters that stand for the word, *come out*] for me by the mark of circumcision, by not cutting the corners of the head [in line with Lev. 19:27], and by wearing show-fringes.

2. A. *[...and welcome] King Solomon:*
   B. The king to whom peace belongs.

3. A. Another interpretation: *and welcome King Solomon:*
   B. The King [meaning God] who brings peace through his deeds among his creatures.
   C. He made the fire make peace with Abraham, the sword with Isaac, the angel with Jacob.
   D. It is the king who brings peace among his creatures.
   E. Said R. Yohanan, *"Merciful dominion and fear are with him* (Job 25:2) [that is, are at peace with him]."
   F. Said R. Jacob of Kefar Hanan, "*Merciful dominion* refers to Michael, and *fear* to Gabriel.
   G. "*With him* means that they make peace with him and do not do injury to one another."
   H. Said R. Yohanan, "The sun has never laid eyes on the blemished part of the moon [the black side], nor does a star take precedence over another one, nor does a planet lay eyes on the one above it."
   I. Said Rabbi, "All of them traverse as it were a spiral staircase."

4. A. It is written, *Who lays the beams of your upper chambers in the waters, who makes the flaming fires your ministers* (Ps. 104:2-3):
   B. R. Simeon b. Yohai taught, "The firmament is of water, the stars of fire, and yet they dwell with one another and do not do injury to one another.
   C. "The firmament is of water and the angel is of fire, and yet they dwell with one another and do not do injury to one another."
   D. Said R. Abin, "It is not the end of the matter [that there is peace between] one angel and another. But even the angel himself is half fire and half water, and yet they make peace."
   E. The angel has five faces – *The angel's body was like beryl, his face as the appearance of lightning, his eyes as torches of fire, his arms and feet like in color to burnished brass, and the sound of his words like the sound of a roaring multitude* (Dan. 10:6) – [yet none does injury to the other].

5. A. *So there was hail and fire flashing continually amid the hail* (Ex. 9:24):
   B. R. Judah says, "There was a flask of hail filled with fire."
   C. R. Nehemiah said, "Fire and hail, mixed together."
   D. R Hanin said, "In support of the position of R. Judah is the case of the pomegranate in the pulp of which seeds can be discerned."
   E. R. Hanin said, "As to Nehemiah's, it is the case of a crystal lamp in which are equivalent volume of water and oil, which together keep the flame of the wick burning above the water and the oil."

6. A. *[So there was hail and fire flashing continually amid the hail* (Ex. 9:24)]: What is the meaning of *flashing continually?*

   B. Said R. Judah bar Simon, "Each one is dying in their [B&K, p. 10:] determination to carry out their mission."

   C. Said R. Aha, "[The matter may be compared to the case of] a king, who had two tough legions, who competed with one another, but when the time to make war in behalf of the king came around, they made peace with one another.

   D. "So is the case with the fire and hail, they compete with one another, but when the time has come to carry out the war of the Holy One, blessed be He, against the Egyptians, then:*So there was hail and fire flashing continually amid the hail* (Ex. 9:24) – one miracle within the other [more familiar one, namely, that the hail; and fire worked together]."

7. A. *[Come out, daughters of Jerusalem, you daughters of Zion, come out and welcome King Solomon,] wearing the crown with which his mother has crowned him, on his wedding day, [on his day of joy]* (Song 3:11):

   B. Said R. Isaac, "We have reviewed the entire Scripture and have not found evidence that Beth Seba made a crown for her son, Solomon. This refers, rather, to the tent of meeting, which is crowed with blue and purple and scarlet."

8. A. Said R. Hunia, "R. Simeon b. Yohai asked R. Eleazar b. R. Yose, 'Is it possible that you have heard from your father what was the crown with which his mother crowned him?'

   B. "He said to him, 'The matter may be compared to the case of a king who had a daughter, whom he loved even too much. He even went so far, in expressing his affection for her, as to call her, "my sister." He even went so far, in expressing his affection for her, as to call her, "my mother."

   C. "'So at the outset, the Holy One, blessed be He, expressed his affection for Israel by calling them, "my daughter": *Hear, O daughter, and consider* (Ps. 45:11). Then he went so far, in expressing his affection for them, as to call them, "my sister": *My sister, my bride* (Song 5:1). Then he went so far, in expressing his affection for them, as to call them, "my mother": *Attend to me, O my people, and give ear to me, O my nation* (Is. 51:4). The letters that are read as "my nation" may also be read as "my mother."'

   D. "R. Simeon b. Yohai stood and kissed him on his head.

   E. "He said to him, 'Had I come only to hear this teaching, it would have been enough for me.'"

9. A. R. Joshua of Sikhnin in the name of R. Levi: "When the Holy One, blessed be He, said to Moses, 'Make me a tabernacle,' Moses might have brought four poles and spread over them [skins to make] the tabernacle. This teaches, therefore, that the Holy One, blessed be He, showed Moses on high red fire, green fire, black fire, and white fire.

   B. "He said to him, 'Make me a tabernacle.'

   C. "Moses said to the Holy One, blessed be He, 'Lord of the ages, where am I going to get red fire, green fire, black fire, white fire?'

D.   "He said to him, 'After the pattern which is shown to you on the mountain (Ex. 25:40).'"

10. A.   R. Berekhiah in the name of R. Levi: "[The matter may be compared to the case of] a king who appeared to his household clothed in a garment [B&K, p. 11] covered entirely with precious stones.

B.   "He said to him, 'Make me one like this.'

C.   "He said to him, 'My lord, O king, where am I going to get myself a garment made entirely of precious stones?'

D.   "He said to him, 'You in accord with your raw materials and I in accord with my glory.'

E.   "So said the Holy One, blessed be He, to Moses, 'Moses, if you make what belongs above down below, I shall leave my council up here and go down and reduce my Presence so as to be among you down there.'

F.   "Just as up there: *seraphim are standing* (Is. 6:2), so down below: *boards of shittim-cedars are standing* (Ex. 26:15).

G.   "Just as up there are stars, so down below are the clasps."

H.   Said R. Hiyyya bar Abba, "This teaches that the golden clasps in the tabernacle looked like the fixed stars of the firmament."

11. A.   *[Come out, daughters of Jerusalem, you daughters of Zion, come out and welcome King Solomon, wearing the crown with which his mother has crowned him,] on his wedding day, [on his day of joy]* (Song 3:11):

B.   [B&K, p. 12:] the day he entered the tent of meeting.

C.   *...on his day of joy:*

D.   this refers to the tent of meeting.

E.   Another interpretation of the phrase, *on his wedding day, on his day of joy* (Song 3:11):

F.   *...on his wedding day* refers to the tent of meeting.

G.   *...on his day of joy* refers to the building of the eternal house.

H.   Therefore it is said, *On the day that Moses completed the setting up of the Tabernacle, he anointed and consecrated it* (Num. 7:1).

The exegesis of Song 3:11 now receives attention in its own terms, our point of departure having been forgotten. No. 1 simply provides a play on one of the words of the verse under study. Nos. 2-6 proceed to work on the problem of the name of the king, Solomon. We have a striking and fresh approach at Nos. 2-3: the reference is now to God as King, and the name, Solomon, then is interpreted as God's function as bringing peace both among his holy creatures, the patriarchs and the angels, and also among the elements of natural creation. Both topics are introduced and then, at No. 4-6, the latter is worked out. God keeps water and fire working together and to do his bidding, they do not injure one another. The proof-text, Ex. 9:24, then leads us in its own direction, but at No. 6 discourse returns to the main point.

No. 7 moves us on to a fresh issue, namely, Solomon himself. And now we see the connection between the passage and our broader theme, the tabernacle. The Temple is now compared to a crown. No. 8 pursues the interpretation of the same clause. But the point of interest is the clause, not the theme under broader discussion, so what we have is simply a repertoire of exegeses of the cited verse. No. 9 carries forward the theme of making the tabernacle. It makes the point that Moses was to replicate the colors he had seen on high. I see no connection to the preceding. It is an essentially fresh initiative. No. 10 continues along that same line, now making yet another point, which is that the tabernacle on earth was comparable to the abode of God in heaven. No. 11 brings us back to our original verse. We take up a clause by clause interpretation of the matter. 11.H is an editorial subscript, with no connection to the foregoing except the rather general thematic one. But the original interest in working on the theme of the building of the tabernacle as Israel's wedding day to God is well expressed, beginning to end.

4. Comparison of God, Elijah, and Moses

I:IV

1. A. *Who has ever gone up to heaven and come down again? Who has cupped the wind in the hollow of his hands? Who has bound up the waters in the fold of his garment? Who has fixed the boundaries of the earth? What is his name or his son's name, if you know it?* (Prov. 30:4):
   B. *...Who has ever gone up to heaven:* this refers to the Holy One, blessed be He, as it is written, *God has gone up to the sound of the trumpet* (Ps. 37:6).
   C. *...and come down again: The Lord came down onto Mount Sinai* (Ex. 19:20).
   D. *Who has cupped the wind in the hollow of his hands: In whose hand is the soul of all the living* (Job 12:10).
   E. *Who has bound up the waters in the fold of his garment: He keeps the waters penned in dense cloud-masses* (Job 26:8).
   F. *Who has fixed the boundaries of the earth: who kills and brings to life* (1 Sam. 2:6).
   G. *What is his name:* his name is the Rock, his name is The Almighty, his name is The Lord of Hosts.
   H. *...or his son's name, if you know it: My son, my first born is Israel* (Ex. 4:22).

2. A. Another interpretation of the verse, *Who has ever gone up to heaven:* Who is the one whose prayer goes up to heaven and brings down rain?
   B. This is one who sets aside the tithes that he owes with his hands, who brings dew and rain into the world.
   C. *Who has cupped the wind in the hollow of his hands? Who has bound up the waters in the fold of his garment? Who has fixed the boundaries of the earth?* Who is the one whose prayer does not go up to heaven and bring down rain?
   D. This is one who does not set aside the tithes that he owes with his hands, who does not bring dew and rain into the world.

3. A. Another interpretation of the verse, *Who has ever gone up to heaven:*

B. This refers to Elijah, concerning whom it is written, *And Elijah went up in a whirlwind to heaven* (2 Kgs. 2:11).

C. *...and come down again:*

D. *Go down with him, do not be afraid* (2 Kgs. 1:16).

E. *Who has cupped the wind in the hollow of his hands:*

F. *Lord, God of Israel, before whom I stand* (1 Kgs. 17:1).

G. *Who has bound up the waters in the fold of his garment:*

H. *And Elijah took his mantle and wrapped it together and smote the waters and they were divided* (1 Kgs. 2:8).

I. *Who has fixed the boundaries of the earth:*

J. *And Elijah said, See your son lives* (1 Kgs. 17:23).

4. A. Another interpretation of the verse, *Who has ever gone up to heaven and come down again*:

B. This refers to Moses, concerning whom it is written, *And Moses went up to God* (Ex. 19:3).

C. *...and come down again:*

D. *And Moses came down from the mountain* (Ex. 19:14).

E. *Who has cupped the wind in the hollow of his hands*:

F. *As soon as I have gone out of the city, I shall spread my hands out to the Lord* (Ex. 9:29).

G. *Who has bound up the waters in the fold of his garment:*

H. *The floods stood upright as a heap* (Ex. 15:8).

I. *Who has fixed the boundaries of the earth*:

J. This refers to the tent of meeting, as it is said, *On the day on which Moses completed setting up the tabernacle* (Num. 7:1) – for the entire world was set up with it.

5. A. R. Joshua b. Levi in the name of R. Simeon b. Yohai: "What is stated is not 'setting up the tabernacle [without the accusative particle, *et*],' but 'setting up + *the accusative particle* + the tabernacle,' [and since the inclusion of the accusative particle is taken to mean that the object is duplicated, we understand the sense to be that he set up a second tabernacle along with the first].

B. "What was set up with it? It was the world that was set up with [the tabernacle, that is, the tabernacle represented the cosmos].

C. "For until the tabernacle was set up, the world trembled, but after the tabernacle was set up, the world rested on firm foundations."

D. Therefore it is said, *On the day that Moses completed the setting up of the Tabernacle, he anointed and consecrated it* (Num. 7:1).

The fresh intersecting-verse, Prov. 30:4, is systematically applied to God, to tithing, then Elijah, finally Moses, at which point the exposition comes to a fine editorial conclusion. I cannot imagine a more representative example of the intersecting-verse/base-verse exposition. No. 5 is tacked on because it provides a valuable complement to the point of No. 4.

5. Moses set up the tabernacle and took it down day by day,
    until he finally left it standing. What came to an end on the
    Day that Moses finished setting up the tabernacle.

I:V

1. A. Another interpretation of the verse: *On the day that Moses completed the
        setting up of the Tabernacle, he anointed and consecrated it* (Num. 7:1):
    B. The letters translated as "completed" are so written that they be read
        "bridal," that is, on the day on which [Israel, the bride] entered the bridal
        canopy.

2. A. R. Eleazar and R. Samuel bar Nahmani:
    B. R. Eleazar says, *"On the day that Moses completed* means on the day on
        which he left up setting up the tabernacle day by day."
    C. It has been taught on Tannaite authority: Every day Moses would set up
        the tabernacle, and every morning he would make his offerings on it and
        then take it down. On the eighth day [to which reference is made in the
        verse, *On the day that Moses completed the setting up of the Tabernacle,
        he anointed and consecrated it*] he set it up but did not take it down
        again.
    D. Said R. Zeira, "On the basis of this verse we learn the fact that an altar
        set up on the preceding night is inavlid for the offering of sacrifices on
        the next day."
    E. R. Samuel bar Nahmani says, "Even on the eighth day he set it up and
        took it apart again."
    F. And how do we know about these dismantlings?
    G. It is in line with what R. Zeira said, *"On the day that Moses completed*
        means on the day on which he left up setting up the tabernacle day by
        day."

3. A. R. Eleazar and R. Yohanan:
    B. R. Eleazar said, *"On the day that Moses completed* means on the day on
        which demons ended their spell in the world.
    C. "What is the scriptural basis for that view?
    D. *"No evil thing will befall you, nor will any demon come near you* [B&K
        p. 15] *by reason of your tent* (Ps. 91:10) – on the day on which demons
        ended their spell in the world."
    E. Said R. Yohanan, "What need do I have to derive the lesson from another
        passage? Let us learn it from the very passage in which the matter
        occurs: *May the Lord bless you and keep you* (Num. 6:24) – keep you
        from demons."

4. A. R. Yohanan and R. Simeon b. Laqish:
    B. R. Yohanan said, *"On the day that Moses completed* means on the day on
        which on the day on which hatred came to an end in the world. For
        before the tabernacle was set up, there was hatred and envy, competition,
        contention, and strife in the world. But once the tabernacle was sert up,
        love, affection, comradeship, righteousness, and peace came into the
        world.
    C. "What is the verse of scripture that so indicates?

D. *"Let me hear the words of the Lord, are they not words of peace, peace to his people and his loyal servants and to all who turn and trust in him? Deliverance is near to those who worship him, so that glory may dwell in our land. Love and fidelity have come together, justice and peace join hands* (Ps. 85:8-10).

E. Said R. Simeon b. Laqish, "What need do I have to derive the lesson from another passage? Let us learn it from the very passage in which the matter occurs: *and give you peace.*

5. A. *[On the day that Moses completed] the setting up of the Tabernacle, [he anointed and consecrated it]:*

B. R. Joshua b. Levi in the name of R. Simeon b. Yohai: "What is stated is not 'setting up the tabernacle [without the accusative particle, *et*],' but 'setting up + *the accusative particle* + the tabernacle,' [and since the inclusion of the accusative particle is taken to mean that the object is duplicated, we understand the sense to be that he set up a second tabernacle along with the first].

C. "What was set up with it? It was the world that was set up with [the tabernacle, that is, the tabernacle represented the cosmos].

D. "For until the tabernacle was set up, the world trembled, but after the tabernacle was set up, the world rested on firm foundations."

We work our way through the clause, *on the day that Moses completed* . No. 1 goes over familiar ground. It is a valuable review of the point of stress, the meaning of the word *completed*. No. 2 refers to the claim that from day to day Moses would set up and take down the tent, until on the day at hand, he left it standing; so the "completed" bears the sense of ceasing to go through a former procedure. The word under study bears the further sense of "coming to an end," and therefore at Nos. 3, 4, we ask what came to an end when the tabernacle was set up. The matched units point to demons, on the one side, and hatred, on the other. No. 5 moves us along from the word KLT to the following set, *accusative + tabernacle.*

6. Anointing and consecrating the utensils.

I:VI.

1. A. *On the day that Moses completed] the setting up of the Tabernacle, [he anointed and consecrated it:*

B. Since it is written, *he anointed and consecrated it* , why does it also say, *he anointed them and consecrated them* (Num. 7:1)?

C. R. Aibu said, "R. Tahalipa of Caesarea, and R. Simeon:

D. "One of them said, 'After he had anointed each one, he then anointed all of them simultaneously.'

E. "The other of them said, *'And he anointed them* refers to an anointing in this world and another anointing in the world to come.'"

2. A. Along these same lines: *You shall couple the tent together* (Ex. 26:11), *You shall couple the curtains* (Ex. 26:6):

- B. R. Judah and R. Levi, R. Tahalipa of Caesarea and R. Simeon b. Laqish:
- C. One of them said, "Once he had coupled them all together, he went back and coupled them one by one."
- D. The other said, *"You shall couple the curtains and it shall be one* meaning, one for measuring, one for anointing."

The exposition of the verse continues to occupy our attention, with the problem clear as stated.

7. The meaning of the number six, as in the six covered wagons brought by the princes to the dedication of the tabernacle.

I:VII.

1. A. *The chief men of Israel, heads of families – that is, the chiefs of the tribes, [who had assisted in preparing the detailed lists –] came forward and brought their offering before the Lord* (Num. 7:2):
   B. [(Following B&K, p. 16:) The word for *tribes* can mean *rods*, so we understand the meaning to be, they had exercised authority through rods] in Egypt.
   C. *...who had assisted in preparing the detailed lists –* the standards.

The clause by clause interpretation of the base-verse does not vastly differ in intent from the interpretation generated by leading the intersecting-verse into the base-verse. That is to say, in both cases we have a highly allusive and wide-ranging reading of the matter, in which we construct meanings deriving from eternal categories, not one-time events but paradigms, as I said earlier. That trait of the exegetical-eisegetical mind of the later document emerges most strikingly in what follows.

2. A. *...came forward and brought their offering before the Lord, six covered wagons [and twelve oxen, one wagon from every two chiefs and from each one an ox]* (Num. 7:2):
   B. The six corresponded to the six days of creation.
   C. The six corresponded to the six divisions of the Mishnah.
   D. The six corresponded to the six matriarchs: Sarah, Rebecca, Rachel, Leah, Bilhah, and Zilpah.
   E. Said R. Yohanan, "The six corresponded to the six religious duties that pertain to a king: *He shall not have too many wives* (Deut. 17:17), *He shall not have too many horses* (Deut. 17:16), *He shall not have too much silver and gold* (Deut. 17:17), *He shall not pervert justice, show favor, or take bribes* (Deut. 16:9)."

3. A. The six corresponded to the six steps of the throne. How so?
   B. When he goes up to take his seat on the first step, the herald goes forth and proclaims, *He shall not have too many wives* (Deut. 17:17).
   C. When he goes up to take his seat on the second step, the herald goes forth and proclaims, *He shall not have too many horses* (Deut. 17:16).

D. When he goes up to take his seat on the third step, the herald goes forth and proclaims, *He shall not have too much silver and gold* (Deut. 17:17).

E. When he goes up to take his seat on the fourth step, the herald goes forth and proclaims, *He shall not pervert justice.*

F. When he goes up to take his seat on the fifth step, the herld goes forth and proclaims, *...show favor.*

G. When he goes up to take his seat on the sixth, step, the herald goes forth and proclaims, *...or take bribes* (Deut. 16:9).

H. When he comes to take his seat on the seventh step, he says, "Know before whom you take your seat."

4 . A. *And the top of the throne was round behind* (1 Kgs. 10:19):

B. Said R. Aha, "It was like the throne of Moses."

C. *And there were arms on either side of the throne by the place of the seat* (1 Kgs. 10:19):

D. How so? There was a sceptre of gold suspended from behind, with a dove on the top, and a crown of gold in the dove's mouth, and he would sit under it on the Sabbath, and it would touch but not quite touch.

5 . A. The six corresponded to the six firmaments.

B. But are they not seven?

C. Said R. Abia, "The one where the King dwells is royal property [not counted with what belongs to the world at large]."

We proceed with the detailed exposition of the verse at hand. The focus of interest, after No. 1, is on the reason for bringing six wagons. The explanations, Nos. 2 (+3-4), 5, relate to the creation of the world, the Torah, the life of Israel, the religious duties of the king, and the universe above. The underlying motif, the tabernacle as the point at which the supernatural world of Israel meets the supernatural world of creation, is carried forward.

8 . The exegesis of Num. 7:2.

I:VIII.

1 . A. *[...came forward and brought their offering before the Lord , six] covered [wagons and twelve oxen, one wagon from every two chiefs and from each one an ox]* (Num. 7:2):

B. The word for covered wagons may be read to yield these meanings:

C. like a lizard-skin [B&K, p. 17: "it signifies that the outer surface of the wagons' frames was as delicately reticulated as the skin of a lizard"];

D. [and the same word may be read to indicate that the wagons were] decorated, or fully equipped.

E. It has been taught in the name of R. Nehemiah, "They were like a bent bow."

2 . A. *...twelve oxen, one wagon from every two chiefs ...:*

B. This indicates that two chiefs would together bring one wagon, while each tribe gave an ox.

3. A. *These they brought forward before the tabernacle* (Num. 7:3):
    B. This teaches that they turned them into their monetary value and sold them to the congregation at large [so that everyone had a share in the donation].

4. A. *And the Lord spoke to Moses and said, [Accept these from them: they shall be used for the service of the tent of the presence"]:* (Num. 7:5):
    B. What is the meaning of the word, *and said?*
    C. R. Hoshaia taught, "The Holy One, blessed be He, said to Moses, 'Go and say to Israel words of praise and consolation.'
    D. "Moses was afraid, saying, 'But is it not possible that the holy spirit and abandoned me and come to rest on the chiefs?'
    E. "The Holy One, blessed be He, said to him, 'Moses, Had I wanted them to bring their offering, I should have said to you to 'say to them,' [so instructing them to do so], but *Take – it is from them [at their own volition, not by my inspiration]* (Num. 7:5) is the language that meaning, they did it on their own volition [and have not received the holy spirit].'"

5. A. And who gave them the good ideas [of making the gift]?
    B. It was the tribe of Simeon who gave them the good idea, in line with this verse: *And of the children of Issachar came men who had understanding of the times* (1 Chr. 12:33).
    C. What is the sense of *the times?*
    D. R. Tanhuma said, "The ripe hour [*kairos*]."
    E. R. Yose bar Qisri said, "Intercalating the calendar."
    F. *They had two hundred heads* (1 Chr. 12:33):
    G. This refers to the two hundred heads of sanhedrins that were produced by the tribe of Issachar.
    H. *And all of their brethren were subject to their orders* (1 Chr. 12:33):
    I. This teaches that the law would accord with their rulings.
    J. They said to the community, "Is this tent of meeting which you are making going to fly in the air? Make wagons for it, which will bear it."

6. A. Moses was concerned, saying, "Is it possible that one of the wagons might break, or one of the oxen die, so that the offering of the chiefs might be invalid?"
    B. Said to Moses the Holy One, blessed be He, *They shall be used for the service of the tent of the presence* (Num. 7:5).
    C. "To them has been given a long-term existence."

7. A. How long did they live?
    B. R. Yudan in the name of R. Samuel bar Nahman, R. Honia in the name of Bar Qappara, *"In Gilgal they sacrificed the oxen* (Hos. 12:12)."
    C. And where did they offer them up?
    D. R. Abba bar Kahana said, "In Nob they offered them up."
    E. R. Abbahu said, "In Gibeon they offered them up."
    F. R. Hama bar Hanina said, "In the eternal house [of Jerusalem] they offered them up."

G. Said R. Levi, "A verse of Scripture supporting the view of R. Hama bar Hanina: *Solomon offered a sacrifice of peace-offerings, which he slaughtered for the Lord, twenty two thousand oxen* (1 Kgs. 8:63)."

H. It was taught in the name of R. Meir, "They encure even to now, and they never produced a stink, got old, or produced an invalidating blemish."

I. Now that produces an argument *a fortiori*:

J. If the oxen, who cleaved to the work of the making of the tent of meeting, were given an eternal existence, Israel, who cleave to the Holy One, blessed be He, how much the more so!

K. *And you have cleave to the Lord your God are alive, all of you, this day* (Deut. 4:4).

The exegesis of the verse in its own terms leads us through the several phrases, No. 1, 2, 3. No. 4, continuing at No. 6, with an important complement at No. 5, goes on to its own interesting question. No. 7 serves No. 6 as No. 6 serves No. 5.

V. The Program of Sifre to Numbers and the Two Pesiqtas on Num. 7:1

A brief reprise of the topical program of the three documents will permit us to draw a simple conclusion. To show the relationships among the programs of the three compilations, I present in bold-face type what is unique to a given compilation, in italics what is shared by Pesiqta Rabbati and Pesiqta deRab Kahana, and in underlining what is shared by Pesiqta de Rab Kahana and Sifré to Numbers. No topic occurs in all three documents.

Pesiqta Rabbati:

1. **The Torah's oral part is unique to Israel.**

2. **The tabernacle was credited to Moses, because he was prepared to give his life for it.**

3.. *Moses is comparable to God. Cf. Pesiqta deRab Kahana No. 4.*

4. **The children of Noah offered peace-offerings [and not whole-offerings].**

5. **The tabernacle is comparable to the marriage canopy, in which God and Israel were united. While this theme occurs at Pesiqta deRab Kahana No. 3, the articulation of the theme is particular to Pesiqta Rabbati.**

6. **Bezalel made the tabernacle, but Moses got credit for it.**

7. *The tabernacle marked the reunion of God with the world, from which, in the sin of Adam, God had departed. Cf. Pesiqta deRab Kahana No. 1, 2.*

8. **Diverse meanings of the words, *And it came to pass.***

9. **The juxtaposition of the account of the tabernacle with the account of the priestly blessing is to show that the tabernacle brought a blessing.**

The authorship of Pesiqta Rabbati has learned nothing from Sifré to Numbers, but at two points has taken over materials in Pesiqta deRab Kahana. The upshot is that the bulk of the topical program of Pesiqta Rabbati on Num. 7:1 is particular to its authorship.

Sifré to Numbers:

1. Moses set up the tabernacle every day and took it down every night, until he finally left it standing. Cf. Pesiqta deRab Kahana No. 5.
2. **Events on the first day of the month.**
3. As the utensils were anointed, they were not sanctified. That was a separate operation. The manner of anointing. The effect.

Some of the details of No. 3 are shared at Pesiqta deRab Kahana No. 6. But – as I shall presently emphasize – the comparison of the two compilations over all shows that the bulk of Pesiqta deRab Kahana goes its own way. The points in common are trivial in the larger composition of Pesiqta deRab Kahana.

Pesiqta deRab Kahana:

1. *In building the tabernacle, Moses has brought God down to earth. Cf. Pesiqta Rabbati No. 7.*
2. *The tabernacle was the place of God's presence on earth. Cf. Pesiqta Rabbati No. 7.*
3. **Exegesis of Song 3:9-11. Pesiqta Rabbati V:XI.1 alludes to the theme of this matter.**
4. *Comparison of God, Elijah, and Moses Cf. Pesiqta Rabbati No. 3.*
5. Moses set up the tabernacle and took it down day by day, until he finally left it standing. What came to an end on the Day that Moses finished setting up the tabernacle. Cf. Sifré to Numbers No. 1.
6. Anointing and consecrating the utensils. Cf. Sifré to Numbers No. 3.
7. **The meaning of the number six, as in the six covered wagons brought by the princes to the dedication of the tabernacle.**
8. **The exegesis of Num. 7:2**

It seems superfluous at this point to observe that the one group of exegetes exhibits little in common with the other, even though, at some few points, the exegetes of Pesiqta deRab Kahana go over ground covered by those in Sifré Numbers, and those of Pesiqta Rabbati share interests with those of Pesiqta deRab Kahana. What one set of sages wishes to know in the verse of Scripture at hand scarcely coincides with the program of the other. But the details should not obscure the character of the whole. As we read one document in its own terms, we find ourselves far from the other two. The comparison of *midrashim* as exegeses of particular verses and all the more so as compilations of exegeses in this case yields a picture of differences so profound as to call into question the premise with which we started. The real question before us is not how to explain commonalities, but why to adopt the premise that the documents emerge from a coherent and on-going, traditional world. Comparison of topics yields an odd result. Once we undertake the comparison we find so little in common among the documents as find new emphasis upon the simple question: what, apart from a few adventitious and not patterned points of intersection, justifies our treating the three compilations as components of a single canon.

VI. What Comparison Teaches

The upshot is that the three authorships go their respective ways, with little to say to one another. They may be characterized as different people talking, to be sure with reference to the same subject, about fundamentally different things – and therefore also to different people, we know not whom. That is because the approach of each set of exegetes to the base-verse derives from a clearly-defined program of inquiry, one that imposes its issues on the base-verse and responds to the base-verse only or principally in terms of the verse's provision of exemplary *detail* for the main point already determined by the exegetes. Accordingly, the first two of the three documents do far more than merely to assemble this and that, forming a hodgepodge of things people happen to have said. In the case of each of the first two documents, Sifré to Numbers and Pesiqta deRab Kahana, document we can answer the question: Why this, not that? They are not compilations but compositions; seen as a group, therefore, (to state matters negatively) they are not essentially the same, lacking all viewpoint, serving a single undifferentiated task of collecting and arranging whatever was at hand. The third of the three, Pesiqta Rabbati, goes its own way, in that it covers a variety of discrete points. Still, it does lay down a clearly perceptible message about the tabernacle and its importance, one that, for its part, the authorship of Sifré to Numbers has not delivered.

These documents of the Oral Torah's exegesis of the written Torah in the aggregate therefore emerge as rich in differences from one another and sharply defined each through its distinctive viewpoints and particular polemics, on the one side, and formal and aesthetic qualities, on the other. We deal with a canon, yes, but with a canon made up of highly individual documents. But that, after all, is what a canon is: a mode of classification that takes a library and turns it into a cogent if composite statement. A canon comprises separate books that all together make a single statement. In terms of the Judaism of the dual Torah, the canon is what takes scriptures of various kinds and diverse points of origin and turns scriptures into Torah, and commentaries on those scriptures into Torah as well, making them all into the one whole Torah – of Moses, our rabbi. Once more, when we come to the end of comparative study of midrash, we find ourselves raising the canonical question: how do the diverse documents form a single cogent statement.

Chapter Eleven

Comparative Midrash [3]: The Issue of Textuality

From Tradition to Imitation in Leviticus Rabbah, Pesiqta deRab Kahana, and Pesiqta Rabbati

I. The Three Related Compilations

In historical sequence, Leviticus Rabbah, Pesiqta deRab Kahana, and Pesiqta Rabbati reached closure in that order. The authorships of the second and third documents in sequence took over materials of their predecessors. The three compilations therefore intersect, in that the first of the two documents share five *pisqaot,* and, as we have noted, the second of the two share a number – evidently four – as well. Comparison of Midrash-compilations therefore requires us to ask how the three intersecting documents relate to one another. Before proceeding, we review the form-analytical facts on the basis of which the comparison at hand is undertaken. In Chapters Seven and Eight we established these form-analytical premises of the following exercise.

A. **Rhetorical Patterns**: Pesiqta deRab Kahana's authorship resorted to three rhetorical patterns:

1. **The Propositional Form**: The implicit syllogism is stated through the intervention of an contrastive-verse into the basic proposition established by the base-verse.

2. **The Exegetical Form**: The implicit syllogism is stated through a systematic exegesis of the components of the base-verse on their own.

3. **The Syllogistic List**: The syllogism is explicit, not implicit, and is proven by a list of probative examples.

B. **The Fixed Order of the Types of Forms**: The nature of these rhetorical preferences also suggests that the order in which these types of forms occur will be as just now given, first the syllogism generated by the intersection of the contrastive- and base-verses, then the syllogism repeated through a systematic reading of the base-verse on its own, finally, whatever miscellanies the framers have in hand (or later copyists insert).

C. **Comparison of Forms:** When we compare our document with another by examining a *pisqa* of Pesiqta deRab Kahana that is not unique to that composition but is shared with Leviticus Rabbah, we see that the definitive rhetorical traits of our document also prove distinctive – and differ from the rhetorical plan elsewhere shown to characterize that other document.

Rhetorical analysis has yielded the proposition that Pesiqta deRab Kahana consists of twenty-eight syllogisms, each presented in a cogent and systematic way by the twenty-eight *pisqaot,* respectively. Each *pisqa* contains an implicit proposition, and that proposition may be stated in a simple way. It emerges from the intersection of an external verse with the base-verse that recurs through the *pisqa,* and then is restated by the systematic dissection of the components of the base-verse, each of which is shown to say the same thing as all the others. The *pisqa* shared by Pesiqta deRab Kahana with Leviticus Rabbah violates the rhetorical plan characteristic of the twenty-four *pisqaot* that are unique to Pesiqta deRab Kahana but (as I have shown elsewhere) it conforms with great precision to the rhetorical plan characteristic of all of the *parashiyyot* of Leviticus Rabbah.

This review yields important facts. We already have seen that, on rhetorical and logical grounds, we may easily identify an otherwise unidentified *pisqa* as particular to Pesiqta Rabbati, on the basis of its rhetorical and logical program assigning it to that document and distinguishing it from one that occurs, in addition, in Pesiqta deRab Kahana. I shall now demonstrate a corresponding fact. It is that on the *same* rhetorical and logical grounds, we may show that a *pisqa* that occurs in Pesiqta deRab Kahana may be distinguished from one that occurs also in Leviticus Rabbah. Moreover, where a *parashah* of Leviticus Rabbah serves also as a *pisqa* of Pesiqta deRab Kahana, we may easily prove that the rhetorical and logical traits of composition assign that *parashah/pisqa* to priority in Leviticus Rabbah and derivative status in Pesiqta deRab Kahana. We may therefore say that Leviticus Rabbah's rhetorical and logical program is taken up but revised by the authorship of Pesiqta deRab Kahana, just as, in a different way, the authorship of Pesiqta Rabbati has taken up and made its own the rhetorical and logical program of Pesiqta deRab Kahana. That comparison of three distinct but intersecting compilations is the final result of this inquiry. Since we can set the three documents into historical sequence and show how and where each set of authors differs from its predecessors and successors, we may also find justification for the judgment that, when we move from Leviticus Rabbah through Pesiqta deRab Kahana to Pesiqta Rabbati, we follow the progression from tradition to (mere) (uncomprehending) imitation.

II. Leviticus Rabbah and Pesiqta deRab Kahana: The Intersecting *Parashiyyot/Pisqaot*

Of the twenty-eight *pisqaot* of Pesiqta deRab Kahana, five occur also in Leviticus Rabbah. I shall now show that the shared *pisqaot* in fact are distinctive to Leviticus Rabbah and violate the rhetorical preferences characteristic of the twenty-three *pisqaot* that are unique to Pesiqta deRab Kahana. That fact will then close the possibility that materials produced we know not where were chosen at random and promiscuously by the framers of diverse documents. For the case at hand I shall now demonstrate the opposite. The authorships of documents, illustrated here by that of Pesiqta deRab Kahana, followed a clearly-defined rhetorical plan. That plan, moreover, may be shown to be distinctive to the document that the authorship has created by comparison of pericopae of a document that are shared with other documents to those that are unique to the document at hand.

In order to demonstrate these propositions, I have first to review the already-established the traits of the rhetorical plan of Pesiqta deRab Kahana. Then I compare the rhetorical forms of Pesiqta deRab Kahana with the forms of a *parashah* of Leviticus Rabbah that occurs also in Pesiqta deRab Kahana. I am able to demonstrate that the characteristic forms of the latter do not occur in the shared *pisqa/parashah* at all, and that *other* forms do. I am further able to explain the rhetorical differences between the two documents. We begin with our initial exercise, the proposal of a hypothesis on the definitive rhetorical program of the document.

We have already noticed that in the aggregate Pesiqta deRab Kahana states in diverse ways a single important proposition concerning a given topic, while Pesiqta Rabbati tends to say many things about such a topic. So the earlier of the two Pesiqtas clearly undertakes a strikingly cogent mode of discourse. We now shall see, overall, that Pesiqta deRab Kahana presents its syllogisms in a far more powerful and direct medium of rhetoric than does Leviticus Rabbah. The upshot of the comparison in the modes of logical discourse of the three compilations may be stated very simply. A given *pisqa* of Pesiqta deRab Kahana repeatedly expresses an implicit syllogism; that is rarely the case in any *pisqa* of Pesiqta Rabbati; it is not the case to the same extent in each *parashah* of Leviticus Rabbah.

Pesqita deRab Kahana, as we recall, makes use of two forms, the propositional or intersecting-verse/base-verse, and the exegetical. Both are so shaped as to carry out a single purpose, which is to state the implicit syllogism, and to do so with great force and persuasive power. Let me state with appropriate emphasis the rhetorical program represented by the two forms we shall now discern. *Both are ways of stating in the idiom our authorship has chosen, in the media of expression they have preferred, and through the modes of demonstration and evidentiary proof they deem probative, a truth they never spell out but always take for granted we shall recognize and adopt.*

The intersecting-verse/base-verse or propositional form in Pesiqta deRab Kahana: The purpose of this formal mode of composition of Pesiqta deRab Kahana is not to explore the meanings of the contrastive-verse, bringing one of them to illuminate, also, the base-verse. It is to make a single point, to argue a single proposition, through a single-minded repertoire of relevant materials, each of which makes the same point as all the others. We may say that if a principal interest of the components of Leviticus Rabbah is exegetical, another principal interest, syllogistic, the sole interest of the authorship of Pesiqta deRab Kahana in the intersecting-verse/base verse form is to make a single point.

The exegetical form in Pesiqta deRab Kahana: Not only so, but since the effect of the contrastive-verse/base-verse construction is to produce a single syllogism, which then serves to impart to the base-verse the meaning that will be discovered everywhere, in each of its details, the exegetical form also functions in a different way in Pesiqta deRab Kahana from the way it functions in either Leviticus Rabbah or Pesiqta Rabbati. Specifically, the exegetical form will again and again make the same point, while in the two other compilations, it makes diverse points. The reason for the difference is simple. As I pointed out in Chapter Eight, if we have not been given a syllogism on the foundation of the contrast between the external verse and the base-verse, then we also should have no syllogism to emerge from each of the components of the base-verse, and a diversity of (thematically appropriate, but syllogistically diverse) propositions should emerge. We shall now see that that is the case. As I said above, if we have been given no implicit syllogism stated through the intervention of a contrastive-verse into the basic proposition established by the base-verse, we also shall discover no implicit syllogism stated through a systematic exegesis of the components of the base-verse on their own.

We may now comapre the two forms as they occur in Pesiqta deRab Kahana with the utilization of these same forms in Leviticus Rabbah. If we were to draw a contrast between the contrastive- or intersecting-verse/base-verse construction as we know it in Leviticus Rabbah and the counterpart in Pesiqta deRab Kahana, we should have to see them as essentially different modes of organizing and expressing an idea. The difference may be stated very simply.

Leviticus Rabbah's compositors draw on materials that systematically expound the intersecting-verse in a variety of ways, and only then draw back to the base-verse to impute to it a fresh and unusual sense, invited by one of the several possible interpretations laid out by the intersecting-verse. The framers of Pesiqta deRab Kahana, by contrast, draw upon an contrastive-verse in order to make a point – one point – which then is placed into relationship with the base-verse and which imposes its meaning on the base-verse.

What this means is that our document aims at making a single point, and at doing so with a minimum of obfuscation through exploration of diverse possibilities. The function of the contrastive-verse is not to lay forth a galaxy of hermeneutical possibilities, one of which will be selected. It is, rather, to present a single point, and it is that point that we shall then impose upon our base-verse. What that fact means, overall, is that the authorship of Pesiqta deRab Kahana aims at a syllogism, expressed singly and forcefully, rather than at a diversity of explanation of a verse that, in the end, will yield a syllogism. The difference between Leviticus Rabbah's intersecting-verse and base-verse construction and Pesiqta deRab Kahana's contrastive-verse and base-verse construction is sharp and total. The form – one verse, then another verse – looks the same. But the deeper structure is utterly unrelated. That the counterpart use of the intersecting-verse/base-verse form in Pesiqta Rabbati is miscellaneous and not pointed hardly requires proof. Let us turn to a shared *pisqa/parashah* of Pesiqta deRab Kahana and Leviticus Rabbah.

III. Pesiqta deRab Kahana 27 = Leviticus Rabbah 30

If my hypothesis concerning the rhetorical singularity of Pesiqta deRab Kahana is sound, then we should find the formal patterns that serve our document out of phase with those that serve Leviticus Rabbah (not to mention Pesiqta Rabbati, with which we have already dealt). What is particular to the rhetorical plan of Pesiqta deRab Kahana, specifically, is the the Propositional Form – another way of speaking of the intersecting-verse/base-verse form – in which the implicit syllogism is both defined and then stated through the intervention of an contrastive-verse into the basic proposition established by the base-verse. My analysis of the rhetorical plan of Leviticus Rabbah repeatedly produced the observation of one result.

It is that the intersecting-verse in that document was subjected to systematic and protracted exegesis in its own terms and not solely or mainly in terms of the proposition to be imputed, also, to the base-verse at the end. By contrast, in Pesiqta deRab Kahana the contrastive-verse, which forms the counterpart to what I called the intersecting-verse in Leviticus Rabbah, is not subjected *to sustained and systematic exegesis in its own terms.*

Quite to the contrary, the contrastive-verse serves for the sole purpose of imposing upon the base-verse a very particular proposition, which then is repeated through a sequence of diverse contrastive-verses, on the one side, and also through a sustained reading of the successive components of the base-verse, on the other. We now come then to a shared *pisqa* and pay close attention to how the contrastive-verse/intersecting-verse is treated.

XXVII:I

1. A. R. Abba bar Kahana commenced [discourse by citing the following verse]: *Take my instruction instead of silver, [and knowledge rather than choice gold]* (Prov. 8:10)."

   B. Said R. Abba bar Kahana, *"Take the instruction of the Torah instead of silver.*

   C. "Take the instruction of the Torah and not silver.

D. *"Why do you weigh out money? Because there is no bread* (Is. 55:2).

E. "Why do you weigh out money to the sons of Esau [Rome]? [It is because] *there is no bread,* because you did not sate yourselves with the bread of the Torah.

F. *"And [why] do you labor? Because there is no satisfaction* (Is. 55:2).

G. *"Why do you labor* while the nations of the world enjoy plenty? *Because there is no satisfaction,* that is, because you have not sated yourselves with the bread of the Torah and with the wine of the Torah.

H. "For it is written, *Come, eat of my bread, and drink of the wine I have mixed* (Prov. 9:5)."

2. A. R. Berekhiah and R. Hiyya, his father, in the name of R. Yose b. Nehorai: "It is written, *I shall punish all who oppress him* (Jer. 30:20), even those who collect funds for charity [and in doing so, treat people badly], except [for those who collect] the wages to be paid to teachers of Scripture and repeaters of Mishnah traditions.

B. "For they receive [as a salary] only compensation for the loss of their time, [which they devote to teaching and learning rather than to earning a living].

C. "But as to the wages [for carrying out] a single matter in the Torah, no creature can pay the [appropriate] fee in reward."

3. A. It has been taught on Tannaite authority: On the New Year, a person's sustenance is decreed [for the coming year],

B. except for what a person pays out [for food in celebration] of the Sabbath, festivals, the celebration of the New Month,

C. and for what children bring to the house of their master [as his tuition].

D. If he adds [to what is originally decreed], [in Heaven] they add to his [resources], but if he deducts [from what he should give], [in Heaven] they deduct [from his wealth]. [Margulies, *Vayyiqra Rabbah,* p. 688, n. to 1. 5, links this statement to Prov. 8:10.]

4. A. R. Yohanan was going up from Tiberias to Sepphoris. R. Hiyya bar Abba was supporting him. They came to a field. He said, "This field once belonged to me, but I sold it in order to acquire merit in labor in the Torah."

B. They came to a vineyard, and he said, "This vineyard once belonged to me, but I sold it in order to acquire merit in labor in the Torah."

C. They came to an olive grove, and he said, "This olive grove once belonged to me, but but I sold it in order to acquire merit in labor in the Torah."

D. R. Hiyya began to cry.

E. Said R. Yohanan, "Why are you crying?"

F. He said to him, "It is because you left nothing over to support you in your old age."

G. He said to him, "Hiyya, my disciple, is what I did such a light thing in your view? I sold something which was given in a spell of six days [of creation] and in exchange I acquired something which was given in a spell of forty days [of revelation].

H. "The entire world and everything in it was created in only six days, as it is written, *For in six days the Lord made heaven and earth* (Ex. 20:11)

I. "But the Torah was given over a period of forty days, as it was said, *And he was there with the Lord for forty days and forty nights* (Ex. 34:28). [Leviticus Rabbah adds: And it is written, *And I remained on the mountain for forty days and forty nights* (Deut. 9:9).]"

5. A. When R. Yohanan died, his generation recited concerning him [the following verse of Scripture]: *If a man should give all the wealth of his house for the love* (Song 8:7), with which R. Yohanan loved the Torah, *he would be utterly destitute* (Song 8:7).

B. When R. Abba bar Hoshaiah of Tiria died, they saw his bier flying in the air. His generation recited concerning him [the following verse of Scripture]: *If a man should give all the wealth of his house for the love,* with which the Holy One, blessed be He, loved Abba bar Hoshaiah of Tiria, *he would be utterly destitute* (Song 8:7).

C. When R. Eleazar b. R. Simeon died, his generation recited concerning him [the following verse of Scripture]: *Who is this who comes up out of the wilderness like pillars of smoke, perfumed with myrrh and frankincense, with all the powders of the merchant?* (Song 3:6).

D. What is the meaning of the clause, *With all the powders of the merchant?*

E. [Like a merchant who carries all sorts of desired powders,] he was a master of Scripture, a repeater of Mishnah traditions, a writer of liturgical supplications, and a poet.

6. A. Another interpretation of the verse, *Take my instruction instead of silver, [and knowledge rather than choice gold]* (Prov. 8:10): Said R. Abba bar Kahana, "On the basis of the reward paid for one act of *taking,* you may assess the reward for [taking] the palm branch [on the festival of Tabernacles].

B. "There was an act of taking in Egypt: *You will take a bunch of hyssop* (Ex. 12:22).

C. "And how much was it worth? Four *manehs,* maybe five.

D. "Yet that act of taking is what stood up for Israel [and so made Israel inherit] the spoil of Egypt, the spoil at the sea, the spoil of Sihon and Og, and the spoil of the thirty-one kings.

E. "Now the palm-branch, which costs a person such a high price, and which involves so many religious duties – how much the more so [will a great reward be forthcoming on its account]!"

F. Therefore Moses admonished Israel, saying to them, *[On the fifteenth day of the seventh month, when you have gathered in the produce of the land, you shall keep the feast of the Lord seven days...] And you shall take on the first day the fruit of goodly trees, branches of palm trees and boughs of leafy trees and willows of the brook; and you shall rejoice before the Lord your God seven days. You shall keep it as a feast to the Lord seven days in the year; it is a statute for ever throughout your generations; you shall keep it in the seventh month. You shall dwell in booths for seven days; all that are native in Israel shall dwell in booths, that your generations may know that I made the people of Israel dwell in booths when I brought them out of the land of Egypt: I am the Lord your God* (Leviticus 23:39-43).

The notion of an implicit syllogism seems to me not to apply at all, since the point of interest of No. 1 is simply that study of the Torah is the source of Israel's sustenance. The theme of the intervening passages is established at 1.B, namely, Torah and the value and importance of study of Torah. Nos. 2, 3, 4, and 5 all present variations on amplifications of that theme. No. 2 makes that same point. No. 3 complements it, as do Nos. 3, 4, 5. Only at No. 6 do we revert to the intersecting-verse/contrastive-verse, which is now brought to bear upon our base-verse to make the point that the reward for "taking" is considerable, hence the taking of the fruit of goodly trees will produce a reward. That point is totally out of phase with the syllogism of Nos. 1-5, and therefore the rhetorical program at hand is not one in which the contrastive-verse is interpreted solely and finally to impute meaning to the base-verse and so to yield an implicit proposition. The rhetorical plan yields two points, one about the study of the Torah, which is irrelevant to our base-verse, the other about the reward for taking the species of the Festival, which is, then the main point. As I said above, it is only at No. 6 that Lev. 23:39 – with stress on the word "take" – recurs.

XXVII:II

1. A. *You show me the path of life, [in your presence] there is fulness of joy* (Ps. 16:11).
   B. Said David before the Holy One, blessed be He, "Lord of the ages, show me the open gateway to the life of the world to come."
   C. R. Yudan and R. Azariah:
   D. R. Yudan said, "David said before the Holy One, blessed be He, 'Lord of the ages, Show me the path of life.'
   E. "Said the Holy One, blessed be He, to David, 'If you seek life, look for fear, as it is said, *The fear of the Lord prolongs life* (Prov. 10:27)."
   F. R. Azariah said, "[The Holy One, blessed be He], said to David, 'If you seek life, look for suffering (YYSWRYN), as it is said, *The reproofs of discipline (MWSR) are the way of life* (Prov. 6:23)." [Leviticus Rabbah adds: Rabbis say, "The Holy One, blessed be He, said to David, 'David, if you seek life, look for Torah,' as it is said, *It is a tree of life to those that hold fast to it* (Prov. 3:18)." R. Abba said, "David said before the Holy One, blessed be He, 'Lord of the ages, Show me the path of life.' Said to him the Holy One, blessed be He, 'Start fighting and exert yourself! Why are you puzzled? [Lieberman, in Margulies, *Vayyiqra Rabbah*, p. 880, to p. 692]. Work and eat: Keep my commandments and live (Prov. 4:4).'"]

2. A. *The fulness (SWB') of joy in your presence* (Ps. 16:11):
   B. Satisfy (SB'NW) us with five joys in your presence: Scripture, Mishnah, Talmud, Supplements, and Lore.

3. A. Another matter: *In your presence is the fulness of joy* (Ps. 16:11):
   B. Read not *fulness* (SWB') but *seven* (SB'). These are the seven groups of righteous men who are going to receive the face of the Presence of God.

C. And their face is like the sun, moon, firmament, stars, lightning, lilies, and the pure candelabrum that was in the house of the sanctuary.

D. How do we know that it is like the sun? As it is said, *Clear as the sun* (Song 6:10).

E. How do we know that it is like the moon? As it is said, *As lovely as the moon* (Song 6:10).

F. How do we know that it is like the firmament? As it is said, *And they that are wise shall shine as the brightness of the firmament* (Dan. 12:3).

G. How do we know that it is like the stars? As it is said, *And they that turn the many to righteousness as the stars forever and ever* (Dan. 12:3).

H. And how do we know that it is like the lightning? As it is said, *Their appearance is like torches, they run to and fro like lightning* (Nah. 2:5).

I. How do we know that it is like lilies? As it is said, *For the leader: upon the lilies* (Ps. 69:1).

J. How do we know that it will be like the pure candelabrum of the house of the sanctuary? As it is said, *And he said to me, What do you see? And I said, I looked and behold [there was] a candelabrum all of gold* (Zech. 4:2).

4. A. *At your right hand is bliss for evermore* (Ps. 16:11).

B. Said David before the Holy One, blessed be He, "Lord of the ages, now who will tell me which group [among those listed above] is the most beloved and blissful of them all?"

C. There were two Amoras [who differed on this matter]. One of them said, "It is the group that comes as representative of the Torah and commandments, as it is said, *With a flaming fire at his right hand* (Deut. 33:2)."

D. And the other said, "This refers to the scribes, the Mishnah repeaters, and those who teach children in their fear, who are going to sit at the right hand of the Holy One, blessed be He.

E. "That is in line with the following verse of Scripture: *I keep the Lord always before me, because he is at my right hand, I shall not be moved* (Ps. 16:8)."

5. A. Another matter concerning the verse *You show me the path of life, in your presence there is fulness of joy, in your right hand are pleasures for evermore* (Ps. 16:11): *In your presence there is fulness (SWB') of joy* (Ps. 16:11):

B. [Leviticus Rabbah adds: Read only "seven (SB') joys."] These are the seven religious duties associated with the Festival [Tabernacles].

C. These are they: the four species that are joined in the palm branch, [the building of] the Tabernacle, [the offering of] the festal sacrifice, [the offering of] the sacrifice of rejoicing.

6. A. If there is the offering of the sacrifice of rejoicing, then why is there also the offering of the festal sacrifice? And if there is [the offering of] the festal sacrifice, then why also is there [the offering of] the sacrifice of rejoicing?

B. Said R. Abin, "The matter may be compared to two who came before a judge. Now we do not know which one of them is the victor. But it is the one who takes the palm branch in his hand who we know to be the victor.

C.   "So is the case of Israel and the nations of the world. The [latter] come and draw an indictment before the Holy One, blessed be He, on the New Year, and we do not know which party is victor.

E.   "But when Israel goes forth from before the Holy One, blessed be He, with their palm branches and their citrons in their hands, we know that it is Israel that are the victors."

F.   Therefore Moses admonishes Israel, saying to them, *[On the fifteenth day of the seventh month, when you have gathered in the produce of the land, you shall keep the feast of the Lord seven days...] And you shall take on the first day the fruit of goodly trees, branches of palm trees and boughs of leafy trees and willows of the brook; and you shall rejoice before the Lord your God seven days. You shall keep it as a feast to the Lord seven days in the year; it is a statute for ever throughout your generations; you shall keep it in the seventh month. You shall dwell in booths for seven days; all that are native in Israel shall dwell in booths, that your generations may know that I made the people of Israel dwell in booths when I brought them out of the land of Egypt: I am the Lord your God* (Leviticus 23:39-43).

The intersecting-verse – Ps. 16:11 – leads us to the base-verse, after a long and majestic sequence of exegeses of the three elements of the intersecting-verse. But the implicit syllogism associated with the base-verse does not form the sole and principal interest of the exegesis of the intersecting-verse/contrastive-verse. When we do reach the base-verse, the connection turns out to be tight and persuasive. The original repertoire of key words – Torah, commandments, and the like – is reviewed. Nos. 5-6 go over the same verse with respect to Israel, introducing the matter of the New Year, Day of Atonement, and Festival. Then each clause suitably links to the several themes at hand. No. 6 of course is tacked on, since the composition concludes properly with No. 5, at which point the intersecting-verse has reached the base-verse.

XXVII:III

1.   A.   *He will regard the prayer of the destitute [and will not despise their supplication]* (Ps. 102:17):

B.   Said R. Reuben, "We are unable to make sense of David's character. Sometimes he calls himself king, and sometimes he calls himself destitute.

C.   "How so? When he foresaw that righteous men were going to come from him, such as Asa, Jehoshaphat, Hezekiah, and Josiah, he would call himself king as it is said, *Give the king your judgments, O God* (Ps. 72:1).

D.   "When he foresaw that wicked men would come forth from him, for example, Ahaz, Manasseh, and Amon, he would call himself destitute, as it is said, *A prayer of one afflicted, when he is faint [and pours out his complaint before the Lord]* (Ps. 102:1)."

2. A. R. Alexandri interpreted the cited verse *He will regard the prayer of the destitute [and will not despise their supplication]* (Ps. 102:17) to speak of a worker: "[Margulies, *ad loc.*, explains: The one afflicted is the worker. The word for faint, 'TP, bears the meaning, *cloak oneself*, hence in prayer. The worker then has delayed his prayer, waiting for the overseer to leave, at which point he can stop and say his prayer. So he postpones his prayer.] [So Alexandri says], "Just as a worker sits and watches all day long for when the overseer will leave for a bit, so he is late when he says [his prayer], [so David speaks at Ps. 102:1: *Hear my prayer, O Lord; let my cry come to you*]."

   B. "That [interpretation of the word 'TP] is in line with the use in the following verse: *And those that were born late belonged to Laban* (Gen. 30:42)."

   C. What is the meaning of *those that were born late*?

   D. R. Isaac bar Haqolah said, *"The ones that tarried."*

3. A. [Another interpretation: *He will regard the prayer of the destitute [and will not despise their supplication]* (Ps. 102:17):] Said R. Simeon b. Laqish, "As to this verse, the first half of it is not consistent with the second half, and vice versa.

   B. "If it is to be, 'He will regard the prayer of the destitute [individual],' he should then have said, 'And will not despise *his* supplication.'

   C. "But if it is to be, 'He will not despise *their* supplication,' then he should have said, 'He will regard the prayer of *those* who are destitute.'

   D. "But [when David wrote,] *He will regard the prayer of the individual destitute*, this [referred to] the prayer of Manasseh, king of Judah.

   F. "And [when David wrote,] *He will not despise* their *supplication*, this [referred to] his prayer and the prayer of his fathers.

   G. "That is in line with the following verse of Scripture: *And he prayed to him, and he was entreated (Y'TR) of him* (2 Chron. 33:13)."

   H. What is the meaning of the phrase, *He was entreated of him*?

   I. Said R. Eleazar b. R. Simeon, "In Arabia they call a breach an *athirta* [so an opening was made for his prayer to penetrate to the Throne of God]" (Slotki, p. 385, n. 3).

   J. *And he brought him back to Jerusalem, his kingdom* (2 Chron. 33:13).

   K. How did he bring him back?

   L. R. Samuel b. R. Jonah said in the name of R. Aha, "He brought him back with a wind.

   M. "That is in line with the phrase [in The Prayer], *He causes the wind to blow*."

   N. At that moment: *And Manasseh knew that the Lord is God* (2 Chron. 33:13). Then Manasseh said, "There is justice and there is a judge."

4. A. R. Isaac interpreted the verse *He will regard the prayer of the destitute [and will not despise their supplication]* (Ps. 102:17) to speak of these generations which have neither king nor prophet, neither priest nor Urim and Thummim, but who have only this prayer alone.

   B. "Said David before the Holy One, blessed be He, 'Lord of the ages, do not despise their prayer. *Let this be recorded for a generation to come* (Ps. 102:18).'

C. "On the basis of that statement, [we know that] the Holy One, blessed be He, accepts penitents.

D. *"So that a people yet unborn may praise the Lord* (Ps. 102:18).

E. "For the Holy One, blessed be He, will create them as a new act of creation."

5. A. Another interpretation: *Let this be recorded for a generation to come* (Ps. 102:18):

B. This refers to the generation of Hezekiah, [Leviticus Rabbah adds: which was tottering toward death].

C. *So that a people yet unborn may praise the Lord* (Ps. 102:18): for the Holy One, blessed be He, created them in a new act of creation.

6. A. Another interpretation: *Let this be recorded for a generation to come* (Ps. 102:18):

B. This refers to the generation of Mordecai and Esther, which was tottering toward death.

C. *So that a people yet unborn may praise the Lord* (Ps. 102:18): for the Holy One, blessed be He, created them in a new act of creation.

7. A. Another interpretation: *Let this be recorded for a generation to come* (Ps. 102:18):

B. This refers to these very generations [in our own day], which are tottering to death.

C. *So that a people yet unborn may praise the Lord* (Ps. 102:18):

D. For the Holy One, blessed be He, is going to create them anew, in a new act of creation.

8. A. What do we have to take [in order to reach that end]? Take up the palm branch and citron and praise the Holy One, blessed be He.

B. Therefore Moses admonishes Israel, saying, *[On the fifteenth day of the seventh month, when you have gathered in the produce of the land, you shall keep the feast of the Lord seven days...] And you shall take on the first day the fruit of goodly trees, branches of palm trees and boughs of leafy trees and willows of the brook; and you shall rejoice before the Lord your God seven days. You shall keep it as a feast to the Lord seven days in the year; it is a statute for ever throughout your generations; you shall keep it in the seventh month. You shall dwell in booths for seven days; all that are native in Israel shall dwell in booths, that your generations may know that I made the people of Israel dwell in booths when I brought them out of the land of Egypt: I am the Lord your God* (Leviticus 23:39-43).

This is a fine example of how the framers of a perciope of the intersecting-verse/base-verse classification dwell on the intersecting-verse and provide an ample picture of its diverse meanings. The difference between this rhetorical pattern and the one dominant in Pesiqta deRab Kahana proves blatant, since the implicit syllogism to be imputed to the base-verse is simply not to be found in any aspect of the intersecting-verse/contrastive-verse – not at any point! The established pattern – the tripartite exegesis of Ps. 102:17, 18 – is worked out at Nos. 1 (supplemented by Nos. 2 and 3), then Nos. 4-7. Until the very final lines, No. 8, we have no reason at all to associate the exegesis of Ps. 102:17-18 with the theme of the Festival. On the contrary, all of the materials stand autonomous of the present "base-verse," and none of them hints at what is to come at the end.

XXVII:IV

1. A. *Let the field exult and everything in it. [Then shall all the trees of the wood sing for joy before the Lord, for he comes, for he comes to judge the earth]* (Ps. 96:12-13):
   B. *Let the field exult* refers to the world, as it is said, *And it came to pass, when they were in the field* (Gen. 4:8) [and determined to divide up the world between them].
   C. *And everything in it* refers to creatures.
   D. That is in line with the following verse of Scripture: *The earth is the Lord's, and all that is in it* (Ps. 24:1).
   E. *Then shall all the trees of the wood sing for joy* (Ps. 96:12).
   F. Said R. Aha, "The forest and all the trees of the forest.
   G. *"The forest* refers to fruit-bearing trees.
   H. *"And all the trees of the forest* encompasses those trees that do not bear fruit."
   I. Before whom? *Before the Lord* (Ps. 96:14).
   J. Why? *For he comes* on New Year and on the Day of Atonement.
   K. To do what? *To judge the earth. He will judge the world with righteousness, and the peoples with his truth* (Ps. 96:13).

Ps. 96:12-14 supplies direct connections to the theme of Tabernacles, with its reference to trees of the wood, exultation and rejoicing, judgment, and the like. These topics are explicitly read into the intersecting-verse at the end, but I am inclined to see the whole as a single and unified construction, with 1.F-H as an interpolated comment. But the base-verse makes no appearance at all, on the one side, and among the holy days mentioned, The Festival is not one. So the passage is included for less than self-evident reasons.

XXVII:V

1. A. *I wash my hands in innocence [and go about your altar, O Lord, singing aloud a song of thanksgiving, and telling all your wondrous deeds]* (Ps. 26:6-7):
   B. [What I require I acquire] through purchase, not theft.
   C. [Leviticus Rabbah adds:] **For we have learned there: A stolen or dried up palm branch is invalid. And one deriving from an *asherah* or an apostate town is invalid** (M. Suk. 3:1A-B).
   D. *And go about your altar, O Lord* (Ps. 26:7).
   E. That is in line with what we have learned there: **Every day they circumambulate the altar one time and say, "We beseech you, O Lord, save now. We beseech you, O Lord, make us prosper now** [Ps. 118:25]. **R. Judah says, "I and him,**

save now."   On that day they circumambulate the altar
seven times (M. Suk. 4:5).

2.   A.   *Singing aloud a song of thanksgiving* (Ps. 26:7) – this refers to the
offerings.

     B.   *And telling all your wondrous deeds* (Ps. 26:7):

     C.   Said R. Abun, "This refers to the *Hallel* Psalms [Ps. 113-118], which
contain [praise for what God has done] in the past, also [what he has
done] during these generations, as well as what will apply to the days of
the Messiah, to the time of Gog and Magog, and to the age to come.

     D.   *"When Israel went forth from Egypt* (Ps. 114:1) refers to the past.

     E.   *"Not for us, O Lord, not for us* (Ps. 115:1) refers to the present
generations.

     F.   *"I love for the Lord to hear* (Ps. 116:1) refers to the days of the Messiah.

     G.   *"All the nations have encompassed me* (Ps. 118:10) speaks of the time
of Gog and Magog.

     H.   *"You are my God and I shall exalt you* (Ps. 118:28) speaks of the age to
come."

I see no formal counterpart in Pesiqta deRab Kahana's other *pisqaot* – those
not shared with Leviticus Rabbah – to this rather odd composition. The
elements are quite discrete and in no way convey demonstrations of a single
syllogism, quite the opposite. No. 1 makes a point distinct from No. 2. "The
innocence" of Ps. 26:6 refers to the fact that one must not steal the objects used
to carry out the religious duty of the waving of the palm branch at Tabernacles.
I assume that the allusion to Tabernacles in Ps. 26:6-7 is found in the referring
to circumambulating the altar, such as is done in the rite on that day, as 1.C
makes explicit. No. 2 then expands on the cited verse in a different way. To be
sure, the *Hallel* Psalms are recited on Tabernacles, but they serve all other
festivals as well. Only No. 1 therefore relates to the established context of Lev.
23:40. It follows that the exegeses of Ps. 26:6-7 were assembled and only then
utilized – both the relevant and also the irrelevant parts – for the present purpose.
The syllogisms are worked out in terms that are otherwise alien to our
document.

Now we reach the more familiar territory of the clause by clause exegesis of
the base-verse, with the syllogism imputed through the reading of each of those
discrete components. But the intersecting-verse/contrastive-verse exercises have
not yielded a single and paramount syllogism. If my thesis is correct, that the
rhetorical preferences of Leviticus Rabbah dominate here and those of Pesiqta
deRab Kahana make no impact, then we should uncover no cogent syllogism
read consistently into one component after another of the base-verse. Rather, we
should anticipate quite the opposite, namely, a diverse program of syllogisms,
all of them relevant to the established theme, but none of them deeply engaged
with any other of them in the set.

For the effect of the contrastive-verse/base-verse construction is to produce a single syllogism, which then serves to impart to the base-verse the meaning that will be discovered everywhere, in each of its details. If we have not been given a syllogism on the foundation of the contrast between the external verse and the base-verse, then we also should have no syllogism to emerge from each of the components of the base-verse, and a diversity of (thematically appropriate, but syllogistically diverse) propositions should emerge. We shall now see that that is the case. Let me state with emphasis the operative criterion together with the reason for it: *We have been given no implicit syllogism stated through the intervention of an contrastive-verse into the basic proposition established by the base-verse. We therefore shall discover no implicit syllogism stated through a systematic exegesis of the components of the base-verse on their own.*

XXVII:VI

1. A. *And you will take for yourselves* (Lev. 23:40):
   B. R. Hiyya taught, "The act of taking must be accomplished by each and every one of you."
   C. "For yourselves" – for every one of you. They must be yours and not stolen.

2. A. Said R. Levi, "One who takes a stolen palm branch – to what is he comparable? To a thief who sat at the crossroads and mugged passersby.
   B. "One time a legate came by, to collect the taxes for that town. [The thug] rose before him and mugged him and took everything he had. After some time the thug was caught and put in prison. The legate heard and came to him. He said to him, 'Give back what you grabbed from me, and I'll argue in your behalf before the king.'
   C. "He said to him, 'Of everything that I robbed and of everything that I took, I have nothing except for this rug that is under me, and it belongs to you.'
   D. "He said to him, 'Give it to me, and I'll argue in your behalf before the king.'
   E. "He said to him, 'Take it.'
   F. "He said to him, 'You should know that tomorrow you are going before the king for judgment, and he will ask you and say to you, "Is there anyone who can argue in your behalf," and you may say to him, "I have the legate, Mr. So-and-so, to speak in my behalf," and he will send and call me, and I shall come and argue in your behalf before him.'
   G. "The next day they set him up for judgment before the king. The king asked him, saying to him, 'Do you have anyone to argue in your behalf?'
   H. "He said to him, 'I have a legate, Mr. So-and-so, to speak in my behalf.'
   I. "The king sent for him. He said to him, 'Do you know anything to say in behalf of this man?'
   J. "He said to him, 'I do indeed have knowledge. When you sent me to collect the taxes of that town, he rose up before me and mugged me and took everything that I had. That rug that belongs to me gives testimony against him.'

K.   "Everyone began to cry out, saying, 'Woe for this one, whose defense
     attorney has turned into his prosecutor.'

L.   "So a person acquires a palm branch to attain merit through it. But if it
     was a stolen one, [the branch] cries out before the Holy One, blessed be
     He, 'I am stolen! I am taken by violence.'

M.   "And the ministering angels say, 'Woe for this one, whose defense
     attorney has turned into his prosecutor!'"

The theme of the preceding, the prohibition against using a stolen palm
branch, is given two further treatments. Except in a formal way none of this
pretends to relate to the specific verses of Lev. 23:40ff., nor do we find an
intersecting-verse.

XXVII:VII

1.   A.   *On the fifteenth day of the seventh month, when you have gathered the
          produce of the land, you shall keep the feast of the Lord seven days;]* on
          the first day *[shall be a solemn rest]* (Lev. 23:40).

     B.   This in fact is the fifteenth day, yet you speak of the first day!

     C.   R. Mana of Sheab and R. Joshua of Sikhnin in the name of R. Levi said,
          "The matter may be compared to the case of a town which owed arrears to
          the king, so the king went to collect [what was owing]. [When he had
          reached] ten *mils* [from the town], the great men of the town came forth
          and praised him. He remitted a third of their [unpaid] tax. When he came
          within five *mils* of the town, the middle-rank people came out and
          acclaimed him, so he remitted yet another third [of what was owing to
          him]. When he entered the town, men, women, and children, came forth
          and praised him. He remitted the whole [of the tax].

     D.   "Said the king, 'What happened happened. From now on we shall begin
          keeping books [afresh].'

     E.   "So on the eve of the New Year, the Israelites repent, and the Holy One,
          blessed be He, remits a third of their [that is, Israel's] sins. On the ten
          days of repentance from the New Year to the Day of Atonement
          outstanding individuals fast, and the Holy One, blessed be He, remits
          most of their [that is, Israel's] sins. On the Day of Atonement all Israel
          fasts, so the Holy One, blessed be He, forgives them for all their sins
          [Leviticus Rabbah: says to Israel, 'What happened happened. From now
          on we shall begin keeping books afresh].'"

2.   A.   Said R. Aha, *"For with you there is forgiveness* (Ps. 80:4). From the
          New Year forgiveness awaits you.

     B.   "Why so long? *So that you may be feared* (Ps. 80:4). To put your fear
          into creatures.

     C.   "From the Day of Atonement to the Festival, all the Israelites are kept
          busy with doing religious duties. This one takes up the task of building
          his tabernacle, that one preparing his palm branches. On the first day of
          the Festival, all Israel they take their palm branches and citrons in their
          hand and praise the Holy One, blessed be He. The Holy One, blessed be
          He, says to them, 'What happened happened. From now on we shall
          begin keeping books [afresh].'"

D. Therefore Scripture says, *On the first day*. What is the sense of the first day? It is first in the task of reckoning sins [done in the future], that is, from the first day of the festival.

Nos. 1 and 2 go over the same matter. It seems to me that Aha's version puts into concrete terms the basic point of Levi's. 2.D is out of place, since it ignores the antecedent materials and takes as its proof-text a formula in no way important in the preceding. There can be no doubt that we have an implicit syllogism, which is that the Festival is an occasion for forgiveness, and that that fact derives from the wording of the base-verse. If we were in a composition particular to Pesiqta deRab Kahana, we should now expect further expositions of other clauses of the base-verse to demonstrate this same proposition – an important and powerful one. But that is not what we shall now find.

XXVII:VIII

1. A. *On the first day* (Lev. 23:40):
    B. By day and not by night.
    C. *On the...day* – even on the Sabbath.
    D. *On the* first *day* – only the first day [of the Festival] overrides the restrictions [of Sabbath rest. When the Sabbath coincides with other than the first day of the Festival, one does not carry the palm branch.]

2. A. *[And you shall take...] the fruit of a goodly tree [branches of palm trees and boughs of leafy trees and willows of the brook]* (Lev. 23:40).
    B. R. Hiyya taught, "A *tree*: the taste of the wood and fruit of which is the same. This is the citron."
    C. *Goodly (HDR)*: Ben Azzai said, "[Fruit] that remains [HDR] on its tree from year to year."
    D. Aqilas the proselyte translated [HDR] as, "That which dwells by water (Greek: *hudor).*"
    E. *Branches of a palm tree* (Lev. 23:40): R. Tarfon says, "[As to branch of palm tree (KPWT)], it must be bound. If it was separated, one has to bind it up."
    F. *Boughs of leafy trees*: The branches of which cover over the wood. One has to say, "This is the myrtle."
    G. *Willows of the brook*: I know only that they must come from a brook. How do I know that those that come from a valley or a hill [also are valid]? Scripture says, "*And* willows of a brook."
    H. Abba Saul says, "'*And* willows of the brook' refers to the requirement that there be two, one willow for the palm branch, and a willow for the sanctuary."
    I. R. Ishmael says, "'The fruit of goodly trees' indicates one; 'branches of palm tree' also one; 'boughs of leafy trees,' three; 'willows of the brook,' two. Two [of the myrtles] may have the twigs trimmed at the top, and one may not."
    J. R. Tarfon says, "Even all three of them may be trimmed."

We have a mass of exegetical materials, linking laws of the Festival to the verses of Scripture at hand. There is no pretense of interest an any implicit syllogism. Quite to the contrary, we might as well be in the deepest heart of Sifra or Sifré to Numbers,with their rather discrete exposition of verses, clause by clause. No. 1 conducts an inquiry into law, and No. 2 provides a word-for-word exegesis of the cited verse. Pages such as the present one in Pesiqta deRab Kahana are few and far between.

XXVII:IX

1. A. R. Aqiba says, *"The fruit of goodly (HDR) trees* refers to the Holy One, blessed be He, concerning whom it is written, *You are clothed with glory and majesty (HDR)* (Ps. 104:1).
    B. *"Branches of palm trees* refers to the Holy One, blessed be He, concerning whom it is written, *The Righteous One shall flourish like a palm tree* (Ps. 92:13).
    C. *"Boughs of leafy trees* refers to the Holy One, blessed be He, concerning whom it is written, *And he stands among the leafy trees* (Zech. 1:8).
    D. *"And willows of the brook* refers to the Holy One, blessed be He, concerning whom it is written, *Extol him who rides upon the willows, whose name is the Lord* (Ps. 68:5)."

2. A. Another interpretation: *The fruit of goodly (HDR) trees* (Lev. 23:40):
    B. This refers to Abraham, whom the Holy One, blessed be He, honored (HDR) with a goodly old age,
    C. as it is said, *And Abraham was an old man, coming along in years* (Gen. 24:1).
    D. [Leviticus Rabbah adds:] And it is written, *And you will honor (HDR) the face of an old man* (Lev. 19:32).
    E. *Branches (KPWT) of palm trees* (Lev. 23:40):
    F. This refers to Isaac, who was tied (KPWT) and bound upon the altar.
    G. *And boughs of leafy trees* (Lev. 23:40):
    H. This refers to Jacob. Just as a myrtle is rich in leaves, so Jacob was rich in children.
    I. *Willows of the brook* (Lev. 23:40):
    J. This refers to Joseph. Just as the willow wilts before the other three species do, so Joseph died before his brothers did.

3. A. Another interpretation: *The fruit of goodly tree* (Lev. 23:40):
    B. This refers to Sarah, whom the Holy One, blessed be He, honored with a goodly old age, as it is said, *And Abraham and Sarah were old* (Gen. 18:11).
    C. *Branches of palm trees* (Lev. 23:40): this refers to Rebecca. Just as a palm tree contains both edible fruit and thorns, so Rebecca produced a righteous and a wicked son [Jacob and Esau].
    D. *Boughs of leafy trees* (Lev. 23:40): this refers to Leah. Just as a myrtle is rich in leaves, so Leah was rich in children.
    E. *And willows of the brook* (Lev. 23:40): this refers to Rachel. Just as the willow wilts before the other three species do, so Rachel died before her sister.

4. A. Another interpretation: *The fruit of goodly trees* (Lev. 23:40) refers to the great Sanhedrin of Israel, which the Holy One, blessed be He, honored (HDR) with old age, as it is said, *You will rise up before old age* (Lev. 19:32).

   B. *Branches (KPWT) of palm trees* (Lev. 23:40): this refers to disciples of sages, who compel (KWPYN) themselves to study Torah from one another.

   C. *Boughs of leafy trees* refers to the three rows of disciples who sit before them.

   D. *And willows of the brook* (Lev. 23:40): this refers to the court scribes, who stand before them, one on the right side, the other on the left, [and write down the opinions of those who vote to acquit and those who vote to convict].

5. A. Another interpretation: *The fruit of goodly trees* refers to Israel.

   B. Just as a citron has both taste and fragrance, so in Israel are people who have [the merit of both] Torah and good deeds.

   C. *Branches of palm trees* (Lev. 23:30): refers to Israel. Just as a palm has a taste but no fragrance, so in Israel are people who have [the merit of] Torah but not of good deeds.

   D. *Boughs of leafy tree* refers to Israel. Just as a myrtle has a fragrance but no taste, so in Israel are people who have the merit of good deeds but not of Torah.

   E. *Willows of the brook* refers to Israel. Just as a willow has neither taste nor fragrance, so in Israel are those who have the [merit] neither of Torah nor of good deeds.

   F. Said the Holy One, blessed be He, "Utterly to destroy them is not possible.

   G. "Rather, let them all be joined together in a single bond, and they will effect atonement for one another.

   H. "And if you have done so, at that moment I shall be exalted."

   I. Therefore Moses admonishes Israel: *[On the fifteenth day of the seventh month, when you have gathered in the produce of the land, you shall keep the feast of the Lord seven days...] And you shall take on the first day [the fruit of goodly trees, branches of palm trees and boughs of leafy trees and willows of the brook; and you shall rejoice before the Lord your God seven days. You shall keep it as a feast to the Lord seven days in the year; it is a statute for ever throughout your generations; you shall keep it in the seventh month. You shall dwell in booths for seven days; all that are native in Israel shall dwell in booths, that your generations may know that I made the people of Israel dwell in booths when I brought them out of the land of Egypt: I am the Lord your God* (Leviticus 23:39-43).

The base-text is systematically read in line with intersecting-verses referring to God. The species are read as symbolizing, in sequence, God, the patriarchs and matriarchs, Torah institutions, and Israel. The powerful result of the exegesis at Nos. 2, 3, is to link the species of the Festival to the patriarchs and matriarchs of Israel. It is continuous with the foregoing, linking the species to God, and with what is to follow, as the species will be compared to Israel's leadership, on the one side, as well, finally, to ordinary people, on the other. The reading of the symbols of the Festival at No. 4 as a parable of Israel's life continues, as noted above, now with reference to the (imaginary) national government. The final exegesis reaches its climax here, concluding, then, with the redactional subscript. The composition follows a single program, beginning to end, as it rehearses the several intersecting realms of Judaic symbol systems. Always at the climax come Torah and good deeds. The base-verse in the present composition yields diverse propositions and the notion of an implicit syllogism stated through a systematic exegesis of the components of the base-verse on their own has no bearing upon this interesting composition.

XXVII:X

1. A. R. Berekhiah in the name of R. Levi: "[God speaks], 'Through the merit [attained in fulfilling the commandment], *And you will take for yourself on the first day . . .* (Lev. 23:40), lo, I shall be revealed to you first; I shall exact punishment for you from the first one; I shall build for you first; and bring to you the first one.'"

    B. "I shall be revealed for you first, as it is said, *I the Lord am first* (Is. 41:4).

    C. "I shall exact punishment for you from the first one refers to the wicked Esau, as it is written, *And the red one came forth first* (Gen. 24:24).

    D. "And I shall build for you first refers to the house of the sanctuary, concerning which it is written, *You throne of glory, on high from the first* (Jer. 17:12).

    E. "And I shall bring to you the first one, namely, the king messiah, concerning whom it is written, *The first to Zion I shall give* (Is. 41:27)."

The eschatological-salvific character of the Festival is now spelled out in specific detail. Esau, that is, Rome, will be punished, the Temple will be rebuilt, and the Messiah will come, all by virtue of the merit attained in observing the Festival. That all this is fresh and without preparation in the prior components of the *pisqa* requires no demonstration.

IV. The Shared *Pisqa/Parashah:* Where Does It Belong?

The upshot may be stated very simply. A *pisqa* in Pesiqta deRab Kahana systematically presents a single syllogism, which is expressed through, first the contrast of an external verse with the base-verse – hence, the Propositional Form, in which the implicit syllogism is stated through the intervention of an contrastive-verse into the basic proposition established by the base-verse, and second through the a systematic exegesis of the components of the base-verse on their own, hence through the Exegetical Form. In Leviticus Rabbah's *parashah* 30 which is also Pesiqta deRab Kahana's *pisqa*, we find neither of these forms utilized in this way. Since these forms otherwise characterize Pesiqta deRab Kahana, it follows that *Pisqa* 27 does not fit well with the rhetorical program of

Pesiqta deRab Kahana, so far as the materials distinctive to our document, viewed whole, define that program. What is striking is that both components that prove relevant, *the intersecting-verse/base-verse construction* of Leviticus Rabbah=*the Propositional Form made up of the contrastive-verse/base-verse construction* of Pesiqta deRab Kahana, and also the Exegetical Form shared between both documents, with its clause by clause exegesis of the base-verse, prove remarkably disparate.

On rhetorical and logical grounds we may show that a pisqa that occurs only in Pesiqta deRab Kahana may be distinguished from one that occurs in Pesiqta deRab Kahana and also in Leviticus Rabbah. Moreover, where a *parashah* of Leviticus Rabbah serves also as a *pisqa* of Pesiqta deRab Kahana, we may easily prove on the basis of the rhetorical and logical traits of composition that that *parashah/pisqa* conforms to the preferences common in Leviticus Rabbah and therefore enters derivative status in Pesiqta deRab Kahana.

We may therefore say that Leviticus Rabbah's rhetorical and logical program is taken up but revised by the authorship of Pesiqta deRab Kahana, just as, in a different way, the authorship of Pesiqta Rabbati has taken up and – whether through reworking or imitating what it has received – made its own the rhetorical and logical program of Pesiqta deRab Kahana. *Pisqaot* of Pesiqta deRab Kahana that are shared with Leviticus Rabbah conform to the rhetorical plan of that document and therefore are primary to Leviticus Rabbah and secondary to Pesiqta deRab Kahana. The reason that the authorship of the latter document has made use of these materials requires explanation as part of the larger syllogistic program of Pesiqta deRab Kahana. *Pisqaot* shared between Pesiqta deRab Kahana and Pesiqta Rabbati turn out to exhibit traits otherwise characteristic of *pisqaot* of Pesiqta deRab Kahana and not commonly present in *pisqaot* unique to Pesiqta Rabbati. If each of the three compilations – Leviticus Rabbah, Pesiqta deRab Kahana, and Pesiqta Rabbati – follows its own distinctive rhetorical and logical program of formulation, all three of them pursue a topical program that, at its foundations, appears to be single and uniform. Defining the program that is common to the three documents and shared by many others is a difficult task, well beyond the limits of the comparative study of midrash-compilations undertaken here. For it is not a problem of exegesis of Scripture, but, in the most profound sense, of the exegesis of exegesis.

V. From Tradition to Imitation and The Issue of Textuality

One definitive characteristic of a canon of the sort with which we deal is the (superficially) imitative quality of redaction. One authorship goes through motions of copying the work of a prior authorship – even while introducing striking innovations. The fundamental apologetic of all authorships rests upon the claim of tradition, beginning with Moses at Sinai. That accounts for the – on the surface – aesthetically conservative traits of the editorships. And this brings us to the issue of textuality. What I want to know is how to describe, analyze, and interpret each of the documents of the rabbinic corpus and so to determine how, as Judaism has always insisted, these documents form not only a corpus but a canon. At stake in the issue of textuality is how we may know when a document constitutes a text and when it is merely an anthology or a scrapbook. The problem is whether or not a rabbinic document to begin with stands by itself or right at the outset forms a scarcely differentiated segment of a larger uniform canon.

Since people rarely wonder why a given composition should *not* be described by itself, let me spell out the basis for the contrary view. The reason one might suppose that, in the case of the formative age of Judaism, a document does not exhibit integrity and is not autonomous is simple. The several writings of the rabbinic canon of late antiquity, formed from the Mishnah, ca. A.D. 200, through the Talmud of Babylonia, ca. A.D. 600, with numerous items in between, share materials – sayings, tales, protracted discussions. Some of these shared materials derive from explicitly-cited documents. For instance, passages of Scripture or of the Mishnah or of the Tosefta, cited verbatim, will find their way into the two Talmuds. But sayings, stories, and sizable compositions not identified with a given, earlier text and exhibiting that text's distinctive traits will float from one document to the next.

When I frame matters in terms of the problem of the rabbinic document, I therefore ask what defines a document as such, the text-ness, or, as I prefer, the textuality, of a text. How do we know that a given book in the canon of Judaism is something other than a scrapbook? The choices are clear. One theory is that a document serves solely as a convenient repository of prior sayings and stories, available materials that will have served equally well (or poorly) wherever they took up their final location. In accord with that theory it is quite proper in ignorance of all questions of circumstance and documentary or canonical context to compare the exegesis of a verse of Scripture in one document with the exegesis of that verse of Scripture found in some other document. The other theory is that a composition exhibits a viewpoint, a purpose of authorship distinctive to its framers or collectors and arrangers. Such a characteristic literary purpose – by this other theory – is so powerfully particular to one authorship that nearly everything at hand can be shown to have been (re)shaped for the ultimate purpose of the authorship at hand, that is, collectors and arrangers who demand the title of authors. In accord with this other theory context and circumstance form the prior condition of inquiry, the result, in exegetical terms, the contingent one. To resort again to a less than felicitous neologism, I thus ask what signifies or defines the "document-ness" of a document and what makes a book a book. I therefore wonder whether there are specific texts in the canonical context of Judaism or whether all texts are merely contextual. In framing the question as I have, I of course lay forth the mode of answering it. We have to confront a single rabbinic composition, and ask about its definitive traits and viewpoint. When we investigate the textuality of a document, we therefore raise these questions: is it a composition or a scrapbook, a cogent proposition made up of coherent parts, or a collage?

The answers help us to determine the appropriate foundations for comparison, the correct classifications for comparative study. Once we know what is unique to a document, we can investigate the traits that characterize all the document's unique and so definitive materials. We ask about whether the materials unique to a document also cohere, or whether they prove merely miscellaneous. If they do cohere, we may conclude that the framers of the document have followed a single plan and a program. That would in my view justify the claim that the framers carried out a labor not only of conglomeration, arrangement and selection, but also of genuine authorship or composition in the narrow and strict sense of the word. If so, the document emerges from authors, not merely arrangers and compositors. For the same purpose, therefore, we also take up and analyze the items shared between that document and some other or among several documents. We ask about the traits of those items, one by one and all in the aggregate. In these stages we may solve for the case at hand the problem of the rabbinic document: do we deal with a scrapbook or a collage or a cogent composition? A text or merely a literary expression, random and essentially promiscuous, of a larger theological context? That is the choice at hand.

My first project has been to find out whether the documentary lines made a difference, that is to say, whether a given composition exhibited distinctive and definitive traits of its own. The alternative was to take the view that pretty much everything in every holy book circulated on its own, without reference to the particular piece of writing in which it made its appearance. In my study of Leviticus Rabbah and Genesis Rabbah I proposed to demonstrate in the case of that compilation of exegeses of Scripture that a rabbinic document constitutes a text, not merely a scrapbook or a random compilation of episodic materials. A text – in the present context – is a document with a purpose, one that exhibits the traits of the integrity of the parts to the whole and the fundamental autonomy of the whole from other texts. I showed that – for those cases – the document at hand therefore falls into the classification of a cogent composition, put together with purpose and intended as a whole and in the aggregate to bear a meaning and state a message. I have therefore disproved the claim, for those compilations, that a rabbinic document serves merely as an anthology or miscellany or is to be compared only to a scrapbook, made up of this and that. In that exemplary instance I pointed to the improbability that a document has been brought together merely to join discrete and ready-made bits and pieces of episodic discourse. A document in the canon of Judaism thus does not merely define a context for the aggregation of such already completed and mutually distinct materials. Rather, I proved, that document constitutes a text. So at issue in the study of any rabbinic document is what makes a text a text, that is, the textuality of a document.

For the case of Pesiqta deRab Kahana and Pesiqta Rabbati, the differences we have noted between the one and the other prove beyond doubt that each editorship or authorship has made and carried out definitive choices. These choices involved indicative traits of rhetorical form and logical cogency of discourse. Since we can fairly easily distinguish one document from the other, and both documents from their closest antecedent, Leviticus Rabbah, it follows that both fall into the category of texts, not scrapbooks. But, as we have also noticed, while Pesiqta deRab Kahana exhibits remarkably coherent discourse, in which a single implicit premise comes to diverse expression, Pesiqta Rabbati does not. It is in some *pisqaot* not so much a propositional statement as – at best – a collage, with discrete items linked to a common and shared canvas of a single theme. And, within our sample, the compilation may also present us with *pisqaot* that are little more than assemblages of material on a common theme. Accordingly, we have found within the rabbinic canon examples not only of well composed texts – into which category I assign both Leviticus Rabbah and also Pesiqta deRab Kahana (not to mention, for quite distinct reasons, Sifré to Numbers), but also compilations that fall somewhere between the classifications of collage and scrapbook. And that interesting literary fact underlines the as yet unresolved theological problem of the canon.

It is how these sharply defined and diverse compilations come together, as they assuredly do, to form a single, vast and cogent statement: a single implicit syllogism, everywhere uniform beneath the uneven surfaces of the discrete and diverse writings. Like the magma that courses upward from the earth's deepest bowels, so that massive, simple syllogism erupts and overwhelms the surfaces – but only irregularly and unpredictably. When we discern the regularity and predict where it will or will not come to expression, we shall have penetrated far more deeply into the heart and soul of the Judaism of the dual Torah than – in these exercises of mine at any rate – the comparative study of midrash has permitted.

Index

BROWN JUDAIC STUDIES SERIES

BROWN JUDAIC STUDIES SERIES

BROWN JUDAIC STUDIES SERIES